THE NEW SCHOOL RULES

k

Previous books by the same author:

I'm a Teacher, Get Me Out of Here!

Teacher on the Run

Yob Nation

THE NEW SCHOOL RULES

The Parents' Guide to Getting the Best Education for Your Child

FRANCIS GILBERT

PORTRAIT

Visit the Portrait website!

PORTRAIT Portrait publishes a wide range of non-fiction, including biography, history, science, music, popular culture and sport.

If you want to:
- read descriptions of our popular titles
- buy our books over the Internet
- take advantage of our special offers
- enter our monthly competition
- learn more about your favourite Portrait authors

VISIT OUR WEBSITE AT: www.portraitbooks.co.uk

Copyright © 2007 by Francis Gilbert

First published in 2007 by **Portrait**
an imprint of Piatkus Books Ltd
5 Windmill Street
London WIT 2JA
e-mail: info@piatkus.co.uk

The moral right of the author has been asserted

*A catalogue record for this book is available
from the British Library*

ISBN 978 0 7499 5127 6

Edited by Carl Cutler
Design and typesetting by Paul Saunders

This book has been printed on paper manufactured with respect
for the environment using wood from managed sustainable resources

Printed and bound in Great Britain by MPG Books, Bodmin, Cornwall

For Tim and Jen – stalwart friends

'*The New School Rules* will be of immense benefit to every parent who wants to understand how to find the ideal school to suit the individual needs of their child. The book is particularly relevant in areas where the choices appear vast but are deceiving! I believe Francis Gilbert's new book will become a well-thumbed "Bible" for parents and a handbook for all good teachers and school governors.'

ANDREA PENDLETON, parent and school governor

Contents

Acknowledgements

Thanks to Alan Brooke and the team at Piatkus, Andrew Boggis, Rebecca Carter, Dom and Suzanne Corrywright, Clare Herbert, Davina Lloyd, Ivan Mulcahy, Alison Murphy, David Parry, Natalie Pecht, Andrea Pendleton, Christopher Smith, the staff at Coopers' and Erica Wagner who helped me great a deal with my research. I would also like to thank everyone interviewed in the book.

Prologue

The phone call came at midnight. I woke with a start and jumped to the receiver. 'Mr Gilbert, your child is about to be born,' a middle-aged woman's voice informed me, adding calmly, 'You should try to get to the delivery room as quickly as you can.'

I was incredibly nervous as I ran through the deserted streets, praying that everything would be all right. I tore down Brick Lane, my heart bumping and my mind racing. For the first time since I had moved into the area, I noticed that hidden in the balmy July darkness there were not only the familiar tired shops and bakeries, tatty blocks of flats and rundown houses, but also a surprising number of schools: a Catholic primary school with a freshly painted playground, a shabbier primary school with a mesh fence towering over my head, an Edwardian primary school with a series of strange ivy-entwined bowers in the bleak playground, an adult education college. In my agitated mood, my mind skittered over what school my child would go to: would I want him or her to go to any of these schools? Would he or she get into any of them?

As I arrived, panting, at the Royal London Hospital, I realised for the first time that the first school I had taught at in London nearly ten years before was just a few minutes walk away. I shuddered. I had had some difficult times there. Suddenly, the corridors of the hospital felt like they were the corridors of that school. I pushed through them, panic rippling through my body. The screams and shouts of the children jabbered around me, the smells of cheesy socks, sweat and school dinners filled my nostrils, and the mocking grins of the nastiest pupils I encountered rose before my eyes. There was no way my child was going there.

But where would he or she go to school?

I was buzzed through to the delivery room.

I pinched myself. I had to stop being so ridiculous. I was ashamed of my own thought processes.

My child would have to get born first.

Introduction

This is the one-stop book for parents who want their children to get the most out of the English education system. You name it, it's in this book: choosing the right school for your child, how to help your child get the best results, how to help them settle into school, what to expect from your school, when and how to make a complaint, how to deal with bullying, drink, drugs. The book is truly comprehensive in that it looks at both primary and secondary schools, state and private, selective and non-selective, single and mixed sex. It is jam-packed with advice and, also, parents' own stories.

But why should you be reading a book written by me, and not one of the other numerous leaflets, books, or websites that offer advice to parents about schools?

The answer to that is simple: I am an insider who tells the truth. What you read in this book is not government propaganda, left- or right-wing rant, cynical sniping or over-optimistic piffle.

In order to know where I'm coming from, you probably need to know a little of my own background. I was educated at state primary schools in the 1970s, attended an insignificant fee-paying school on the outskirts of London in the 1980s, took a degree in English and then trained to be a teacher in 1989. Since then, apart from a break from teaching in the late 1990s, I have been a teacher in a number of state schools. So you can see, I have been obsessed with the state of English education for most of my adult life because I have, for the most part, been involved in it in some way – either as a teacher or a journalist. Schools have dominated my existence to a degree that used to embarrass me. In the early 1990s, I was sometimes ashamed at dinner parties to admit that I was a school teacher at a comprehensive. Most of my other friends from college were either working in the media or lecturing at universities – something they made clear was very different from teaching sweaty adolescents in smelly classrooms.

Before any of us had children, conversations in pubs, bars, cafés, restaurants and at our homes always had focused on our tastes in films and music, our worries about mortgages and relatives, our sneering contempt for the Tory government and the general crappiness of affordable cars, the British and ourselves. In essence, we wanted to be cool – and school just wasn't cool, even to teachers like me.

Then everything changed. Tony Blair strode into Number 10 promising to concentrate on 'Education, Education, Education' – and simultaneously my friends started to have children. People's attitudes towards me at social occasions began to change. Rapidly, things became entirely different. People actually stopped in their tracks, and stared at me with wide eyes. 'So you're a teacher? Tell me what it's like!'

After 1997, no one I met could actually stop talking about England's schools. As soon as it was known that I was a school teacher, the conversation would become infected with the virus of 'school chat': what school would be good for their child at three, at eight, at 11, at 14, at 16, incessant comparing of notes about teachers, about curricula, about the state of the PTA, about head teachers, about bullying, about private versus state, tales of moving house, of marital break-ups, of neighbours' friends falling out, analysis of government policy, and endless suggestions about how things could be so much better.

I became an important person, a sage to be confided in, someone who knew the truth about the secret operations of the nation's schools.

It wasn't until I had a child myself that I realised what the fuss was about. In an instant, I understood. I wanted the very best for him. How could I let him be poorly taught, or bullied, let down by low expectations or force-fed facts? I wanted him to love his school days.

My perspective shifted. In conversations, a degree of uncertainty started to creep into my pronouncements. I no longer felt like the education expert I had set myself up to be, I could no longer make the sweeping assertions that any child would be fine if they went to any state school. I could no longer blandly offer reassurance. Even though I had taught for as many years as I had been a pupil, I was not prepared for putting my child through the system. I wrote a couple of books about my experiences as a teacher – *I'm a Teacher, Get Me Out of Here* and *Teacher on the Run* – which forced me to admit the truth: I had encountered some pretty shoddy schools in my time as a teacher.

Having allowed myself to become an 'education expert' by default, I felt I had to investigate, to shine a light on the parents' side of the education debate. I knew what schools were like from the teacher's perspective but did I really comprehend what the parents thought? I had been through over a thousand parents' evenings during my career, but did I really know what they were thinking and feeling? Did I know how their marriages and relationships were affected by the trauma of trying to give their children a decent education? How should I try to help educate my child? What should I do if he or she was bullied or unhappy? What should I do if it looked like they weren't learning anything?

My head was spinning as the questions rocketed through my mind. There were so many things to consider, so many issues to work out, so many questions to ask and so many answers to find. The truth of the matter is that the English education system is one of the most complicated in the world. It isn't just simply a matter of sending your child to the nearest local school and knowing that they'll be fine. It is far, far more involved than that.

As a teacher, I had written out my own rules for my pupils in order to give them some boundaries, some notions about what to expect when they were taught by me, in order to make them feel safe in my classroom. I felt that now perhaps it was time to write some rules for myself and other parents so that we too could feel more secure. That's why I have written this book: to provide some clear guidelines that would enable me, and other parents, to clear a path through the school jungle.

In order to make the book as accessible and relevant as possible, I interviewed many different parents throughout the country, a huge number of teachers and other significant experts, and a host of pupils – as well as researching the most up-to-date literature and research on the topic. I decided to keep my focus on schools in England and Wales since the Scottish and Northern Irish systems are in many ways quite different from ours.

Chapter 1 of the book concentrates upon the first question all parents ask anyone in the know: about 'Getting Your Child into a Good School'. This chapter takes you through all the stages you need to understand: it helps you work out what kind of parent you are, it tells you about the different types of school, it explains the truth about the league tables and Ofsted reports, it gives you some important guidelines about visiting schools and filling in applications and provides many stories from parents who have gone through the process with varying degrees of success.

Once you've got your child into a school, a number of other problems frequently crop up. Using the latest research, Chapter 2 deals with the thorny issue of 'Getting the Most Out of Your School'. In it I explore what parents want and what schools actually provide: sometimes the mismatch here is rather alarming! I explain how to help your child to settle into their new school, how to deal with complaints from teachers and how to complain yourself. I show you how to decode school reports, survive parent–teacher consultation evenings, what to do about homework, and lastly, show you how to teach your child at home – if you're completely fed up with the system.

Chapter 3, 'How To Tackle the Big Problems', deals with even scarier stuff. I illustrate some of the problems that can occur with bullying, drink, drugs, underage sex, school dinners and night-mare parties. I provide some strategies for improving your own child's behaviour and how to stop him or her becoming a bully; something which is a real parental concern.

Ultimately, these concerns may well be tied in with what is now called your child's 'special needs': when your child finds it difficult to learn properly because of some kind of problem they may have. In Chapter 4, 'Does Your Child Have Special Needs?', I explain how you can get the most of the system by admitting that your child has special needs. I explore what schools are sup-posed to do with special needs children and tell the truth about various government policies in this area. It is a real eye-opener even for parents who think their child doesn't have special needs.

Chapter 5, 'Getting Involved with Your Child's Education', covers all aspects of involvement with your child's schooling. I show how the greatest motivation is praise, and offer some strategies for making your child more motivated to work and succeed. I show how parental enthusiasm is vital if your child is going to do well at school. I then go on to talk about other ways of getting involved, such as becoming a member of the Parent–Teacher Association or a school governor.

Much of a parent's attitude towards their child's schooling is determined by what happened to them at school. In Chapter 6, 'Your Experience and Your Child's Experience', I show how it is important to analyse your own school days in order to help your own child properly.

Sometimes if parents are not sufficiently analytical they can become involved in many different kinds of confrontations. In Chapter 7, 'When Schooling Causes Conflict', the chapter which succeeds the reminiscences, I detail all the different rows and conflicts that can occur over school.

If both parents agree about what makes a good school, this can really avoid conflict. Chapter 8, 'What Makes a Good School', explores this issue: I examine a mixture of bad and good schools, hearing the stories of parents and teachers, and give a vivid picture of schools in England and Wales today. I also talk about what makes a good 'private tutor' and offer some important guidelines. Since over a quarter of parents employ private tutors to educate their children, this chapter will be of great interest to many of you.

Chapter 9, 'Getting the Most Out of the National Curriculum' highlights all the important subjects that your child will need to study, and explains how to help him achieve his best. I supply important tips on how to study and revise properly and provide some excellent questions to test your child's knowledge.

In Chapter 10, I suggest 'Some New School Rules for the Government', and finally, Chapter 11 is a brief summary of the key 'Five Essential Rules'.

There are also a number of Appendices which include reading lists, a list of the key New School Rules and a Glossary. I have also posted an entertaining slide-show of the most important New School Rules on my website, www.francisgilbert.co.uk, or you can look at my website specifically devoted to parents and schools, www.schooladviceforparents.co.uk.

The book is designed so that it can either be dipped in and out of, or read straight through.

CHAPTER 1

Getting your child into a good school

For most parents this is the really big issue. You hope that once your child is in a good school, everything else will be smooth sailing. But the tricky bit is getting him or her into a good school in the first place.

In the current climate, there are a number of pitfalls. This chapter takes you through all of them, interweaving vital advice with the true stories of parents who have suffered and triumphed. It gives you crucial advice about the questions you should be asking of yourself and your child before you look at different schools, and the different types of school on offer. It shows you how to spot a good school, and gives lots of tips on how to play the system to your own benefit.

At the end of the book, in Appendix C, I have summarised and collated all the 'New School Rules for getting your child into a good school' into a long, continuous list so that you don't have to keep cross referencing to individual chapters: the vital rules are all collected together there. Refer to them once you have read this chapter. You can also look at my slideshow of the New School Rules on my website www.francisgilbert.co.uk.

What kind of parent are you?

It was a month after my son was born but Niall, an old school friend, was getting jittery on my behalf. In the smoky pub, he sipped at his pint of Directors and tipped his head in my direction. 'So what are you going to do about schools then?' he asked.

I blinked. Since my mad dash to the hospital, I hadn't given schools a second thought: the first month after James's birth had been so frenetic, so full of the typical traumas of having a new baby, that I hadn't had time to think about the issue of schools at all. 'I don't know,' I said.

Sensing my discomfort, our other friend, Tim, interjected in my defence: 'What are you doing about Martin?' Tim and I laughed. Niall's son Martin was three months old. Niall swallowed more of his beer. 'I'm going to church,' he confessed as he played tentatively with his earlobe.

I nearly spat out my white wine. Niall was one of the most virulent atheists I had ever come across. During the days when he was at university, he had fulminated at length about the evils of the church: its arbitrary rules, its hypocrisy, and its asinine fictions posing as truths. 'You hate Christianity. You haven't got a good word to say about it.'

Niall curled his lip. We were right, but he was the sort who always defended his decisions aggressively. 'You don't understand, you guys, do you? This is serious. This is our children's education we are talking about. I've been checking out the schools in my local area, and there's only one good one, where all the good teachers are, and where all the concerned parents send their children. The others are shit. They get shit results. And they look terrible. It just so happens it's a church school. You need a good report from your local vicar to get in there. So that's why me and Vicky are going to church. I'm not having Martin going to a terrible school where he learns nothing and gets beaten up all the time.'

I was flabbergasted. After he had calmed down a little, Niall convinced me that he was right to be worried. If the vicar didn't say that he had completed four years of dutiful service at his local church, then he would almost certainly fail to get his child into the only good local school.

Niall told us, 'The vicar explained to me that he used to write a character reference, but they've had so many people coming to church recently that the only way that the school has been able to differentiate between the truly devout and the fly-by-night characters is to get everyone signed in and signed out. So there's a register, and the parents have to sign in every Sunday.'

There was a pause in the conversation. Niall buried his head in his hands again. I could tell he was very uneasy about going to church. I asked him gently if he had really worked out what kind of parent he was, if he had really sat down and discussed with his partner about what kind of education he wanted for his child.

He conceded that he hadn't really. He'd panicked and heard that the Church of England school was good, and saw that it came top of the league tables in the area, and assumed that he had to get his child in the school because everyone else did. I told him that he needed to take things one step at a time.

'Before you do anything, you have to work out what kind of parent you are,' I said, 'so that you're confident that you're sending your child to the right school for him and for you. It's a real jungle out there and you need to know what kind of animal you are in it before you can work out the best way to survive.'

I spelled out to Niall the different types of animal I had encountered in the school jungle so far. I told him:

Giraffe parents have very long necks – they can peer over the top of the school jungle and gain a long-distance perspective. Having their feet on the ground but their heads high in the air, giraffe parents want their child to go to a state school but want him or her to do academically well in it. They are troubled by some of the stories they read in the press about schools but they are not brainwashed by them. They are quite happy for their children to mix with any social class but they have definite expectations that their child will go to a good university and ultimately have a rewarding career. Giraffe parents don't panic because they know, having read all the research, that finally it is parental support that is the most important factor in a child's attainment at school. I like to think of myself as being a giraffe parent, although, frighteningly, there are moments when I am:

An eagle parent who contrasts with a giraffe parent, his nearest social ally in the school jungle, in that he wants his child to do very well academically, but he also wants to remove his child from society which might 'coarsen' him or her. Eagle parents send their children to state or private schools with social cachet, and want to use the system to fly up the social ladder.

Leopard parents want to put their child into some sort of serious training of one sort or another so that he or she can run very fast in his chosen field. Leopard parents train their children to be footballers, athletes, or tennis players from a very early age and expect their children to go to a school that will assist them with this project, such as a specialist sports school.

Wildebeest parents want their children to muck in with everyone else. They send their children to local community schools and feel that the most a child can get out of school is to be a 'fully rounded' human being who is part of the benevolent herd. They never feel happier than when they see their children playing with their friends from around the corner. Academic achievement, although a concern, is secondary to social fulfilment. They will probably hate this book, although they may well read it because they are often the best educated of all of us. Famous wildebeest parents are scary people like Fiona Millar (*Education Guardian* columnist and TV programme presenter), Phil Beadle (Teacher of the Year), and John O'Farrell, author of the excellent novel *May Contain Nuts*. I have interviewed the last two to give them a fair hearing. I also have spoken to a number of older wildebeest parents who have come to rue their earlier attitudes. These people are highly educated liberals who sent their children to comprehensives on principle, only to find that their children grew up totally uninterested in the academic pursuits of their parents. Life at a wildebeest school gave their children great social skills but very little in the way of academic qualifications or interests. This was now a source of great regret to their parents, who felt they had little connection with their children. This is perhaps the biggest reason why I have rejected the wildebeest mentality – although I know it is probably the most morally proper position to hold.

Anteater parents keep their noses to the ground, eat the ants in front of them and never look up to get a good view of what is really going on. This makes them prone to be victims of the system; they assume that the school jungle is benign when it is not.

'Arsehole' parents (Well, perhaps an animal name is too good for this kind of parent.) One frustrated parent and observer of many parents over the years in the area (Upminster) where I teach, Mike Robinson, memorably posed the rhetorical question to me, 'Why are so many parents arseholes?' Now, what you have to understand here is that Mike does not live in an area of high deprivation, full of hideous social problems, he lives in one of the most affluent areas in the country, and yet he has seen during his many voyages to parents' evenings – he has two teenage sons – and various social functions that many parents are just simply arseholes! Most importantly, he is not a teacher – but his thoughts are surprisingly in tune with the majority of teachers I interviewed as well. He explained to me:

> There are many parents around who feel a lot of antagonism towards teachers. Everything is always the teachers' fault. They think that teachers are nearly always wrong, that they don't understand young people. They think that teachers are there to bully their children. They use the phrase 'she's a good girl really' a great deal, which is basically a euphemism for 'she's an absolute pain in the backside'. They have no respect for education, for books, for newspapers, for museums, for culture in general: they

just believe in making money. And don't get me wrong, 'arsehole' parents aren't poor. They've often made a lot of money by setting up their own businesses and what have you, but the bottom line is they don't have a book in the house and yet they expect their children to be properly educated without any input from them.

I have to confess I have come across a few such parents in my career – as has any experienced teacher; such parents are very quick to blame and complain, even threaten and shout, but rarely are they willing to pay much attention to their own children.

Niall was grateful for my advice because by the end of the conversation, he'd worked out he was definitely a giraffe parent: someone who wasn't hugely ideological but wanted to have a larger perspective on what was going on.

'I'm not going to panic,' Niall said determinedly, 'I'm actually going to research properly what is going on at the different schools before I start madly praying to God for assistance.'

THE NEW SCHOOL RULES
about the different types of parent

1. **Figure yourself out** It is worth trying to work out what kind of parent you are because it will affect very deeply the choices you make for your child. Leopard, eagle and giraffe parents are very different types of parents in many ways but all have common aims. They are looking for very specific schools; you really need a good map of the school jungle before you can work out where might be the best school for your child.

2. **Be honest with yourself** Don't send your child to a school just because your political convictions insist that you should; do what is best for your child.

What kind of child do you have?

It was one of my more shameful escapades. My son, James, was six years old and had been invited to a five-a-side football birthday party. I had never really taught him the rules of the game, other than kicking the ball around in the park on the odd occasion. As a result, he looked totally lost on the pitch, chewing on his sleeve and watching the other boys and girls running after the ball as he stood still. Seeing his bewilderment, I decided to pitch in myself and offered to play. Unfortunately, the supervisor organising the game allocated me to the opposite side to James.

Being the competitive dad that I am, I hijacked the game, hoping to compensate to for James's lack of interest and enthusiasm by showing some passion of my own. Within a few minutes, I had hoards of small girls and boys chasing after me on the pitch as I wove in and out of them, and I scored several goals. Some deluded part of me at the time actually made me think that I was fostering a sportive spirit.

I am not sure the other parents concurred. One of them shouted from the sidelines, 'Hey Francis, you know there's no kudos in beating seven-year-olds!' But some demonic urge to prove myself kept me running on and on, scoring goals and hogging the game. It got so bad that for the final match of the five-a-side tournament, the supervisor relegated me to being goalie, and when I ran out of the goal and scored again, he disallowed the goal!

I kept running up to James, urging him to get involved in the game. 'Come on, it's fun! You just have to play that's all! Come on!' I said. But he remained un-impressed. By the end of the tournament, his main response was to cry. I tried unsuccessfully to hide my impatience: 'Oh come on, you've got to like football, it's a great game.'

This only prompted more tears. After the party, as we were walking home, I told him that we'd play more football in the park, and he'd get good. But at the back of my mind, I knew that he wasn't really the 'sporty' type. He was more of a dreamer. He liked playing imaginary 'games', pretending to be Dr Who and Superman, and I could see already that the more competitive sports were never going to be top of his list. Unless that is, I really pushed him to be like that. At six, he was still malleable. If I implemented a programme of playing football in the park every weekend, maybe he would be good?

This thought occurred to me and appealed to my worst instincts. While I am OK at football – I can beat seven-year-olds when pushed to do so – I am not as good as I would like to be. Maybe James could go one better than me and be the sportsman I never was? I could get him some coaching and maybe he'd acquire the kind of skills I just don't have?

Erica, my wife, wasn't too thrilled. She's American, and doesn't have much affection for soccer. 'That's a ridiculous idea. He's not like that. He's just not the kind of child who's going to enjoy being sent off to a football coach,' she said.

'But we don't know until we've tried,' I said. 'I don't want him to grow up and be a sad case like me. I mean, I can only beat seven-year-olds!'

She shook her head in disbelief. 'He'll grow up with your pathetic competitiveness if you don't watch out. That's all you'll do if you send him off to football coaching. He's not ready for it.'

Her comments gave me real pause for thought. Did I want James to grow up to be the kind of man who was so competitive that he felt compelled to try to beat seven-year-olds at football? I hung my head in shame. No, I didn't! My mother, a music teacher, had trained me from an early age to be a piano player and encouraged me to play in concerts where I could show my prowess in playing Mozart and Beethoven. I had been pretty good at the age of eight, showing off at my primary school with glittering cadenzas, but by the time I was 14 I was utterly fed up with the instrument. Her pushy parenting had backfired because I knew at the back of my mind that her reason for teaching me so fiercely and diligently was so that she could show me off to the other parents. I had never become a very good piano player, but I was left with a fundamental insecurity about my status in life which meant that I felt compelled to beat seven-year-olds at football.

I decided to compromise. I'd gently teach James how to play football in the park on the weekends, but I wouldn't send him off to football coaching. I had to see if he had a natural inclination for the sport. Even though he was young, I had to let him choose for himself.

The more I researched the issue, the more I realised that I had to figure out what kind of child my son was if I was going to give him the best education. Many of the best schools select children who have a particular aptitude for sport, dance, music or drama. While I knew that it wasn't going to do James much good if I pushed him to do a sport that he didn't like, I knew that helping him develop in one of these areas would greatly assist his chances in getting into a good school, state or private – and his chances in life generally. Basically, I could get him to find his 'passion'.

One parent in the 'know', Andrea Pendleton, spelled it out in cold terms for me. She is a parent-governor and has helped a lot of parents get their children into good schools. She said, 'If your child excels in some sort of sport or art, they're much more likely to get a scholarship to one of the top private schools or get into a state school where there's fierce competition for places.' She listed them for me:

- **Dance** An excellent dancer may get a scholarship to Italia Conti, Anna Scher, or the Royal Academy of Dance if you choose this path.

- **Music** A musician may qualify for the Guildhall School of Music, and may also be offered a scholarship or place at a school that specialises in music.

- **Sport** A good all-rounder will be welcome at many private secondary schools and will help towards an all-rounder scholarship, particularly if the child also plays an instrument.

Andrea pointed out that in order to get these sorts of scholarships or get into the top specialist schools, your child had to be really good. She said, 'Please be REALISTIC and find out their level from a recognised professional in the field i.e. director of coaching, or the senior county coach, and not from your after-school club. Are they performing at district, county, national or international level? If they aren't, it's very unlikely that they'll get into the top secondary schools or a scholarship.'

This sort of talk scared me. While James is clever and imaginative, he would much prefer to be pretending to be Superman or reading his comics at the weekend than being drilled to be a dancer or a musician or a football player. He's happy to do some reading homework and practise on his recorder for a little bit, but I don't think he'd really like being coached for hours on end. And besides, even if he was, would Erica and I want that? It would mean we'd hardly ever get to see him, as both of us work during the week.

Nevertheless, I knew I would need to investigate these areas further and see just what aptitude he had in these areas.

THE NEW SCHOOL RULES
for finding out your child's abilities

1. **Discover a talent** Every child is talented, it is just a matter of finding out what those talents are. Talk to your child and find out what they like doing. Try to encourage them to have an enthusiasm, a passion, an area of expertise. At an early age, try to give them a variety of experiences: play sport with them, encourage them to play a musical instrument, see what they're like at acting and dance. Talk to your child's teachers about their abilities and then do what you can to encourage your child to follow their passion.

▶

2. Give your child plenty of time If you're interested in your child getting a scholarship or getting into a top specialist school, you'll need to do your research early and find out what schools there are in your area and what their entry requirements are. Remember, your child will have to excel in a particular specialism or show real promise to get into the top secondary schools.

2. Don't be too pushy Be wary of forcing your child to attend classes/coaching lessons that they really don't enjoy. This can backfire horribly later on, leaving you with a surly, demotivated teenager who is resentful of the unrealistic expectations you have put on them. Bear in mind that children born in the summer are often in classes with children nearly a year older than them and are unfairly compared with them as a result. Don't become paranoid if your summer-born child seems far behind the children in his class who were born in September and are a year older. Most secondary schools are clued up about this now. For example, summer-born boys applying to the City of London Boys' School (one of the best private schools in London) will be considered for a resit a year later if they fail to attain a scholarship the first time.

The different types of state school

So you've worked out what kind of parent you are, now you need to start getting your head around the different types of school in your area. The label given to a school by the government has a huge influence because it effectively determines who goes to the school. If you're in the know you'll be in a much better position to play the system and get into your child into a school that's right for him or her.

Firstly, get to know your Local Education Authority (LEA). This is the authority which is in charge of giving children a good education in their area or borough. Some are hugely influential, and others are not. You will need to know whether the LEA is the admissions authority for the schools in your area. This means does the LEA decide which children go to what school, as opposed to the school deciding itself? Nearly always LEAs attempt to send children to their nearest local school. It is also important to know whether your LEA is any good or not. Some LEAs spend more money on education than others, whereas others are much better at producing good results or new initiatives. The best place to start is by looking at your LEA's website. If your LEA is good, the website will be very informative, lively, and provide all the necessary links to find out more about it.

Most LEAs should be able to educate children of all ages. Before we look at more specialist information, it's worth going over some obvious points about the schools that cater for different ages. The most important definition you need to learn is 'admissions criteria'. This is the rules that schools set for 'admitting' prospective pupils; the entry requirements in other words.

When their child is tiny, most parents opt for some sort of pre-school education. Eagle parents often opt for private nurseries or childminders who actually attempt to teach children some of the basics of reading and writing when the child is between two to five years old. Other parents go for Montessori nurseries, playgroups or state-run nurseries, where the emphasis is on safety and fun – which it should be at this age. All registered pre-school education is now inspected by Ofsted for basic health and safety precautions. There is usually very little comment on the standard of teaching. The government has pledged a part-time place of five morning or afternoon sessions per week for all four-year-olds.

▶ **CHECK OUT**
www.bbc.co.uk/dna/actionnetwork/A1181792. What follows is my unique insider's interpretation of the more

sober information provided by this excellent BBC website which details all the different types of schools as well as a huge amount of other educational information.

Primary schools

Often, primary schools are thought of as small, cosy places full of matronly women who nurture and mother children from the age of four to 11. Don't break the law; every child has to go to school when they are five. However, lots of children go to primary school before their fifth birthday. If your child was born in the summer, he or she could end up going to school shortly after their fourth birthday because most schools take pupils at just one point in the year, normally September. You should talk to the school about this because all the evidence suggests that young children find the academic demands of the curriculum very difficult to cope with when they are four and five. There may be many children who are far more advanced than yours if he or she has started school early. Too often teachers and parents can forget this when they are making judgements about a child's progress at this stage.

A primary school usually has an infant department (5–7 years: Key Stage 1) and a junior department (7–11 years: Key Stage 2).

Secondary schools

Usually, secondary schools are perceived to be far scarier than primary schools: big, impersonal places with masses of ugly adolescents and distressed, dog-eared teachers. The secondary school system takes children either from 11 to 16 or 11 to 18, depending upon whether the school has a sixth form.

Now that sounds very simple, three basic types of school: pre-school, primary and secondary. If only it were that easy. The savvy parents who want to work the system to their best advantage need to get wised up to a few subcategories of school.

It's only then that you'll understand why certain schools have their own particular identity; you see, some schools are effectively able to select their pupils secretly and some are not.

Community schools

These schools definitely are not able to select their pupils. Community schools are local primary schools and 'bog-standard' local comprehensives by any other name, which wildebeest parents might favour because they are controlled by the local authority and take children only from the local catchment area. At their best, they contain a wide variety of different social and ethnic groups and are characterised by liberal, tolerant values and are at the heart of the local community. At their worst, they are sink schools dominated by one social or ethnic group who haven't had the intelligence, power or influence to send their children anywhere else.

Foundation schools and Trust schools

Some commentators believe these schools have the power to select their pupils by the back door if they so choose. Leopard, eagle and giraffe parents are very interested in these types of schools because they set their own admissions criteria, which are devised by the governing body. This means they often 'select' pupils covertly by asking prospective pupils to meet a long list of criteria; this effectively requires very pro-active parents to meet these criteria – more on this later. The government is currently trying to crack down on this with its new School Admissions Code[1] but it remains to be seen whether schools will 'work their way' around the code. Recent legislation aims to give any local authority maintained school the opportunity to behave very like foundation schools and become what will be known as 'Trust schools'. These schools will have to form a link with a charitable organisation (the Trust) which might include universities, businesses, or voluntary or community organisations. Crucially, these schools will be able to set their own entry requirements –

so all the vital tips I offer about 'voluntary-aided' schools in this book will apply to Trust schools as well.

Voluntary-aided schools

These schools are, again, of huge interest to many parents because the governing body sets the admissions criteria, which can effectively mean there is selection by the back door. Most voluntary-aided schools have some sort of connection with the church, but that doesn't necessarily mean that they insist upon proof of huge religious commitment. The land and buildings are normally owned by a charitable foundation.

Voluntary-controlled schools

Although these sound like voluntary-aided schools they are quite different. Voluntary-controlled schools tend to be church schools that don't select their pupils. Yes, there are still quite a few around! This is because the LEA employs the school staff and has responsibility for admissions, and since most LEAs favour local catchment area schools, this means that pupils are drawn from the local community whether they are religious or not. The land and buildings are almost always owned by a charitable foundation.

> ▶ **CHECK OUT**
> www.teachernet.gov.uk/educationoverview/uksystem/
> structure/schooltypes/, for more information.

Within these different categories of school, there are more specialised schools:

Specialist schools

These schools teach the normal range of subjects but specialise in certain areas like languages, sports and the performing arts. Leopard parents love these schools if they cater for the particular specialism the leopard has chosen for his child – whoops, if they cater for the area their child is interested in. But the huge problem is that there is never a proper specialism in the area when you need one. However, you should be aware that many schools now are offering second specialisms in another subject – if your child excels in this particular subject he could be at a distinct advantage if it is on the admissions criteria. Specialist schools can select 10 per cent of their intake based on a child's aptitude for that specialism. Whether they do or not remains a very, very vague point. Having talked to a number of parents and pupils now, it appears that schools interpret this rule very loosely, taking pupils they like the look of, and using this rule as their excuse. So it is well worth your while 'bigging up' your child's aptitude on the admissions form for a specialism if you can possibly do so. For example, if you're trying to get your child into a specialist music school in the state sector, a nice note from your child's music teacher and an estimate of where she is at will usually do. This compares very sharply with music schools in the independent sector where your child will have to have passed Grade 3 or above in order to get in.

> ▶ **CHECK OUT**
> www.specialistschools.org.uk/, and for the truth, talk to parents of pupils who have got into your chosen school.

City Technology Colleges

These were set up by the Conservative administration of the 1990s, usually in areas of social deprivation. These schools are strange creatures: they are already historic relics from the Tory era. They can be a little rigid in their approach and perhaps have a little too much focus upon vocational subjects for some parents' tastes. They usually specialise in Information Technology and science. CTCs have developed close links with employers and offer a wide range of vocational qualifications.

▶ **CHECK OUT**
www.standards.dfes.gov.uk/academies/ctcs/?version=1

Academies

These are the schools that so many parents love at the moment, but so many left-wing politicians hate – even if they are trying to get their children into them. They usually have replaced failing schools in areas of deprivation. Their aim is to lure back middle-class parents into the state system with their wonderful resources and promise of high academic standards. Whether they are doing this or not is questionable: the data indicates that their achievements so far are patchy, but it is early days. Both on an anecdotal and statistical basis, I have seen how parents are falling over themselves to get their children into these schools. They look so spanking new and delicious, and have become irresistible even to some eagle parents I have spoken to. If a substantial majority of middle-class parents is putting its faith into the school, it appears they are being successful: this seems to be the case in Hackney where academies such as the Mossbourne Academy are thriving. However, in other areas, where a mass of low-achievers and Special Educational Needs (SEN) pupils are in attendance and where middle-class parents are opting for other schools, it appears that the schools remain poor. The Labour government has set a target of 200 academies by 2010. For more information: see pages 297–299.

▶ **CHECK OUT**
www.standards.dfes.gov.uk/academies/ and
www.mossbourne.hackney.sch.uk/

Extended schools and child and family centres

These schools are open much longer than normal schools (usually from 8.00 am to 6.00 pm) and offer a range of extracurricular and community activities: breakfast clubs, homework clubs, a range of sporting activities, parenting classes, health services. The government is proposing that all schools should become extended schools by 2010. Some primary schools are being asked to become Child and Family Centres, offering a number of different services to parents including after-school child care, medical provision and so forth. You need to check in the school's prospectus exactly what activities are available: some schools are much better in this regard than others.

> ► **CHECK OUT**
> www.everychildmatters.gov.uk/ete/extendedschools/

Grammar schools

Definitely the state school of choice for the eagle parent – but many other parents, from the wishy-washy to the very left wing, secretly take out a licence to kill to get their children into these schools. Private tutors are hired, practice papers are completed on the kitchen table, and, hey presto, a parent whom you thought had sworn blind their child would never go to a school that perpetuated 'educational apartheid' is saying, 'Well, he did so well in his eleven-plus that it seems a shame to pass up this opportunity!' Some local authorities such as Kent still run a selective secondary school system with grammar schools, while other boroughs have grammar schools dotted here and there. There are more than you think: approximately 150 state grammar schools in England alone. Pupils in these areas take the eleven-plus test; the results of this test determine whether or not they gain entry to the local grammar school. For more log on to: www.ngsa.org.uk/. This is the website of the National Grammar Schools Association. It is particularly good for helping you locate the relevant schools in your area and gives a lot of information about the wonders of grammar schools. Be wary of thinking that grammar schools are absolutely spiffing – as we shall see, some of them are not – but if your child is very academic, they are definitely good schools to attend.

Faith schools

These schools are really on the rise in England because many schools have found that religion can be a good way of selecting pupils. However, as has been said before, find out what type of faith schools are in your area. Nearly half of faith schools are voluntary-controlled, which means they teach the locally agreed religious syllabus and the LEA is the admissions authority: they often have no admissions policy other than being in the local catchment area. Voluntary-aided faith schools are responsible for setting their own admissions policies and teach religious education according to their religious precepts: these schools tend to have much more complex admissions criteria. Faith schools admit pupils on religious affiliation but many admit those who are not of the school faith.

> ▶ **CHECK OUT**
> www.cesew.org.uk (The Catholic Education Service),
> www.cofe.anglican.org (The Church of England website).

Special needs schools or 'Special' schools

The government now has a policy of 'inclusion' which means any child with physical or behavioural problems has the right to be taught in a mainstream school. As a result, many special schools have closed, which is a shame because a great many of them did a wonderful job and were loved by parents and pupils alike. But since an estimated one in five children has some form of SEN, if everyone with a special need was catered for, a great many special schools would have to be opened. Clearly, it is only pupils with extreme special needs who should be in a special school, those with 'mild' special needs are far better off in the mainstream. There are still about 1,200 special schools for pupils with special needs. Some of these are run by voluntary organisations and others are in hospitals. See Chapter 4, Does Your Child Have Special Needs?, for more about this.

> ▶ **CHECK OUT**
> www.specialneedsuk.org/parents/index.htm – a website dedicated to helping parents find the right school for their child as well as offering a wealth of information about special needs for parents and professionals.

Pupil Referral Units (PRUs)

These schools have fought hard not to be labelled 'sin bins'. They are for pupils who would not receive a mainstream education unless they went to this kind of school: so pupils who have been permanently excluded from school or teenage mothers might attend them. PRUs are a type of school established and maintained by the LEA. They attempt to get pupils back into mainstream education with varying degrees of success. I have spoken to a number of teachers at PRUs who say the worst problem is attendance: pupils often don't come to school. They are surprisingly pleasant places to visit: very few pupils, and lots of friendly and engaged staff. Often the pupils who do turn up genuinely want to learn because they know it is their last chance. They are run by a management committee made up of a range of people from school governors to representatives from social services.[2]

> ▶ **CHECK OUT**
> www.dfes.gov.uk/exclusions/alternative_provision_policies/pupil_referral_units.cfm

State boarding schools

There are a few, too few in my mind, state boarding schools which provide a high-quality academic education for the lowest possible costs. UK and other European Union nationals and others with the right of residence in the UK pay only for the cost of boarding, while the education is free. This means that these schools are much cheaper than your average independent boarding school.

Such schools are very good at making pupils feel at home: they are warm and friendly places. They also achieve some of the best results in the country. No wonder parents have been stampeding to get their children into them.

Many pupils opt for sixth-form boarding because it is a good preparation for university. All these schools have a mix of boarding and day pupils.

> ▶ **CHECK OUT**
> www.sbsa.org.uk/about.htm

Independent schools

You have to shell out considerable sums to pay for your child to attend even the most nondescript of independent schools. Independent schools are truly 'independent': they are not bound by most of the regulations that schools in the state sector have to abide by, but they usually make their pupils take GCSEs and A levels. Some schools also pay for their pupils to take the Key Stage tests, the compulsory tests taken at the ages of seven, 11 and 13 in state schools, but most don't. There is huge variability in this sector: some schools are great, but others are awful. Don't be deceived by all the tradition and the pomp, investigate the school very carefully before making your decision. (See pages 80–3 for more on private schools.)

Independent primary schools

They fall into two main categories: pre-preparatory, for age two to seven and junior or preparatory schools to age 11–13. The 'prep' school is so named because these institutions prepare pupils for the Common Entrance examination, an extremely demanding entrance test, which is required for many independent secondary schools.

▶ **CHECK OUT**
www.iaps.org.uk/school/default.asp, the website of the Incorporated Association of Independent Preparatory Schools.

Rudolf Steiner schools

These schools follow the precepts laid down by the eccentric mystical philosopher Rudolf Steiner. Their overwhelming emphasis is on a 'holistic' education, which means that where possible pupils have the same teacher year after year, and are taught the connections between the different subjects. I have observed Steiner schools in action and was disappointed because Steiner had some very complex ideas which need a great deal of explanation. This meant that I saw a lot of lecturing going on, and not a huge amount of hands-on learning. There is much emphasis on creating spiritual 'art'; again this was something I felt was restricting rather than liberating since much of the art had to follow the Steiner precepts.

▶ **CHECK OUT**
www.steinerwaldorf.org.uk/

Foreigners' schools

Have you ever considered sending your child abroad in England? Foreigners' schools are predominantly for foreigners' children who are living in England. There are a number of respected Anglo-American schools which are generally more liberal and enlightened than their English independent counterparts. The French Lyceés in England tend to operate both French and English streams. Fees vary: they can be very expensive. They are very academic in emphasis and a little dry in approach.

> ▶ **CHECK OUT**
> www.ecis.org/index.asp. This is the website of the European Council of International Schools. It has an excellent search facility.

Montessori schools

Many nursery schools claim that they are Montessori but in reality they are not. The name is not copyrighted so anyone can open a school, slap the name Montessori on it and, bingo, they're pulling in the punters. Look for schools which are affiliated to accredited Montessori associations such as the International Montessori Association. Most importantly you should be looking for cosy and warm classrooms that are a cross between a laboratory, a kitchen, a playhouse and a library where children are determinedly and purposefully doing their own thing either in groups or by themselves. Classrooms should be uncluttered and laid out in such a way that a child will learn about different subjects while exploring them: science, art, maths, literacy. There should be no rows of desks in a Montessori classroom, and absolutely no rote learning. Maria Montessori was a brilliant educationalist who pioneered many ideas which have affected every school in the world, such as little chairs for little people. She believed that a child should never be forced to learn anything but should be guided by being placed within a suitable learning environment. This meant that all objects should be at a child's height and should be there to encourage and foster learning.

> ▶ **CHECK OUT**
> www.montessori.org.uk/schools.php

Choir schools

These are schools attached to cathedrals, churches and college chapels throughout the country that train the pupils to be choristers in the choir. There are 21,000 pupils at chorister schools, with most schools taking pre-pubescent boys and a few accepting girls. Most are independent schools but three are state funded. One of the requirements may be a talent for singing: if your child is in the choir (not all children are) he will have to sing in the numerous services throughout the year at weekends and during religious holidays. Pupils can be either board or be day pupils, depending on how near they live to the school.

> ▶ **CHECK OUT**
> www.choirschools.org.uk

Music, dance and drama schools

There are a plethora of music, dance and drama schools throughout the country which offer after-school and weekend lessons in their chosen specialisms. If you are serious about getting your child a scholarship to a top private school, you probably should enrol your child at one of these schools and give them plenty of practice! There are many music schools in the country but only a small number with really good reputations and, as a result, they are very difficult to get into. The website www.musiclessonsonline.co.uk is a good place to start looking for music lessons, while the Royal Academy of Music (www.ram.ac.uk/), the Guildhall of Music and Drama (www.gsmd.ac.uk/) and Trinity College of Music (www.tcm.ac.uk/) remain the top schools in the country.

Dance schools abound and can be easily found at www.dance schools-uk.co.uk/. Again the top schools are in London, such as the Royal Ballet School (www.royal-ballet-school.org.uk/). Meanwhile, stage schools purport to cater for any budding actors and actresses. Usually they offer an academic curriculum during the morning and drama lessons in the afternoon. The academic lessons are usually very traditional in emphasis, but the drama lessons can be exceptionally good. They appear to be good at motivating some difficult children who are desperate to be celebrities. For information log onto: www.stageregister.co.uk/FullTime.htm. At the time of writing, the website is extremely poor with poor design and not enough links. Let's hope they improve it!

The quality of such schools varies considerably. You will need to be vigilant about what exactly your child is learning, using the other pointers in this book to assist you in judging whether the education they are getting is a good one.

Kumon schools

These are schools which are devoted to teaching the Kumon method. They nearly all run as after-school institutions. The Kumon method in English and maths basically operates by giving pupils repetitive exercises which are easy for the child at first but become progressively harder. A child will be given a worksheet in English and maths to complete and will not go onto the next level unless they have answered all the questions correctly on the sheet. It is quite similar to old-fashioned rote learning where children were asked in schools of yesteryear to complete endless practice exercises in English and maths. The advantages of the method are that it does build up confidence and it is good at drilling children in the basics. The disadvantage is that it does not encourage much independent thought.

▶ **CHECK OUT**
www.kumon.co.uk/

When considering any independent school, you should investigate the various scholarships, bursaries and government grants that are on offer to the wised-up parent. A third of all pupils at independent schools receive help with their fees, but very few actually have all of their fees paid. Scholarships are awarded for many different reasons: special ability in music, art or some other specialism or for all-round merit. Some schools give awards for drama, sport, design and technology. Usually, your child will have to take an exam in order to prove his or her abilities. Unlike a scholarship, a bursary is not tested by exam and is a grant from the school to help you pay the fees, after the school has seen the details of your income.

▶ **CHECK OUT**
The Independent Schools Council website:
www.isc.co.uk/index.php

THE NEW SCHOOL RULES

for researching schools

1. **Do your research** Find out about the different ages the schools in your area cater for by looking at your LEA's website or getting hold of their prospectuses. Googling the relevant name and area should take you straight there. How does the schooling system cater for the different ages in your area? Remember, some areas still operate a First (5–8-year-olds), Middle (9–13-year-olds) and Upper School (14–16) system which will affect your choices profoundly. Most areas follow the primary and secondary model, in which case, it is important to find out whether secondary school is from 11 to 16 or from 11 to 18 years. Again, this is crucial because a school which

▶

takes 18-year-olds will have a sixth form, and this will affect the atmosphere of the school. It may be, though, that the area operates with an 11–16 secondary school system, and then has sixth-form colleges.

2. **Get those council taxes working for you** Get the most out of your LEA. A few LEAs, too few in my mind, have parent helplines to assist with the whole process. If they have nothing, give them a ring anyway and complain!

3. **Wise up on selective and religious schools in your area** Find out if there are any selective schools that you could send your child to. Is there a grammar school system in your area? If there is, it is very likely that your child will take an eleven-plus exam in Year 6 which will decide whether he or she goes there or not. Find out about the religious schools in your area. Many of the best schools are religious in foundation but their admissions criteria vary hugely depending upon what type of school it is. See below for more information.

    www.direct.gov.uk/EducationAndLearning/fs/en goes into more depth about the different types of school (and much else besides) but is a government website so will not give you the vital inside information I have given you.

4. **Plan early** This is particularly the case if you are thinking about sending your child to an independent school and wish to receive help with the fees. Research the various scholarships, bursaries and government grants on offer by looking at the Independent Schools Council website: www.isc.co.uk/index.php/. For the top state and independent schools, the Good Schools' Guide website is definitely worth a look: www.schoolsguidebook.co.uk/index.html. It offers some free evaluations of the schools and links, but you will probably need to pay for more in-depth commentaries.

The league tables

Sometimes, parents used to look at only the league tables in order to choose a good school. This is a mistake. My old school is now one of the 'most improved' in the country. Yet I'm not sure it's so different from a decade ago. I will never forget the day when I learned that the secondary school in which I was teaching had come bottom of the School Performance Tables. That was more than ten years ago, but the publication last week of the latest league tables reminded me of the utter demoralisation I felt at the time.

It was my first year of teaching, and it was also in the early years of the league tables. There was an atmosphere of mild hysteria in the school, which was in a very poor area of the inner city. The Tory government of the time had been threatening to close down failing schools and our establishment seemed to be clearly at risk. Some of the staff were wandering around in a daze wondering if they were soon going to be out of a job.

Many of the teachers had no idea that the school was so bad at getting its pupils through their exams. Only three per cent of pupils had achieved five GCSE passes at A–C level. Quite a lot of the staff felt sad; it was as if they had lost their innocence. The smoky staffroom was a particularly bleak place on the morning that we received the news. The piles of exercise books strewn across the tables seemed to be accusing us of negligence, the mouldy coffee cups were symbols of our laziness, the slovenly atmosphere somehow suggested that we were reprobates.

Normally the staff were quite jokey, but no one was laughing that morning. Hunched over their stained coffee mugs, they were being forced to reflect that they were working in the school whose distinction was that it had been identified as the nadir of all educational establishments.

Some grew angry and outspoken, peppering their complaints about the government with expletives. Others wryly accepted their position. I remember particularly one young teacher, a football fan, who jokily punched his fist into his palm exclaiming, 'We're like Millwall, we're bottom, but we're hard!' The majority of the pupils were the children of immigrant families and few understood the significance of the statistics – their English was too poor – but the brighter ones certainly did.

'Does this mean we're a really bad school, sir?' I tried to reassure them that it didn't, but they weren't convinced because I couldn't convince myself. I left the school shortly after that and now, more than ten years later, having worked in a variety of other establishments, I have been able to put that dismal experience into a wider context. I realise that the statistics that put that school at the very bottom of the list gave a false impression.

Discipline, while not exemplary, was not terrible, and there were many hard-working teachers who achieved remarkable things with the pupils. However, the school's position in the league tables did have an effect. Within a couple of years of their publication the head was replaced by a new man who was much cannier about how to play the system.

He identified the potential high-flyers among the children – the ones who he felt could pass GNVQs (vocational qualifications that count for statistical purposes as GCSEs). He taught them himself and gave them special attention. He also took the cynical but, in the circumstances, entirely understandable decision that most of the pupils should study Bengali and take the GCSE in it.

There was a very high pass rate which improved the results enormously. It was hardly surprising: these kids were Bengali. The head's new measures produced the desired result: the school rose steadily in the league tables and last week it was named as one of the most improved in the country.

However, in January 2007, when the new, revised school league tables were published by the DfES, the school was back near the bottom again. This was because a school's position in the league table is now judged upon its English and maths scores at GCSE. My old school only scored 27 per cent A–C passes in English and maths. Effectively seven out of ten pupils are not very competent at the 3 Rs. This is not their fault: for most pupils English is their second language.

Although it's tough on the school, the new league tables give parents a more accurate impression of what is going on there. The intake is pretty much unchanged from when I taught there, many of the children don't speak English when they arrive, and there are still the same kinds of social problems.

But the term 'league table' is in itself misleading. It suggests transparency and simplicity in the process of assessing schools – as though measuring their performance were as simple as comparing football teams in the Premiership. This is far from true. Schools can be very clever at playing the statistics game; some head teachers know which qualifications will help send their school soaring up the tables.

They can insist that pupils take modular exams at GCSE which allow them to retake certain sections if they fail first time round. Even the 'value-added' scores can be misleading. These measure how much 'value' the school has added to the child's achievement. Every child arrives at a secondary school with a set of results from primary school, but these are notoriously inaccurate and can render the 'value-added' score worse than useless.

I've come across many teachers who have been goggle-eyed about the scores that some of the new intake of pupils achieved in their primary school. 'How on earth did she get top marks in her tests? She can't even write a sentence,' I heard one teacher groan, before adding, 'The "value-added" scores are going to make me look like a terrible teacher!'

I always advise parents not to take the league tables too seriously. Instead, I encourage them to read the Ofsted report. This usually, if not always, gives a fairly accurate picture of a school. Its terms are quite precise and if it has judged a school to be 'good' or 'outstanding', the school will be well worth considering.

The parents should visit the establishment several times and insist on looking in on lessons – even if the head teacher is reluctant (see below on this). They should ask about staff-pupil ratios and pass rates in English and maths, two vital indicators of performance. These provide a much sounder basis for choosing a school than the mad lottery of league tables.[3]

THE NEW SCHOOL RULES
for league tables

1. **Check out the English and maths scores** The most reliable scores to look at in the league tables are the English and maths scores. If a primary school is scoring below 50 per cent at Level 4 in English at Key Stage 2 (the tests taken by 10-year-olds) that means that less than half the pupils are reading and writing at the level expected for their age. This could spell trouble: it means there may be a critical mass of pupils who are really struggling with their literacy. In 2006, the DfES will publish the English and maths results at GCSE as a separate column: this is extremely useful information which will give you a good idea about how many pupils can read, write and are numerate in the school. If less than 50 per cent of pupils are attaining A–C grades in English and maths, then be concerned.

2. **Check out the A–C grades** With secondary schools most parents look at the percentage of pupils attaining five or more A*–C GCSE grades: this is known now as Level 2 data. Don't confuse this with Level 1 data, which is the number of pupils attaining five or more A*–G grades; it is very easy to get a G grade at GCSE and so this data is more or less worthless. Be cautious about trusting this grade because it may be the school has done well by getting their pupils to take vocational qualifications which are really much easier to get higher grades in because they are assessed entirely by coursework: this can be re-submitted up to three times. The best schools encourage their pupils to take 'difficult' GCSEs on top of English and maths: English literature, modern languages and sciences.

▶

3. **Check the number of SEN pupils** Look at the number of pupils with Special Education Needs on the table. This can tell you a lot! If there are a lot of SEN pupils this can mean that the school has many pupils who are struggling to cope with the work. If the school is scoring high results with a high percentage of SEN pupils, then it is probably a very good school.

4. **Get a long-term perspective** Look at the results of a school over a period of four or five years. Sometimes, schools can have had a fantastic year but be generally mediocre for most of the time. Casting your eye over the school's results for a number of years will probably give you the best idea as to the direction the school is heading, whether it is upward or downward, or static. Generally, results are rising year on year, so the best schools should be improving.

5. **Beware of dodgy statistics** Be wary of 'value-added scores' in the league tables. The ways of measuring value-added scores seem to change year on year; I am generally suspicious of them, as they often make the hair-raising schools look good compared with the nicer ones. Schools in areas of high social deprivation score very highly because many of the pupils enter from such a low benchmark, whereas schools in more prosperous areas struggle to have good value-added scores because their children have scored highly in the first tests. That said, it is worth taking them into account with the other statistics.

6. **Trawl the best websites** The most exhaustive website for explaining school league tables is the government website (www.dfes.gov.uk/performancetables/). However, the BBC website gives a good summary of the major issues and a breakdown of the crucial results: news.bbc.co.uk/1/hi/education/league_tables/default.stm.

Getting the most out of Ofsted

When my son was three, I started where most parents start, looking at the schools in my local area. I had looked at the league tables for all the schools in the area and saw that nearly seven out of ten pupils in the primary schools attained the expected levels in English and maths when they were 11: a Level 4. This wasn't bad. However, as I have explained, I am a little distrustful of the league tables: I needed to know more, much more.

I looked at the brochures for the different schools: pupils in sunlit playgrounds smiled up at me, classrooms blazed with beautiful displays, teachers were full of enthusiasm, parents gathered happily at the school gates. I read through the list of schools that he could go to and felt sick. I had no idea which one to send him to. I had to write down three schools in rank order on the form. Oh my God, what was I going to do?

What should I be looking for in a school? I was an experienced teacher and I did not know. I knew it meant quite a bit of work on my behalf. I took a deep breath and started my research.

First, I talked to Erica about what kind of school we wanted for James. Luckily, we both agreed on the sort of school we were looking for: many couples don't. We wanted a local, mixed-sex school if possible, but we also wanted an academic school that could offer music and drama lessons. We thought it would be great if he could study a modern foreign language, such as French, before secondary school.

We realised that the state was unlikely to be able to offer what we wanted, but before we looked at the private sector, I felt it was worth checking out state provision in our area properly.

I looked at the Ofsted reports (www.ofsted.gov.uk) of my favoured schools, seeing which ones were judged to be Grade 1: outstanding, Grade 2: good, Grade 3: satisfactory, Grade 4: inadequate. I was a little confused because my primary schools were not judged on the scale laid out on the Ofsted website, and instead were judged on a slightly different scale which ranged from outstanding, very good, good, satisfactory and not satisfactory. It became clear from checking the date of the reports that these were old reports from a time when Ofsted graded schools differently.

One of our local schools was judged to be very good. The report stressed that the school was very good at teaching English and maths, and although it took pupils who were well below the national average when they entered the school, it raised their game sufficiently so that they were broadly in line with the national average when they left the school. It also judged the school to have very good discipline and behaviour.

However, the school that we were most likely to be allocated, as it was directly in our catchment area, was judged to be good. It was less mixed than my favoured school: that school had 75 per cent of pupils from ethic minorities, this school had an astonishing 97 per cent from Muslim backgrounds. Also, Ofsted had judged the reception classes there to be unsatisfactory, which was not good. Both schools had problems with the recruitment of staff. They did not offer music lessons per se, but my favoured school did a lot of extracurricular activities based around drama, music and art. The others did not.

I checked the value-added figures for the core subjects. These were the figures that said how much value had been added to a child by the school, how good the school was at improving the child's academic abilities over and above what was expected of them. My favoured school did very well on this, scoring A grades in English and maths: that meant that compared with other schools in the country it was doing very well in the value it was adding to the pupils as they went through the school. However, my most local school scored D grades, revealing it to be unsatisfactory. This was worrying, although it had been judged to be a good school. It was clearly not doing as well as the school just down the road.

Overall, the Ofsted reports were difficult to read and decipher, even for me. They were very long, amounting to 50 pages of single-spaced type. I navigated my way around them by focusing upon the key points: whether the school was judged to be an outstanding or good school, the levels attained in English and maths compared with the rest of the country, the levels of discipline, and the turnover of staff – which all the schools had issues with according to the Ofsted reports.

Having read the Ofsted reports, I knew what position the schools were in the league tables, but I glanced at the tables too (www.dfes.gov.uk/performancetables/).

I read the schools' Key Stage 2 results with some care and saw that my favoured school, considering its intake, was teaching English and maths to a high standard. In the final tests marked externally, over 85 per cent of pupils achieved a Level 4 or above, which meant the majority of the school was attaining the national average in English and maths. My other two schools results were not as good, and the value-added data suggested that compared with other schools they weren't doing that well at all.

My top school was judged to be very good, and my other two were judged to be good. Unfortunately, I knew for a number of reasons that if James didn't get into my top school, I wouldn't be happy. Good was not good enough for me. Having looked closely at the reports and data, I realised that for a number of reasons the other two schools were not up to scratch. As a white, middle-class student, James would be in a minority in all the schools, but in the two less-favoured schools, he would probably be the only white boy in the class. He would also not be paid much attention to – because the reports had noted that high attainers, which he would be simply because English was his first language, were not catered for very well by a staff devoted to bringing on those who had English As An Additional Language. Added to which, the lack of extracurricular activities would make for a rather dull experience in my view.

Nevertheless, having double-checked all this data, I felt I had a definite top three schools to put down on the LEA form. As I filled in the forms I wondered: did all parents endure this sort of rigmarole? My wife and I had spent the best part of two weekends getting to our top three – and we hadn't even visited the schools yet.

The Ofsted report on a school is definitely the most useful document you will read about a school. The reports are wonderfully accessible now. All you do is go to the website (www.ofsted.

gov.uk), type in your postcode and bingo, the reports on your local schools will arrive. This is particularly useful for another reason because it will tell you which school is nearest in your catchment area.

THE NEW SCHOOL RULES
for Ofsted reports

1. **Beware of out-of-date information** Check the date of the report. Schools change very quickly and if the Ofsted report is more than two years old, it may not be reliable.

2. **Check out the overall effectiveness of the school** Look very carefully at the section on the overall effectiveness of the school. A sentence will summarise this and go on to make a judgement about the teaching and learning, the curriculum, the behaviour of the pupils, the progress and achievement, the way it cares for its pupils and their safety, the quality of the head teacher and the senior management team, and the social and personal development of the pupils. The report will tell you if there are any areas of weakness. Alarm bells should ring if it highlights a core subject like English, maths or science as being 'inadequate'.

3. **Make sure you understand the grading systems** It is important to realise that the inspectors arrive at their grades from 1 to 4 by looking at a number of different aspects of the school, such as the achievement and standards, the quality of the teaching and learning, the curriculum and other activities, the leadership and management, the health and safety issues of a school, and the contribution of the pupils. Then, taking all these different components into account, they arrive at their overall judgement. The problem with this is that a school

▶

may be great on health, curriculum, and contribution of the pupils, but have poor discipline; they may still attain a good grading because of all the things they are doing right. Unfortunately, though, if you want a school with good discipline first and foremost you may feel the report is misleading unless you read it very carefully.

4. **Beware special measures** Think twice about sending your child to a school which is in 'special measures': this means the school has serious failings and the inspectorate is considering closing it down. This is an institution which is 'failing or likely to fail to give its pupils an acceptable standard of education' (School Inspections' Act 1996). This information will be clearly stated in the sentence on the overall effectiveness of the school. Be equally wary of a school which is judged to have 'serious weaknesses'. If at any point in the report you see this phrase, look at what the inspectors mean very carefully.

5. **Beware dodgy statistics** In particular, be cautious about leaping to agree with inspection reports which have criticised a school for achieving badly on the PANDA (Performance and Assessment Data) or for having poor CVA (Context-Value-Added). The PANDA purports to tell you how a particular school compares with schools with similar intakes, giving the school an overall grade and the different subjects grades as well; A is the best grade and E the bottom. The CVA is similar in that it attempts to take into account the social background of the pupils and see whether the school has added 'value' to them; in other words has the school helped its pupils achieve better results than could be expected? Sometimes the figures are quite accurate, but sometimes they are not. There have been a number of high-profile cases recently where schools which have had nothing but great inspection reports have been judged to be failing

▶

because of these statistics. These statistics are all about measuring how much a school adds to a pupil's performance in exams compared with how they achieved in previous exams, while taking into account the social background of the school as a whole. Schools which have a lot of children from prosperous backgrounds can do very badly even though they get good results, while schools where the pupils and the results are poor can do very well. Frequently, secondary schools opt to do 'vocational' qualifications to boost their PANDA and CVA. You will need to look carefully at the rest of the report to get an idea as to whether this is happening.

6. **Beware of political correctness** Look at the key points and bear in mind Ofsted can be too either kind or too harsh. Remember, inspectors look at a whole range of factors before coming up with their overall judgement as to whether a school is good or satisfactory or failing. It may be that the school has scored very highly in categories you don't value: it's been found to be very good at catering for SEN pupils, for example. However, it may have been not so good at disciplining the children. It may be that the school has an overall good report because of its ability to meet criteria you think are not important. Inspectors often have their own politically correct agenda and if a good school has not provided the pupils with enough experience of 'other cultures' or is not 'inclusive' enough, they can be very critical. Similarly, if a school has been wonderfully politically correct, it can get away with a good report – but it may be a hotbed of poor behaviour and indiscipline. My instinct is to look at the judgements on the behaviour and safety of the pupils with real care.

7. **Squeeze the juice out of the report** Scan the report for vital pieces of information. What is the staff recruitment

▶

situation like? What are the definite extras of the school? Does it offer instrument lessons by trained specialists? Does it have specialists teaching maths and science? Look at how the quality of teaching and learning is rated, the ability of the school to cater for pupils with special needs, and most crucially, the comments on the behaviour of the pupils. If the report says that there is quite a bit of 'low-level disruption' in the school, then alarm bells should be ringing. This means that lessons are often disrupted and spoilt by pupils chatting, calling out, and annoying each other. Look at Ofsted's description of the school: this is very interesting and informative. It will give you an idea of the social background of the pupils, the numbers on free school meals and so on.

8. **Beware self-assessment** Be a little wary of schools assessing themselves. The latest fad of inspectors is the School Improvement Plan (SIP) and Self-Evaluation Form (SEF). In the new regime of Ofsted reports, schools have been asked to assess themselves. Common sense tells you that these forms are not going to be entirely reliable: schools will always try to present themselves in the best possible light.

9. **Look at the pupils' opinions of the school** Ofsted have a new emphasis on asking pupils for their views of the school. There appears to be no particular methodology to this, but the inspectors are able to question many more pupils than you are on a quick whip round the school so it is worth seeing what the pupils say about the school in the report.

10. **Read Ofsted's letters to the pupils** Do look at the letters that Ofsted write to the children of the school after their report; these can very informative and put into simple, clear language what the inspectors really think.

School profile – propaganda or useful information?

Many Ofsted reports can be out of date within a very short space of time, so it is worthwhile looking at the school profile. This is an annual report for parents written by schools themselves which contains information on their successes, details of extracurricular activities, health and safety information, their response to the latest Ofsted report. They can be read online at schoolsfinder.direct.gov.uk/.

Whereas much of each report may well be self-congratulatory puffery, there are some interesting points to look for. In particular, see what the school says about its successes, the progress its pupils make from 11 to 16 compared with other schools, and the activities available to pupils.

Much of this information will be available on the school's website or in its brochure, but the school may be a little more honest and up to date in the school profile since it is a 'government-approved' document which has to be produced every year. You will need to read all of these documents with a somewhat sceptical eye but obviously if a school presents itself well to you, it may well be presenting itself well to the pupils, which is always a good sign. Half the battle in a school is to convince its pupils that it's a great place to be and it is a success once it has passed on this message.

However, sometimes a school can create a 'cover-up culture' if it is not honest with its parents. If the school suggests there are loads of extracurricular activities going on when, in fact, there are comparatively few, if a school makes out that it is a very well-disciplined place with no bullying when, in fact, yobbery is rife, then the brochure, the school profile and the website are no more than false propaganda. It is very difficult to know what the truth is in this situation other than talking to parents who have children at the school, and the pupils themselves – see what I have called the DEATH analysis for more on this.

A parent who was duped by the bumpf – and one who was not

Anna, who lives in a small town in Yorkshire, was in a state of real distress. She'd obviously been crying. Her voice cracked with emotion as she told me:

> But it looked like such a wonderful school. I really did my best to send my daughter, Lillian, to what I thought was a lovely Church of England primary. The brochure said it was a very welcoming, caring place, the website looks amazing! It's full of lovely colours and pictures the children had done. It said that standards of discipline were very high. It was for that reason that I didn't send Lillian to the local primary and went to church every Sunday – even though I am not that religious.
>
> But the school isn't like what it says it is at all. Lillian has been bullied quite badly by several other girls in the class. The school said in the brochure that it was caring, but when I talked to the head teacher about it, she said it was Lillian's problem and that there was no bullying in the school. I've found out that a lot of the time, Lillian is bored stiff in class. All she does is copying or practise SATS papers. She seems to have a different teacher every day. She hates going there. I have to almost drag her into school. I am losing sleep over what to do.

Anna had been suckered in by the bumpf the school produced but hadn't read the school's Ofsted report recently which had graded the school as 'adequate' with some 'serious weaknesses' in English and maths. None of this was mentioned in the brochure, of course, and had been quickly glossed over as an area for improvement in the annual report to governors – this was in the days before the school profile. If she had read the Ofsted reports carefully then she would have probably realised that it was best to send Lillian to her local primary which did not have these weaknesses. However, she'd been overly influenced by some unfounded gossip about her local primary and opted for the Church of England school instead. Anna admitted to me:

> I wish I had never listened to those other parents. They moaned about our local primary over what I now know are trivial things such as it not having a proper Christmas Fayre and looking a bit scruffy, but if I had looked beyond the surface things, I would have seen that it was a nice school. I was dazzled by the displays and website of the other school, and didn't look under the surface.

In the same town, I spoke to Louisa who had sent her son to the local primary which Anna had rejected.

> I know it looks a bit shabby and its website isn't up to much, but I spoke to quite a few of the pupils there and they seemed really happy. And I also talked to their parents a lot. They did have their moans and groans but they weren't huge ones. They told me that there were three really good teachers there who genuinely liked children and were very good at teaching the 3 Rs. They were old-fashioned teachers who didn't know much about websites and technology, but they did the business and, for me, that's what counted. I also saw that in the Ofsted report, the teaching and learning was graded as 'good' so I decided to ignore all the complaints about the school and send my son there. It proved to be exactly the right decision. It is a lovely school and it has really brought my son on.

Most crucially, Louisa saw that the local primary school focused on the basics and ignored all the trendy stuff that can get in the way of good teaching. She ignored the school's somewhat scruffy appearance and trusted the judgement of other parents (and the Ofsted report) about the quality of teaching.

How parents choose their primary schools

When I started interviewing parents throughout the country about deciding what primary school to send their children to, I found a big variation between London and the rest of England. By and large, most parents outside of London send their children to their nearest state primary and there aren't huge rows about it.

I felt very envious of the parents I interviewed in Northumberland. In Embleton, an idyllic, ancient village on the Northumbrian coast, all the young children in the village went to the beautifully tended village primary school. Many of the parents there explained to me that it was simply what everyone did. There wasn't any choice about the matter: they were in the catchment area for the school and that's where their children went. They didn't have a list of nearly 20 possible primaries to choose from as I did in my London borough. They were not bamboozled by choice. Every parent I spoke to was very happy about the school. They told me that they had glanced at the league tables and were pleased about the school's good results, but more than this, they loved what I would term the 'accessibility' of the school.

'You can just drop in there and talk to the teachers if you like. I knew one of them before I sent my daughter there, and I know a lot of parents who send their children there,' one parent told me. 'It's a small village so everyone knows everyone and the school is at the heart of the community really. We have jumble sales and fêtes, and everyone gets a good look at it well before they send their children there. I was very happy to send my daughter there.'

Where there were choices conflict could arise. In Ebbw Vale, Wales, Dylan, a local youth worker, told me about how he had become entangled in a row with his fiancée's family about where to send his daughter. He said:

I grew up in this area, you see. When I was a little boy, I went to Beaufort Primary School. My mother got really involved with the school and became a dinner lady there. She loves it and wouldn't have wanted me to go anywhere else. It is part of the family if you like. There was a real problem then when my fiancée insisted that we sent my daughter, Lily, to Willow Tree, the other local primary school. My fiancée's reasoning was that it was where Lily knew some friends from nursery. This led to a dispute between me and my fiancée about what would be best for Lily. I felt that because my mum was at Beaufort she would be able to keep an eye on her and she would settle in quickly. My fiancée won and she went to Willow Tree. There is still some resentment about it though.

Most of the parents I interviewed in the south-west, in the Chippenham and Bristol area, seemed fairly unfazed about the admissions process to primary schools, usually opting for their local primary school, unless they were religious, and following the recommendations of other parents. Likewise, even in Leeds, which has huge issues about secondary school admissions, primary admissions seemed straightforward: parents appeared happy about sending their children to the local primary.

Atmosphere and distance – two parents' stories

However, all the major cities in England have issues about admissions because there are many choices and various social issues, which cause parents huge anxieties. My overwhelming impression was that it wasn't so much the Ofsted reports, the league tables, the value-added scores that were at the back of parents' minds when they visited a prospective primary school but the general atmosphere of the place. Peta Pryor's story illustrates this point.

6 We live on a council estate which is close to ten schools. When my daughter, Phoebe, was three we began to look for primary schools. One of the top state primary schools is on our doorstep, in addition to a very nice prep school. At the time Phoebe went to an excellent, if small, playgroup for local residents. Most people who

lived on our council estate did not send their children to the play-group because it was too 'posh'.

I had looked at a couple of other nurseries and I was horrified. In some I disliked the language, effing and blinding by both staff and pupils. Others were oversized with too few staff to provide individual attention to the toddlers. They were not caring for the pupils. These state primaries could not bring out the abilities and interests of the children.

We started at the playgroup by taking Phoebe to a drop-in toddler group. That was where it truly dawned on me that there was a peck-ing order in education. I grew up abroad and had no real notion of the complexities of the English education system. I went to a prep school in England until the age of eight, but then moved overseas, where having passed my eleven-plus I was sent to a strict, high-achieving Irish convent grammar school.

Parents who were at the playgroup took their children to musical groups. It astonished me to see three-year-olds banging drums and dancing to nursery rhymes. It felt liberating and I thought it was lovely, and it reminded me of my childhood, which was very happy. These parents were also interested in reading to their young children as well as helping them to write and paint and explore the world.

The education in that playgroup was gentle and encouraging of all abilities. It was a very mixed group of children: Guyanese, Danish, Dutch, English, and American children freely mixed and got on with each other. Phoebe went there until she was five and she flourished. The teachers taught her to read without pushing her, but always encouraging her to do her best. She achieved some remarkable things before she was even five.

We found our primary school while walking around just outside our area one afternoon, and liked the look of the building, with its red brick walls and spacious rooms – the building is listed. We applied to get her in when she was four. It is a Church of England primary and as we are regular local churchgoers, there was no problem about getting her in there.

The primary school at that time was a very mixed, with many chil-dren having English As An Additional Language going to the school.

However, I felt that the whole ethos of the school was supportive and felt sure that Phoebe wouldn't feel out of place there. I believed that there she would develop the ability to mix with everyone socially. I also promoted the primary school with the playgroup. I heard some stories about the local prep school which expected children to be very well behaved and study hard at a very early age. They were doing rote learning and timetables at four years old and I didn't feel this would be right for us. Anyway we didn't have the money for one child to attend prep school, let alone two. **9**

Peta's story is typical of so many parents because she made judgements about the primary school she chose for her daughter not on the school's position in the league tables, but on its 'atmosphere' – which appeared to include its architecture, the demeanour of the children and the supportiveness of the staff. It was the atmosphere of the other schools that put her off in various degrees: the stifling, 'hot-house' atmosphere of the prep school, and the coarse, yobbish atmosphere of the state-run nurseries. Her decision to choose the primary school was a combination of observation and intuition. She appeared less concerned about the issue of 'distance' which is, in essence, the main criteria most parents have for choosing their schools.

In a recent survey conducted by the *Daily Telegraph*, nearly three-quarters of parents wanted to send their child to a local school which was within walking distance of their house.

Pierre's story best illustrates this point. He told me:

6 When my child Peter was three years old, my wife and I started to investigate where to send him to school in England. We knew nothing about the system, having been educated in New York and France respectively. I thought you went up the road to the nearest place and that was it. How wrong I was! When I was a kid my mother just marched me to the local school and that was it.

We had just moved to the country and we started to try to find out what was going on. I didn't differentiate between what were public or private funded schools. I started with the school that was closest to the house – it was in our street. I was put off at first because it was in a Victorian house and didn't appear to be like a school at all. It was like going into someone's home. I mean, it was a nice house and so on, but it hardly felt right to be a school. But as I looked at more schools, I found that this was the norm for private schools and I went back to that first school.

So Peter went to this Montessori training school in our street. He liked it there for the first year, but then Peter's favourite teacher left, and he started to seem unhappy. The teacher that replaced Peter's favourite was not a good person and actually dislocated Peter's elbow after jerking it very hard. Peter was a very straight kid and not disruptive. We were very pissed off. We had to take him to the Royal Free Hospital after the school sent him home.

After that, we started to look for an alternative. We chose this small privately run prep school not because of snobbery about our local state school but purely for reasons of distance. It was the closest school to our house, only a few doors away. I did visit a state primary on an avenue a few blocks away. It was not that far away but they said to me that they were totally full and that Peter would have to go to another state school much further away, which was very inconvenient. Another state school, which was a little closer, was fully booked. **9**

In contrast to Peta Pryor, who was a regular churchgoer and so got into the state school of her choice easily, Pierre's experience of being turned away by two state schools is typical of parents living in areas where there is real competition for state school places. Fortunately, he was able to afford to pay for his child to go to a local private school, but if he hadn't been able to he would have had to send Peter to a school a long distance from his home. Having been educated for the most part in France, Pierre was naturally suspicious of private schools. He told me that in France, it is only the no-hopers who go private. He had, of course, been outraged at the dislocation of Peter's arm at the private Montessori school. However, because it was the nearest local school, he opted for the private prep school.

THE NEW SCHOOL RULES

for choosing a primary school

1. **Be cautious** Do trust your intuitions about a school, but don't solely rely on them. If the evidence from an inspector's report or your own further investigations show that the school is not that good, your intuition may have been wrong. Peta was lulled into a false sense of security about her daughter's primary school and her daughter's education suffered as a result.

2. **Expect the unexpected** Don't expect that you will be allocated the nearest state school as Pierre had initially trusted would be the case; if you don't meet the admissions criteria or it is full, you will not be let in.

3. **Use DEATH to help you** Learn how to do what I call a DEATH analysis on a school – see pages 59–76 on exactly what this is and how you should do this.

Listening to other parents

As I had experienced with Niall, talking to other parents about schools was a fevered topic. Most conversations were focused around the discussion of local catchment areas. Where was the right place to move to? One mother confessed to me that she felt irresponsible giving birth in such a rough area because it meant that if she didn't move fast, her child might be consigned to a hellish school. Rumours abound that many head teachers have been offered bribes in order to give a child a place at a school,[4] whereas others have been threatened. I found absolutely no evidence for this when I interviewed a number of head teachers. However, I have spoken to parents who claim friends and acquaintances of theirs have lied about their addresses, using friends' and relatives' addresses as their place of residence on the admissions form. Such accusations are very difficult to prove: not surprisingly no one is willing to admit to such behaviour. I certainly know at first hand of a couple of cases where this has happened.

What is certainly true is that these allegations and manoeuvrings only fuel the anxiety that many parents feel about getting their child into the right school. They get into a panic about the whole process, and it appears that normally law-abiding citizens are willing to go to any lengths in order to get their child into the school of their choice.

Amidst this furore, it is best to keep a cool head. Nevertheless, asking other parents about schools is important. But be warned. Parents are not that reliable. Be prepared for the fact that many will be very loyal to the school even if it is a bad one. However, if you put them at their ease, they may be more prepared to be honest with you.

When trying to find out about a school you're interested in, talking to parents who have children at the school can be helpful. Start by asking the obvious questions about the school such as, 'Is your child happy there? What's great about it? What does your child like best about it? What are you most pleased with?'

But once you've got a parent talking in general terms about a school, you can start to ask nitty-gritty questions which may be far more revealing. Ask about how good the school is at communicating with parents. Do they know who to call if there is a problem? What does the school do about bullying? What does the school do if a child is struggling with the work or is finding it too easy? Do they know anything about the practical stuff such as uniform, homework, school dinners, the state of the toilets, the access to phones and drinking water, holidays, assemblies, what is taught in lessons, the rewards and punishments, letters home and news-sheets, turnover of staff?

Once a parent doesn't feel defensive about the school, you can then subtly slide in more challenging questions such as, 'Have you had any problems? Or what's been the biggest let-down?'

THE NEW SCHOOL RULE

for listening to other parents

Don't trust the gossip Listen to what other parents have to say about the schools, and take their views on board, but don't trust blanket opinions such as the school is 'crap' or 'amazing'. Instead try to ask about the practical stuff: about bullying and discipline policies, how the school communicates with parents, what is taught in lessons, the school dinners, the state of the toilets! Remember, when it comes to trying to get a child into a good school, many parents do have ulterior motives but the majority of them do not bribe head teachers or lie about their addresses. Don't become paranoid that your child will fail to get a place at a school because of the machinations of other parents.

Visiting schools

I phoned the schools and made appointments with the secretarial staff for my wife and I to see them and the head teachers over the coming weeks. One of the schools tried to insist that we came on the Open Day – when none of the children would be in school – but I held firm. I knew that it was vital that we saw the school in action, with the pupils fidgeting at their desks and the teachers perspiring by the whiteboards. It was only then that I would find out what the school was really like.

But I knew this was going to be the most nerve-wracking experience of all. It was all very well sitting in the safety of my study, trawling through the Ofsted reports and data, but talking to the staff face to face was a different matter altogether. Even for me, having taught for so many years, there is something intimidating about school.

On my first visit, I had come doubly prepared, having read *The Good Schools Guide* and sifted through their questions to ask about schools, nearly 50 of them. Yet, when I walked through the school gates, a strange thing happened to me. I froze. I felt ashamed to bring out my long list of questions to ask.

In all the schools, it was the head teacher who showed us around. Generally, the head teacher was treated with respect, but in one school, a couple of pupils notably forgot to hold open doors for him, it was almost as though he was invisible. Moreover, he seemed uncomfortable with being around the children. His study was set well away from the rest of the school, and I sensed that he didn't get out much except for the parents and inspectors. At the other two schools, the head teachers were treated with much more familiarity and respect: doors were held open for them, they were greeted as they entered the classroom, the teachers seemed comfortable around them but also anxious to please them.

This is something to look for: a leader who commands an easy respect from both pupils and staff, doesn't seem anxious moving around the school, who knows the pupils by name and has a bearing that suggests someone who enjoys her job.

At my most-favoured school, the head teacher was quite happy for us to look at the pupils' exercise books in a number of classes, but we were quickly directed away from this in the other two schools. It felt like we were prying where we shouldn't be.

The two schools with poorer results were noticeably less keen on putting pupils' work on the walls. There was some but it looked perfectly manicured. However, the best school had loads of display work completed by the children, and it appeared that it was going up and coming down all the time. This is an important clue about what a school is like: if the display work looks like it was been there for years or had been manufactured, then it tells you that the school is not that confident about the pupils' achievements.

All the schools we saw were having new ICT resources put in, but as yet, there weren't many computers for the pupils to work on. This didn't bother Erica and I since we are fairly old-fashioned: pen and paper will do fine. As long as they learn to read and write, everything else follows.

But the classes were big. There were usually 28 in a class; sometimes there was a support teacher but usually not. Each school had a very clear special needs policy which meant that if a child was struggling, he or she would be given extra help. There was also some funding for gifted and talented pupils, thanks to which they could go on extra courses run by the borough.

I asked about the exclusion rate in all the schools. None of them had significant problems. All the schools appeared to be well-disciplined places. However, one of the head teachers was prickly about the issue. She told us that we should expect our child to be sworn at because 'We take children from very deprived backgrounds here and I do get some middle-class parents complaining about what I term "banter". But I always tell them that this is what they can expect.'

That put me in my place. The implication was that it was 'classist' to complain about swearing.

At first, when we were being given the guided tour, I didn't have the nerve to ask for the rates of staff absence and turnover – something I know as a teacher is a key indicator of how well a school is doing. It felt like a cheeky question. After all, there is the feeling in the state sector that teachers are doing you a favour by educating your kid for free – or so it felt as we were being shown around.

But as we finished our tour, I questioned the head teachers about staff absence and turnover. They blinked. They were surprised by the question. The head teacher of the most successful school was able to say that not many teachers left the school, and that very few called in sick. However, I knew from reading the Ofsted report that this was a disingenuous answer. 'But your last Ofsted said you have a problem with temporary staff,' I said.

She sighed. 'Yes, we do. It is a problem throughout the whole of London. Teachers move on very quickly, and you have to get agency staff to fill in their places, and sometimes they can be less than perfect. But we do have schemes of work that they must follow and I keep a close eye on them,' she said.

But the other two were cagey. One school refused to give me the figures, and the other one promised to send me the figures but didn't. Going though the Ofsted reports again, I subsequently found out that there had been significant problems with recruitment across all the years in the school.

Using DEATH to help you in the school jungle

My experiences as a teacher in state schools for the past 15 years, my visits to possible schools and my interviews with head teachers, experts, parents and pupils have helped crystallise into one short, sharp acronym what I think any parent should be looking for in any prospective school, be it primary or secondary, private or state.

You need to use DEATH to help you!

● **D** stands for Discussion, Discipline and Display

● **E** stands for Ethos, Evaluation and Extracurricular Activities

● **A** stands for Assets and Achievement

● **T** stands for Target Setting and Turning Up

● **H** stands for Head Teacher

Let's explain each letter in more detail:

Discussion

This is the most important aspect of your research. Just in the same way that the best plumbers and electricians you'll ever find are the ones who come with good 'word of mouth', the best schools have great 'word of mouth'. Talk to as many parents and pupils as you can and try to get a balanced point of view. We've already seen what questions you might ask other parents (see pages 54–56, Listening to Other Parents), but, if you can, talk to pupils in the school. Apart from the obvious questions about what they like at the school, ask them about what level they are attaining in the main subjects (English, maths and science) and see if they know what they have to do to improve. If they don't know what level they are attaining (from the age of seven all pupils should know the National Curriculum level they are working at) and they don't know what they need to do to improve, this could show you that the school is not giving them a clear idea about how to do better. Try to talk to a cross section of pupils if you can – the open evening can be a good time for this when you are shown around a school. Ask if pupils who work hard are seen as 'boffs' or 'swots' and are ridiculed as a result (see Ethos below).

Discipline

The first and most important question you can ask the staff at a prospective school is: 'Would you send your child here?' The senior management of the school – the head, the deputies, the assistant heads – may not give you a straight answer: after all, they are committed to promoting the school, but the way they reply will tell you a lot. If they immediately say with a smile on their face that they would definitely send their child to the school – or even better tell you that their children are at, or have gone to, the school – then you probably know you are on to a winner. However, if they are hesitant or doubtful in their appro-bation of the school, you may have reason to question them further. Ask them, 'Why would you like your child to go to the school?' Find out whether they are being hesitant because that is just their way or because there are problems with the school.

The best staff to ask this question are the ones who don't have such a stake in the school but look like ordinary people. Try to see if you can spot a moderately junior member of staff who looks like they could be a parent, and see what they say when you ask them the question. Reassure them that you're not going to tell the head if they answer truthfully, just say you want to know the truth about the school. They may well be hesitant, but if you talk a little bit about your child and what he or she is like, that member of staff may well open up. If they tell you that they'd be happy about their child going to the school, you can bet your last Tesco voucher-for-schools that the discipline in the school is pretty good. You see, this is what most teachers are concerned about: they know that if the classes are safe and orderly then most supported children will do OK. If you manage to engage a teacher in a longer conversation, go on to ask about what the children are like, and if you're really friendly, the quality and the commitment of the staff.

If you can, visit the school while it is in session and see what the classes are like. Are pupils getting on with the work purposefully? Are teachers shouting too much – or ignoring misbehaviour to the class's detriment?

Ask a pupil and teacher about what you do if you know your child is being bullied at the school. Every pupil at a good school will know immediately who to report bullying to, and will know what the consequences of it will be.

A well-disciplined school will have a very clear discipline policy, or code of conduct that may well be put up all around the school. The pupils should be aware of the consequences of certain actions and know that they will be followed through if they misbehave. Talk to the pupils about this and ask them what happens if they misbehave. If the pupils are vague about the issue then you know that there is no clear policy. If they know exactly what will happen, then you've got a well-managed school. Don't be alarmed if there is an 'On-Call' system, which can be great if it works! This is where pupils who are misbehaving in class are sent out to be babysat by a senior member of staff. Some 'On-Call' systems don't work at all because the pupils and teachers never know where the senior staff are: a complicated timetable is published whereby the on-call staff are located in different rooms during the school day. A good 'On-Call' system has a central location, and there are consequences for being sent 'On-Call' – such as a detention or letter home. I have seen some very rough schools become great places of learning because the head teacher has instituted a proper 'On-Call' system.

Unfortunately, far too few schools in the country are well managed like this, even the ones with good reputations. If you think the discipline policy in your school looks vague and unclear, bear in mind that it will be unclear to the pupils – and there may well be mayhem as a result. I have been attacked by many teachers and educationalists for highlighting the shoddy discipline in many of our schools. For me, it is a national scandal and much of it is due to poor management where teachers are left to fight their battles alone in the classrooms without any support from senior management. A cover-up mentality then occurs whereby teachers are attacked for highlighting poor behaviour and so end up not reporting it. However, don't be deceived. It is a major problem. In a recent survey by Teachers' TV, 66 per cent of teachers felt there was a discipline crisis in our schools.

Display

You can actually tell an awful lot about a school from the different displays that are put up around the school. First – the worst form of display – graffiti may well be your first clue that the discipline in the school isn't great. Have a look in the children's toilets: the general atmosphere of them will tell you a lot about how the school cares for the pupils. If they are scrawled with graffiti, obviously this is a bad sign. If the desks are scarred with it, if the walls are scrawled in gang tags and abuse, then obviously you know you've got trouble. Meanwhile, a school that values the pupils will have displays posted around the classroom and in the corridors. They won't be manicured or perfect, but they will be recently completed and not curling at the edges. They won't be finished by the teacher and there won't be lots of mass-produced posters; the overwhelming emphasis should be on what the pupils are learning.

Ethos

This relates to the previous point about discipline but it cannot be stressed enough that this is the crucial area to look for in a school. Does this school have an ethos where children can get on with the work if they want to? The school will have a mission statement, but how many of the pupils know the mission statement or understand what it means? Is there an ethos where children won't be ridiculed or bullied for working hard, for handing their homework in on time?

Evaluation

First, as we have seen, look at Ofsted's evaluation of the school and then look at the way the school evaluates the pupils. Look at the pupils' books: are they being marked regularly and in a clear, understandable way? Watch out for: generalised comments such as 'good', 'satisfactory', 'add more detail'; marking which is very difficult to read; merely ticks and crosses; comments that are far too long; comments that have no suggestions for improvement. Teachers should be providing written evaluation of how good a piece of work is by providing precise comments on what they like about it, and then suggesting something to work on in the future.

Extracurricular activities

Most good schools offer more than the curriculum. The best schools have thriving drama, music, sports and arts clubs going on during lunchtime and after school. However, it is important to ask whether the school's attitude to such activities is just tokenism. The best test is their attitude towards music and dance. Do the pupils learn to read music and scales, learn the classical ballet repertoire and so forth, and does the school provide optional external examinations such as the Trinity Board exams and Royal Academy of Dance/Drama awards? It is also worth asking what gifted and talented courses are on offer, either by the school or within the borough, and how easy it is for children to attend them. These are courses which aim to stretch the best pupils, giving them knowledge beyond the everyday curriculum. Perhaps most importantly, you need to ask how much the after-school clubs cost and who gets to decide who attends which club.

Assets

A school's greatest asset is its pupils. As we will see, there is a direct link between social class and the academic achievement of a school. The wealthier, the more prosperous the parents, the better the results are on the whole. However, perhaps the best schools are ones where there is a genuine social mix, where middle-class pupils mingle with working-class pupils, where black sit next to white, where Muslim pupils listen to assemblies with Christians.

Unfortunately, these sorts of schools have never really existed and the few that did are rapidly disappearing as the system becomes ever more fractured. Parents are either moving into areas where they can get their child into a school with a 'socially advantaged' intake or using various dodges with admissions to get their child into such a school, leaving the children of parents who don't care or are not wised up to go to sink schools. It's ghettoisation on a massive scale.

Next, after the pupil intake is the staff. Most importantly, are there trained specialists teaching the core subjects of English, maths and science? Watch out for schools that are cutting back on specialist staff by introducing new subjects like media, technology, 'life skills' and citizenship. If 'catch-all' subjects like humanities are scheduled in the timetable, it may mean there are no specialist geography, history or religious education teachers to teach the separate disciplines. Look at the subjects that are compulsory at GCSE. Many schools are now making modern languages optional because they don't have the staff to fill the posts.

After 2008, all secondary schools will have to offer vocational GCSEs. Even if your child is 11, you will need to think hard about his possible career path. Do you want him to study more 'modern' and vocational subjects like business studies, media studies and health and social care, or do you want her to be doing more academic subjects? This could seriously affect your choice of school. Some schools are very geared up for the new vocational qualifications; others are definitely much more academic. Make sure that you ask about the provision for vocational education, because it may be that your child will be railroaded into doing vocational qualifications at Key Stage 4 – when they are 14 – because the school has invested so much money in instituting these new qualifications.

It is important that you are not too snobbish about vocational subjects. One parent, Chris Fettes, told me:

> In my day if we were very academic you wouldn't have dreamt of being an entrepreneur but my most academic daughter actually didn't go university. She's got this risk-taking mentality which she picked up at school through Young Enterprise and doing vocational subjects. She has got an agency which has helped her to sell jewellery on the Internet.

Other hugely important assets: it is vital to find out where the money is being spent. The school profile (schoolsfinder.direct. gov.uk/) might give you an idea of the school's overall funding and how its money is spent, but don't bet on it: it's actually very difficult to know the precise details of funding, but it's worth asking the head teacher how much of the budget is spent on books.

A good school will allocate a lot of funds for books. Don't get too distracted by all the computers and interactive whiteboards on show, all the evidence reveals that the best lessons are still those where pupils have good, old-fashioned textbooks in front of them. Computers are too often an excuse for pupils to footle around on the Internet and play games while the teacher isn't looking, but books keep them on task. Believe me, I know as a teacher myself. Is your school heaving and bulging at the seams with freshly minted, up-to-date textbooks or are they looking tired and unappealing? How good is the library and how much is it used? Talk to the librarian. Often, they know more about the children's real reading habits than anyone else.

Achievement

Find out about your prospective school's results by looking at them on the league tables but also find out the crucial data: the results for English, maths and science. (See pages 34–38 on league tables about this.)

Target setting

Every school has to publish what is known as an SIP or School Improvement Plan where they publish targets the school has to achieve over the next few years. Find out what these targets are and whether you think they will help your child's education. Also, on a smaller scale, see whether target setting is taken seriously in the school. In many places, lip service is paid to it and it generates lots of bits of paper, but the crucial test is to ask pupils there: what are your targets? What are you trying to improve upon in, say, English? Do they have a sense of direction?

Turning up: 1 – staff turnover

The figures for this tell you more about a school than any Ofsted report, value-added data, or league table could because they let you know in essence how happy the staff are in the school. Let me explain. First, if there are a lot of supply staff at the school, you know that there is something wrong: this means that either there is long-term staff sickness or lots of short-term sickness or vacancies the school can't fill. It doesn't matter whether they are the most marvellous teachers in the world, if they aren't in school, it is more than likely that a cover teacher is taking the classes and is probably doing 'filler' work with the pupils: stuff to pass the time which is probably not that educational.

Then you have to ask yourself why the staff are calling in sick. Are the classes stressing the teachers out because they are poorly behaved? Are they too difficult to teach given the resources of the school? If a school has a high proportion of special needs children or children with English As An Additional Language, this can be exceptionally draining work for a teacher. I know because I have been both types of teacher.

A related figure to look at is the staff turnover figure. How many staff leave during any given year? Why are they leaving in droves? Why can't vacancies be filled? Teachers leave schools all the time but the best schools have a core of long-standing staff who give the school its backbone, its solidity, its character. Does your school have this? Or are the majority of the staff newly qualified who are leaving nearly as soon as they join?

At a primary school, and indeed at any school but particularly when children are young, children need to form a decent relationship with their teacher, to learn to rely on them and to trust them, and obviously they can't do that if the teacher is barely there. Consistently, throughout my career, the teachers that children feel most let down by are the ones who are always taking days off work and leaving them with a cover teacher who gives them copying or colouring to do.

The most telling statistic of all, however, is the number of head teachers a school has had in the last five years. This was most shockingly illustrated at Dunmore Junior School in Abingdon, Oxfordshire. Since its long-standing head Eric Bird departed in 2000, the school went through 13 head teachers, 10 of whom left within three years. The National Association of Head Teachers' General Secretary, Mick Brookes, said, 'This is the extreme end of what is happening nationwide. We know of heads who have walked into schools on Wednesday thinking everything was fine, had a visit from inspectors, and then been considering their position by the weekend.'

Be prepared for the unexpected! A parent who had their child admitted to the school in 2000 may have, quite rightly, been extremely pleased that they were part of one of the most successful primary schools in the country – under Bird the school was one of the best – only to find that the school slumped miserably for the next six years. Aileen Jones, 40, whose 11-year-old daughter Abigail attends Dunmore, said:

We knew the heads were changing because every time my daughter was in a choir performance there would be a different person standing in the hall. But I think all the parents were surprised by the Ofsted report – I hadn't noticed any difference in the work

Abby was bringing home from school. This school has gone from beacon status to special measures and it is clear the LEA must be held accountable for this.

A comparison of contrasting Ofsted reports published in the *Times Educational Supplement* says it all:[5]

	2000	**2006**
Status	A beacon school	In special measures
	Same head for 18 years	13 heads in six years
The inspectors said	'Dunmore is a very effective school. It provides very good value for money'	'The school has faced substantial changes in leadership and management and this has led to a decline in standards. It is failing to give pupils an acceptable standard of education'
Leadership rating	Very good	Unsatisfactory
Teaching rating	Very good	Unsatisfactory overall
Combined test results for 11-year-olds out of 300	274	253
Pupils on roll	327	296

Jean Hopkinson, a mother of four daughters in rural Cheshire, gave me a vivid illustration of how an excellent primary school can quickly change if the staff leave.

❝ My eldest daughter, Amelia, went to a local state primary school after we carried out some research. Most importantly, we looked very carefully at how she responded to the school when she looked around. Amelia, who was only four years old, looked up at the teacher and said, 'I like to read.' The teacher was very enthusiastic and asked about what she liked to read and gave her a book that followed on from what she was already reading.

The teachers there were exceptionally good at that time. They were experienced, vivacious people who had the traditional values of the 3 Rs and were very focused on academic success. Overall though, because it was a local school, it had a lovely community feel to it. Our social life quickly came to revolve around the school.

My first two children went happily through it. But by the time our third child was going through it a lot of the mature teachers had retired. Our third child was not taught well because most of the older teachers had retired, and the new teachers were very inexperienced. They were young and settling in. The curriculum seemed to have changed a great deal – this was the late 1990s. What went from being traditional maths and English lessons changed. They were teaching phonics, literacy and numeracy, which all sounds fine and dandy, except that nobody pushed you on if you didn't want to do the work.

My third daughter, Rose, wanted to do football and not much else. She was brilliant at sports. The most salient part of her end of term report was "Rose has really good ball skills." It was funny but it was distressing because she had left the school without achieving academically at that point in time. The teaching was so awful that I felt she had no confidence in her ability in the academic subjects. That lack of confidence has stayed with her until today – and has severely cut down her options at A level and university. ❞

Within a few years, the school degenerated from being a top primary school to a terrible one for one reason: all the good staff left and were replaced by inexperienced teachers who didn't have the know-how to maintain standards.

Turning up: 2 – pupil turnover

Sharp-eyed parents may have detected that there was going to be problems for Dunmore Junior, and not only if they had twigged that Bird was leaving the school. As the last statistic indicates, the school lost over 30 pupils over six years. Some schools lose pupils simply because there are fewer children in the catchment area than there used to be. Other schools lose pupils because parents vote with their feet and take their children elsewhere if they are able to. A bit of both appears to have happened with Dunmore, which had a falling roll anyway and then appears to have suffered because of its woes with head teachers and generally poor teaching standards.

A perceptive parent could have learned in 2000 that the school roll was falling and realised that there would be problems. Fewer pupils means less money for a school, which means fewer staff which can mean that all sorts of structural problems occur.

It is worth asking about the projected roll for the years your child will be at the school because it could affect their education. If the roll is falling, ask why. Is it because parents are voting with their feet? How is the school going to manage its staffing? Will it be losing staff?

Finally, it is vitally important to know how many pupils are being excluded from school and for what reasons. If 20–30 pupils are being excluded for misbehaviour each term, you need to know the reasons why. If it is just a handful, then relax. Remember, exclusion is the last sanction schools have against unruly pupils and that the government has been discouraging schools from excluding pupils for some years now. Exclusions last only a few days at the most, but pupils who are permanently excluded are out for ever! Some schools exclude pupils for smoking in school uniform, whereas others would never dream of doing this because too many pupils would be excluded. Finding out the reasons why pupils are excluded is very useful because it indicates the standards the school expects of pupils.

Head teacher

Having read my book *I'm a Teacher, Get Me Out of Here* a former pupil, Hassan, got in touch with me. I had been his form tutor and I had taught him English when he was 11 in an inner-city secondary school in Tower Hamlets during the early 1990s. He was now in his twenties and working as a financial journalist in the City. I was pleased and relieved that he had been so successful: I knew that most pupils who left that school at that particular time did so with very few qualifications and not many prospects.

He was clearly bitter about the education he'd had there. He explained to me why he thought the school was so bad:

❝ The set-up was poor. There seemed to be a lack of real leadership and direction. If it was difficult for students to learn (and it was!), I can fully accept that even good teachers may have found the atmosphere difficult to teach in. Teachers were infected with the blasé and indifferent atmosphere of the school. There was a blatant lack of determination and will to do anything.

Discipline was poor and that meant kids would meander through lessons learning next to nothing. I can literally count only a handful of things that I truly learned from at the school. I went to a very good primary school and I guess that put me in good stead. The five years at the school were just a hiatus and my brain did not develop as it should have done. There was a culture of not wanting to learn. I deliberately held myself back because I did not want to be ostracised by my peers for being a swot.

My parents didn't have much time to think of the school I attended, they were too busy putting food on the table and ensuring that we had a comfortable life. I guess in the Bengali community as a whole there was an understanding that because it was a British school, it had to be good. Why would a civilised country like Britain allow kids to be taught at inept, poor schools?

I also accept that I have to take a lot of the blame as well and perhaps should have applied myself better. I guess it was a cocktail of issues that ensured our wretched fate. ❞

Hassan complains about the poor behaviour of the pupils, the generally disrespectful attitude towards learning, the blasé attitude of the teachers, and the lack of parental know-how and power which led to him receiving such a poor education.

Much of this was to change when a new head teacher arrived at the school. He improved discipline by separating girls from boys at break-time and enforcing stricter school rules, he greatly boosted the results by introducing vocational qualifications which counted for statistical purposes as GCSEs – although, as I've indicated, they are not the true equivalent of GCSEs – and he rigorously enforced the recommendations of the various inspection reports the school had endured. The school is certainly not the same place where I once taught.

Clearly, dynamic head teachers do make a big difference. Nick Davies, along with many parents and experts I spoke to, echoed this view. Davies is the parent of children who attend schools in Lewes, a large Sussex town, and is the author of a number of books including *The School Report: The Hidden Truth About Britain's Classrooms*. He explained to me why they are so important:

> Head teachers are important not because they are symbols but because they are dictators – they may be benign, most are, or they may be destructive, as some certainly are, but the point is that they have overwhelming executive power in their schools. Governing bodies are supposed to be responsible for corporate governance but my experience, as a former parent-governor, is that governors see their role with the head teacher the way magistrates used to see their role with the police – 'we're here to offer support' and they will try very hard to turn a blind eye to a head teacher's faults. Beyond that, the governors rely almost entirely on the head teacher for information about what is happening inside the school and will often not understand the policy and budgetary issues that lie behind what is going on. Put it all together and you have the head teacher operating without any effective check from the governing body. The LEAs have less and less power over head teachers because they have less and less control over budget and policy, both of which are being passed by central government to the heads; plus, unless something exceptional goes wrong, LEAs also tend to 'support' the head teacher, right or wrong.

The staffroom may moan and groan about the head teacher but they are not going to be asked to set policy and, if a head teacher senses rebellion, he or she can make life very nasty for individual teachers, simply by messing with the timetable and their duties. The parents are even weaker – they can moan and groan in the playground or take their complaints to the governors or the LEA but they are not going to get very far. Heads rule OK.

Davies gave me a shocking illustration of this by telling me the story of a head teacher who got involved with crack cocaine. Mrs Smith was the successful head teacher of a primary school in north London until the culture of the streets outside the school invaded it. She told Davies, 'There is drugs and prostitution day and night. We get drugs stuff in the playground, coming in off the street.' In the late 1990s, after her son had been killed by drug dealers in New York, she became embroiled with a drugs ring, and allowed a number of people to steal from the school in order to pay off her debts to them. Thousands of pounds worth of computers and cash was stolen from the school, and she was frequently absent, once calling in to work to say that she was hiding in a safe house to escape Yardies who were threatening to kill her.

Shamefully none of the authorities that should have stopped her from effectively destroying the school were able to. The LEA, the governing body, Ofsted and the DfES all turned a blind eye to what was going on until an LEA audit revealed that equipment had been stolen from the school and cheques had been falsified. She was then sacked for gross misconduct. She said:

I feel let down by myself actually. I think that I have been a really lousy parent and really lousy to people around me that needed my support. It's obvious I can't teach any more because this thing is going to be round my neck for the rest of my life. I'm a head. A head is not supposed to want help. Everybody else comes to school with problems and I am supposed to sort them out.

What's scary about this case is that Smith was allowed to get away with it for so long. Drug dealers were openly using the school, there was a crisis in staff recruitment, and the head teacher was on the run from dealers, and still no one did anything. Pleas to the LEA from the staff and the chairman of governors were ignored until the very last minute. The governing body was rendered virtually impotent by absences and resignations.

Both exceptionally brilliant and exceptionally awful head teachers are rare. While most head teachers simply do not have the vision, energy, intelligence, influence or luck to turn around a failing school, equally they are not so bad as to embezzle funds, or squander vast sums of money fruitlessly. Most head teachers are, like the rest of us, ordinary people doing a very demanding job, trying their best but not always succeeding.

Here's my guide to the different species of head teacher you might encounter:

The ostrich is relentlessly upbeat and buries his head in the sand before acknowledging bad behaviour or poor results. The ostrich head would rather run a mile than actually criticise the children. However, he will quite shamelessly blame other teachers if they complain about poor discipline or impossible working conditions.

The orchid head looks wonderful, sounds great and persuasive, but is rarely sighted in school because he or she is too busy hob-nobbing at conferences. She is perhaps at her best as an important figurehead but don't think she is really running things. The reason why she's become a head teacher is because the rough and tumble of school is too much for her delicate sensibilities and she would much rather be sitting in a large office sorting out documents and dealing with adults.

The creeper head's roots and tentacles spread everywhere throughout the school. He has excellent surveillance techniques which means he actually knows what is going on around the school. This kind of head teacher may not be very flashy but can be very effective at making everyone else paranoid, which has its advantages: motivated by fear the staff mark their books diligently and are scrupulous about preparing for inspections. However, the creeper can demoralise the staff if he micro-manages too much, and a lot of 'covering up' can occur if he is not too careful. The moment he stops creeping around, the staff and pupils put their feet up because their sole motivation has been fear.

The bamboo head teachers are strict, forceful characters who are not afraid to use the metaphorical stick if they have to. You can tell them immediately. If they are women, they are bustling, slightly forbidding but energetic; if they are men, they wear suits, possibly a gown, and brook no dissent. They can be good at bringing a sense of discipline to a school. Their disadvantages are that they can have favourites and can easily demoralise more creative staff, leaving only the compliant and craven to remain.

The palm tree heads are my favourite. These are head teachers who are genuine leaders. They are always positive because they know they have to be, but they do take their job seriously. Unfortunately, they tend to thrive only in sunny climes and are possibly only happy because they are in a good school anyway. Palm tree heads can only be spotted when you talk to the pupils and other staff; only they know what head teachers are genuinely like.

Just remember, good head teachers are approachable; they are firm about what they want from pupils, staff and parents; they have instituted good discipline policies in school; they have encouraged staff to offer a range of extracurricular activities; they have stable, committed staff who don't disappear in the middle of the term and lose truckloads of coursework; and they have the support of the majority of parents.

A NEW SCHOOL RULE

for visiting schools

Use DEATH to help you Photocopy the DEATH analysis questionnaire sheet at the back of the book (see Appendix A) to take with you around prospective schools.

Filling out the application forms

What initially puzzled me about the application process for primary schools was that you had to apply through your LEA. And you have to apply in good time, nearly a year before your child is about to start school – when your child is three or four years old. I had somewhat naively and ignorantly thought you could apply to the school of choice directly and they would send the application form to the LEA. This is definitely not the case. You have to apply through the LEA and, if the school asks for it, to apply to the school as well.

All schools have admissions criteria. This is a list of rules that you have to meet in order to get your child into a school. Usually, it is simply that people who live closest to the school are preferred, but it can be that having a sibling at the school will favour your child, and in the case of religious schools proof of your faith – something Niall was so hell-bent on proving.

When the admissions criteria are not simply based on local catchment area, usually parents are expected to apply through the LEA and also apply directly to the school. The school then checks to see whether you have met the criteria and sends their list of chosen pupils to the LEA for approval. If you have not applied through the LEA your application will probably be disqualified, particularly if the school is over-subscribed and they need to get rid of people anyway.

Once I investigated these issues, I realised that I was in a real quandary regarding how to fill in the LEA application form for James. Despite living quite close to a good primary school, we did not live in the catchment area, which, because of its popularity, was quite small. This meant that if I put the school down as first choice and he failed to get in, he would be allocated to our second choice, but it was very likely that that school would be full too because the LEA operated the policy of giving first choices where possible. In other words, the parents who had put our second choice down as their first choice would have got in first. Therefore, it would almost certainly be full if it was a popular school. This would be the case for all three schools I was intending to put down on the LEA form; they were all popular schools.

If this happened, the LEA would allocate my child a place in the nearest school with available places, which basically meant we would get the school nobody else wanted and it would probably be miles away.

I was biting my nails by this time. He wouldn't get in, would he? And he would be sent to some hellhole where the kids screamed and fought all day, and the teachers were permanently off with stress-related illnesses, where drug dealers hung around the gates and the parents were abusive to each other in the playground.

I looked at the LEA's admissions policy again. There were some good religious schools in the borough but it was a bit late to start going to church. Besides, Erica was adamant she wasn't going to lie about believing in Jesus. Damn! So that option was blown. Then I saw that children with special needs got preferential treatment. Ah, special needs! That amorphous, woolly term which could mean that your child was severely disabled at one end of the spectrum to being perfectly able-bodied but a pain in the arse at the other.

What special need did James have? I thrummed my fingers against the LEA admissions form. I thought about his behaviour, character, his personality: he liked trains, enjoyed me telling him Cheeky Monkey stories, he wasn't keen on getting his hair wet, he was very chatty about buses, he enjoyed going to a museum, unlike most children he ate broccoli. Damn! Damn! Damn! He had nothing approaching a special need at all.

I knew that it was very unlikely that he would get into the school of our choice and that if I wasn't careful he wouldn't get into a good school at all.

A NEW SCHOOL RULE

for choosing a primary school

Prepare for the unexpected Don't expect to get your first choice school if you don't meet the admissions criteria.

Appeals

We could appeal against the LEA's decision. This would mean that the LEA would examine the case for our child going to the school based on the school's criteria. It would then justify its case in front of two independent lay people. We would then put our case, leaving the lay people to decide whether the LEA had made the right decision.

Ninety per cent of appeals fail largely because the LEA or school (depending upon who is the admissions authority) doesn't usually get things wrong. Sometimes parents neglect to stress their child's special needs which can only be catered for by the school of their choice. The independent observers can overturn the admissions authority's decision if they feel a child meets the school's criteria.

Reverend Shepherd, a veteran of such processes in Harrogate, told me:

I have sat on appeal panels for ten years for the high school. The rules changed four or five years ago, and a governor is no longer allowed, and now it is purely independent people. But I saw, for many years, parents who were very anxious about getting their child into the school. For many of them it was the first time they weren't in control of the situation as regards their child. I kept trying to tell them that they should relax but invariably they didn't listen because they felt the situation was so out of control. The main thing to remember is that it doesn't matter very much where your child goes to school. It is a parent's support and love that is the most important factor in a child succeeding.

THE NEW SCHOOL RULES
for appeals

1. **Appeal if you must** Do appeal to the relevant admissions authority if you have failed get into the school of your choice. Remember, most appeals fail because parents do not meet the admissions criteria.

2. **Appeal against the appeal** If you are rejected think about going to the ombudsman who can overturn the appeal panel's decision. For more information see: www.lgo.org.uk/index.php

---

Resolution?

Niall had managed to resolve the nightmare issue of converting to Christianity by moving house to an area where there was a decent school – or so he thought. But now that Martin, his son, was placed there, Niall wasn't happy – and neither was his child. Martin was in the reception class, but, according to Niall, he wasn't learning anything.

'The whole place is like one big playground. The kids rush around on their trikes, bashing each other. Martin hates it. He never gets a go on the trikes,' Niall complained. 'And as for him doing any reading, forget it! I have to do reading with him when he gets home.'

I asked Niall whether he had complained to the teachers, but Niall had said that he hadn't. 'I don't want to look like a moaner,' he said ruefully. 'If the teachers think that you are a moaner, they make sure that your child really doesn't get any help.'

'How do you know that?'

'I've heard the other parents talking about it. That's what happens.'

The truth was that Niall was a bit of a whiner. All parents tend to whine on the subject of schools because they feel powerless against the system. They rarely know what is going on and they often receive a negative picture about school from their children. But schools resent being criticised and complained about, and can find ways to take revenge on those they judge to be persistent whiners like Niall.

In a suitably inquisitorial voice, Niall questioned me about what I was doing with my son, James, who was now in nursery. I explained that Erica and I had looked around some schools, and that the good primary school in our area couldn't take James because we weren't in the catchment area. So we had managed to get James into a fee-paying, Christian school.

Niall exploded. 'So you are telling me that after all that piss-taking about me going to church, and all your protestations about the value of state education, you are sending James to a private Christian school!'

I nodded shamefacedly, protesting feebly that I just wanted what was best for James. Niall calmed down a little when he saw I was embarrassed.

'Hey, listen mate, it's nothing to be ashamed of, but what made you do it? I mean, you've been teaching in the state sector for all these years and yet you go private. It doesn't show much faith, does it?'

I explained somewhat apologetically: not only is sending your child to a private school regarded as selfish by people like Niall but also fundamentally 'sinful' – harmful to society at large.

As I have said, Erica and I had looked at a number of schools, including the local state primary schools in our area of east London. Once I realised that we probably wouldn't get our child into the best local primary in our area, we then looked at private schools and saw a few places that brought home the divide between the private sector and the state. Classes were much smaller – a maximum of 20 compared with 32 in the state sector. Staff turnover was much lower – in both local state schools I saw there were problems with staff absences and staff leaving. We saw a couple of dreadful private schools which appeared to drill the kids from an early age, expecting them to sit in silence for long periods of time, asking them to learn spelling lists and times tables by rote. There appeared to be a lot of copying from the board going on. They were very bad schools, schools which could have never survived in the state sector because Ofsted would have been on them like a ton of bricks.

However, there were two enlightened schools that we found. When one offered us a place, we accepted. We still hadn't been told by the local state primary which we liked whether we had got a place or not. They were first making offers to the parents in their catchment area. Rather than risk ending up with the bad state school choice, we quickly accepted the place at the private school.

It was a Christian school but appeared liberal in its ethos. We had been asked on the application form whether we were practising Christians and we said no. That didn't appear to harm our chances. Unlike Christian state schools it didn't demand written proof from the local vicar that we were regular churchgoers. On the admissions form, we told them we were atheists.

The teachers at the school observed James at his nursery school, and interviewed us before granting a place.

It was not cheap, but both of us were working and were able to cover the cost of the fees, as well as employing a nanny to pick James up at the end of school, when it finished at 3.15 p.m. The total cost of all of this consumed most of my teacher's wage. For most people, it would be far too expensive.

When we went for drinks in the headmaster's study – how many state schools have such a thing? – it was quite interesting to see that a number of parents there were visibly left-leaning characters (journalists, writers, academics) who had all fled the state system. Among them was Fenella Greenfield, who is the general secretary of her local Labour Party. She told me:

I feel astonished that I have sent Fynnie to a private school. I think of myself before Fynnie was born and I don't know what I would have thought of myself if I had known that I would send my child to a private school. There is a good state primary near where we live but it is totally Roman Catholic. I know a great deal about it because I am a governor there. There are prayers before the governors' meeting and prayers every morning in the school; it not the sort of atmosphere I want my child to grow up in.

There is another school near us but it is Anglican and quite religious too. There is a list of eight criteria for getting in there. Top of the list is having your child baptised in a local church. Bottom of the list is living near the school.

I talked to one of the head teachers at the school and told him, 'Sorry, I am not going to pretend that I am Christian. I am a committed atheist.' He replied that he knew that a lot of parents came into the school with their fingers crossed behind their backs.

The third school that I could have sent Fynnie to is a pretty rough school which services all the council estates in the area. It's a good school but I felt hesitant about sending Fynnie there because I felt he would be such a fish out of water. Most of the parents there live in council accommodation whereas I own my own flat.

Following some parents' advice I loitered outside the school at picking up time and observed the parents. I kid you not, but I heard one parent say, 'Here, did you hear that Ginny's just got out of prison?'

So I went private! And here I am!

A NEW SCHOOL RULE

for getting your child into the best schools

Understand that the financial cost can be high Many schools have ways of helping you plan out your finances. See www.isc.co.uk/ and lose your principles if you have to!

Getting your child into a good prep school

Be warned, there are a lot of terrible private schools around – read some of the stories later on in the book. You need to use the DEATH analysis to have a good look at them. Don't trust the Independent School Council's reports on the school; they do not have the same independence as Ofsted and are usually far too forgiving as a result. The private sector is entirely unregulated and you can be taken for a real ride.

In major cities like London, because there are so many desperate parents out there and comparatively few schools – especially good ones – it is a seller's market, but don't be conned into sending your child to a private school you are not sure about. You are probably far better off sending them to the school the LEA provides which at least has the benefit of being closely monitored.

Make sure that you visit the school first and, if you like it, register your name with the school. Usually, you need to fill in a detailed form with your particulars on it, and pay a registration fee. Once this has been done, the school will nearly always test your child in some sort of way to gauge their ability.

Private schools are quite ruthless in creaming off the best pupils but they also want a mix of pupils. The best schools, like the one James went to, now observe very young prospective pupils in their nursery settings or talk to them with their parents. It is very important that your child acts as naturally as possible in these situations. Don't prime your child with historical dates and useless information so that they sound clever. Let the school decide for themselves whether your child will fit in.

If you are aiming to get your child into a prep school, he or she will usually have to sit an exam. You will probably need to hire a tutor to assist them with this at the beginning of Year 2 if they are going to a state primary school – see the timetable at the end of this chapter. State primaries do not train pupils for such exams. The transition from a state primary to a prep school is probably the most difficult of all transitions because most privately educated pupils are brought on much more quickly than their state-educated counterparts.

Once you have been offered a place, then you have to pay the fees, but make sure that you read the contract you sign very carefully before you do so.

THE NEW SCHOOL RULES
for private schools

1. **Remember, private schools are a law to themselves** Bear in mind that private schools are much more ad hoc in their admissions procedures. They don't have to justify their decisions to the ombudsman or anyone except themselves.

2. **Don't become bitter** If your child isn't selected by your favoured private school, it may be to your benefit: the teachers observing them may well have felt that he or she wouldn't have thrived in the school. Private schools are strange places with their own eccentricities, bizarre rituals and foibles. Many are snobbish places that use their reputations like weapons to attack any parent or pupil who challenges them and not every child is suited to them.

▶

3. **A good school will take a good look at your child**
   Realise that a good private school will observe a young child in a classroom rather than interviewing him or her formally.

4. **Get in early** Putting your child in a pre-prep school can be advantageous if you want them to pass the entrance exam to prep school: most pre-preps groom their children to pass the exam. Moving from the state sector to the private at seven can be a real trauma: state pupils probably need extra coaching to pass the exam.

Getting your child into a good secondary school

While many parents find getting their child into a satisfactory primary school relatively straightforward, the same cannot be said about secondary schools. The admissions procedures for state secondary schools are generally more complicated; children are older, social and gender divisions seem wider and secondary schools are much bigger and more impersonal than their cosy primary school counterparts. It is a scary time. Parents become obsessed with doing the right thing. They think if their child doesn't get into the right school, all will be lost. One parent whose daughters were about to go to secondary school in the north of England told me:

> As the girls are eleven, I'm bracing myself, ready to face the nightmare zone. So far there have only been a couple of things. What school? This was a nightmare, I became hysterical. My natural train of thought led me from … I make the wrong decision = girls unhappy = do badly in school = leave at 16 with no qualifications = a life of deprived misery on the dole drinking homebrew surrounded by a brood of filthy children who don't know what melon is. This may seem ridiculous but it's a horrible

time when the pressure of this enormous decision gets too much and you can go a bit mental. It's a bit like doing badly in an exam and you think the world has caved in and the gate to your preferred path in life is well and truly bolted.

THE NEW SCHOOL RULES

for getting into a good secondary school

1. **Do your research** (See below.)

2. **Visit them** Visit your preferred four choices of school in Year 4 and get the feel of their ethos and ensure you like them. In Year 5, shadow a Year 6 parent going through the process and take your child to see only your top choices and see what they think. Discuss your thoughts with your whole family.

3. **Involve your whole family** If you have younger children, think about where they may go when you are making the choices for your first child. So, for example, if you send your oldest child, your daughter, to a single-sex school then obviously your son will not be able to go there. If you want your younger child to attend the same school, you'll have to opt for a mixed-sex school. Remember that many schools favour siblings. It is important to discuss this when making your choices.

Meeting the criteria

I see them flocking into my school in their hundreds every September, parents clutching their prospectuses and their children, desperate to get their child into the school, but I know that only a chosen few will make it. One parent, a hard-working nurse, had tears in her eyes as she said to me, 'Is there any chance that my son will get in?' I didn't have the heart to tell her that she didn't have a hope and just said that she needed to read the admissions criteria carefully. However, I knew that she hadn't read the criteria early enough: it stipulated that a child had to have attended clubs for two years. Her son hadn't. If she had known this years ago, she might have managed to get her child a place. But she didn't.

New Labour has supplied a lot of misinformation about admissions to schools in recent years. They have proudly proclaimed that they have eradicated covert selection by stopping all schools interviewing and testing pupils before entry, or demanding that buying expensive uniforms are prerequisites for joining the school. Yes, they have done this, but they have also allowed schools to apply certain demands to their admissions criteria which only very organised, clued-up parents can meet.

In truth, the admissions system has been made more complicated by New Labour – and selection by postcode or religious faith has thrived as a consequence. The rules change from year to year, from borough to borough, from region to region but there are some general points that are worth bearing in mind.

Where you live

First and foremost, living as close as you can to your preferred school will give you an advantage, but you should be aware that it is not the be-all and end-all to school admissions – it's a lot more complicated than that. Some schools operate a banding system which means they take a cross section of pupils who reflect the different ability ranges in the area, supposedly with a representative number of pupils from each ability range. This can widen the catchment area of the school as it searches for a broad cross section of pupils.

Religion

As we have seen with primary schools, your religion can help significantly to get your child into a good school: many secondary schools with the best results favour pupils of a particular religion on entry.

Being 'special'

Any special ability that your child has may help. There are still 200 grammar schools in England, and every specialist school has the discretion to select pupils who have particular abilities in their specialism, which can be in languages, science, sports, music, technology, and so on. Many schools will also favour children with special needs. As we have seen before, this is an amorphous term, but if your child has been assessed by a specialist and judged to be dyslexic, have particular learning difficulties or be mentally or physically disabled, many schools will favour this kind of child.

Lastly, many admissions criteria favour siblings, but this is likely to disappear in the coming years because it is increasingly viewed to be against equal opportunities and discriminating against only children. However, at the moment, it is a criterion that remains on many schools' admissions codes.

On the surface it sounds so organised and highly regulated – but don't be fooled. Admissions criteria vary hugely throughout the country. It is a chaotic system. The DfES informs parents proudly that there is a system of 'co-ordinated admissions' for the whole of England but this doesn't mean there is a uniform policy. It simply means that you must apply to any state school through your LEA, even if your chosen school is not in the LEA.

THE NEW SCHOOL RULE

for school admissions: vital questions to ask your LEA

Ask the right questions Does your preferred school get to know what's on your admissions form? This is crucial

▶

because some comprehensives become very shirty when they see you've put down a grammar school as first choice – and may well reject your application out of hand as a result. In some areas, schools that want to know which parents have put them as their first choice are provided with this information by the LEA. If your child fails the eleven-plus, and has failed to receive any of your other choices, the LEA will then allocate the nearest available school with spare places – which can be, alas, the local failing school. Does your LEA allow parents to hold multiple offers? This is fantastic for you if it does because you don't have to make an immediate decision when you receive your first offer – you can hang on until you've got all your offers in. Most LEAs are moving away from this system because it can cause chaos. It's good for savvy parents, but it's terrible for the less popular schools. Some parents hold on to multiple places until very late in August, and, as a result, some schools are not filled come September because the schools and the LEA hadn't been able to allocate all the available places.

The school lottery

The concept of choice was always supposed to be one of the central plans of the government's education policy. Over the last decades, Tony Blair and a succession of Labour education secretaries have trumpeted their commitment to increased parental power over schools admissions. So in a much hyped speech in 2005, the Prime Minister heralded his plans to introduce much greater choice into the system. 'Where parents are dissatisfied,' he promised, 'they need a range of good schools to choose from; or where there is no such choice, [sic] able to take the remedy into their own hands.'

But, like so much feelgood New Labour rhetoric, this pledge

has turned out to be hollow. When it comes to expanding parental rights over schooling, the government has presided over growing disappointment. In early 2007, it was revealed that over 200,000 pupils missed out on their first choice of secondary school that year, while it is estimated that in some parts of Britain a third of children were denied their preferred place.

Because of the increasing pressure and frustration, one local authority, Brighton in Sussex, in March 2007, resorted to the drastic measure of introducing a lottery system for over-subscribed schools in its area. Under Brighton's scheme, where the demand outstrips supply places will allocated by numbers drawn from an electronic ballot. It was the first time that such a method for deciding school rolls had been used, but other local authorities could soon follow, particularly because the government is supportive of this approach. Indeed, the official new code on admissions, which will apply to pupils transferring to secondary schools from September 2008, claims that lotteries are an effective way of promoting fairness and reducing the middle-class dominance of certain good schools. 'Random allocation can widen access to schools for those unable to afford to buy houses near to favoured schools and create greater social equity,' says the code, displaying the bureaucratic enthusiasm for social engineering.

But all this talk about fairness is missing the point. Random allocation might satisfy the pen-pushers with their loathing for middle-class ambition, their hatred of anything that smacks of elitism and their obsession with deprivation, but it will do nothing to raise educational standards. Lotteries are not about justice but about hitting the middle-class. And they are a guaranteed way of bringing more resentment and chaos into a system that is already facing a crisis over low achievement.

Teaching as I do in a London comprehensive, I am deeply disturbed by the message given out to pupils if the lottery approach is widely adopted. It is an absurd way to decide the life chances of thousands of children. Education is far too important to be left to a lottery. The whole idea represents the trivialisation of schooling, reducing it to the status of a game of cards or the spin of a roulette wheel. Perhaps we are seeing New Labour's famous addiction to gambling at work again here, with the government encouraging the belief that our futures should be decided by mere chance rather than ability or hard work or genuine needs.

It is hard to imagine a more dubious or dangerous way of deciding allocations. There are plenty of other criteria that could be used which are more pertinent to a child's education, such as geographical proximity or intellectual attainment or interest in a certain subject or parental involvement in the community. But these have been ignored because of the eagerness to avoid any hint of recognising talent or achievement. According to this mindset, it is better to create a shambles in the name of egalitarianism than to encourage pupil success.

But in reality there is nothing fair about a lottery. It will undermine families and schools, as well as making a mockery of Labour's promises on parental choice. Community schools, which presently have no control over their admissions policy but take their pupils entirely from their local catchment area, may be hit because they could be forced to take randomly selected pupils from outside, thereby weakening their neighbourhood ethos, which is surely meant to be one of their virtues. The government dislikes the emphasis on geographical location because it is said to favour middle-class families buying up properties near a good school. But to go to the extreme of a lottery system, forcing schools to take pupils from a far wider area, could be more damaging. We could end up in the absurd situation where a child, living next door to a school, would have to take up a place miles away, while others are brought in from far afield. As well as weakening the spirit of community, such a change would also create horrendous transport problems, which could only be met by expensive bussing arrangements or parental car journeys, which our green government is supposed to be discouraging.

Equally worrying is the case of schools, such as city academies and voluntary-aided establishments, which have some say over their own admissions policies. My own establishment, a long-standing faith school, has a distinctive ethos, since our allocations are decided partly by criteria such as the demonstration of a musical or sporting interest.

Again, Tony Blair has often talked of encouraging schools like ours, with the aim of bringing more diversity and flexibility to the education sector. Yet lottery-based admissions and the admissions code which will be applied from 2008 onwards could destroy our good work. In our case, there will be no guarantee that the chosen pupils will have any interest in music or sport.

There are a host of other difficulties. Families could find that siblings will be forced to go to different schools if one of them has, so to speak, drawn the short straw. The ballots could be open to serious abuse, as favoured parents or corrupt heads or bureaucrats try to subvert the system. In recent years, we have seen the electoral system in urban local government become seriously tainted by widespread postal voting fraud. It is highly possible that the same could happen in education authorities. The administration of the ballot itself, involving checks on parents, is bound to create more municipal bureaucracy, wasting funds that could be used on schools.

So is there anything that parents can do to beat the crazy system? There are some small steps that they can take which may help their child get into a good school. The new school admissions code means that schools can no longer ask prospective pupils to meet a long list of criteria such as attending clubs for two years or playing a musical instrument, but specialist schools do have the discretion to select ten per cent of pupils in their chosen specialism. So if parents can prove that their child is good at their prospective school's specialism, they will stand a much better chance of being selected. However, this will refer to only one in ten students.

Most schools will retain the 'sibling' rule on their admissions code, although this may disappear soon. If you have a child already at the school, his or her sibling will be bumped up the waiting list. Religious schools will still be able to pick students who believe in their faith. However, most students will be chosen by how close they live to the school, with the pupils outside the immediate catchment area being chosen either by lottery or a 'banding' system.

The 'banding' system is where students within a chosen area

– usually defined by the school or LEA – are given Intelligence Quotient (IQ) tests by the school and then a certain proportion of students from the bottom of the band (the less able ones), the middle of the band (the average ones), and the top of the band (the bright ones) are allocated places so that the school has a genuine mix of abilities. Many parents get very confused with schools that 'band' their students because they think their children are being selected for being clever: although this is how it seems, it's more complicated than that. Your child may actually benefit from scoring badly on the test because the school needs to fill the places at the bottom of the band, while a bright child may have a great deal of difficulty making it into the top band because there are too many bright children taking the test.

In certain areas of the country, there are still state-funded grammar schools so if your child is bright enough they can pass the eleven-plus – the entrance exam for grammar schools – and get into a grammar. However, competition for such schools is fierce and you'll need to have your child tutored to get them in (see http://www.elevenplusexams.co.uk).

Other students can be legitimately picked by the school if they have a special need which the school can uniquely cater for. So, for example, if the school specialises in assisting pupils with dyslexia and your child is dyslexic, you will receive preferential treatment. If you like the look of a school, you should examine whether your child has a special need which you think this school can help with. Remember that special needs is a very subjective term which means that a child has some form of 'learning difficulty'. Savvy but unscrupulous parents have already started to use this entrance criterion (which is on many schools' admission criteria) to their advantage by finding a school they like well ahead of time and 'inventing' a learning difficulty for their child which means they will receive preferential treatment. So, for example, I came across one parent who claimed their child was 'dyspraxic' (a term used to describe pupils who have trouble co-ordinating their bodies) and needed to study drama and dance in order to enhance their co-ordination and social skills – two subjects that the parents' favourite school offered.

They were able to support the claim with documentary evidence from an educational psychologist, who happened to be a family friend, and, bingo, their child was admitted to the school.

My former headteacher, Dr Davina Lloyd, a veteran of thousands of applications, told me:

> Parents don't say everything they should on the application form. Governors are very sympathetic to disabilities, medical conditions or other issues but often are not told. Parents often feel ashamed about revealing key details. Recently, we turned down a prospective pupil even though the child was looking after a disabled sister and an ill parent. The first we heard about it was when it was brought up at appeal. The child was then admitted to the school but I felt much trauma could have been avoided if these details had been written down on the admissions form in the first place.
>
> The main advice I would give parents is to be realistic. They know the sort of school their child would be happy at and this may well be the school down the road where all their friends are going. The key to success at GCSE is to have parents who are supportive of their child and the school. If this is the case and the child is happy in school, the school makes relatively little difference. The best school in the world can't make an unhappy, unmotivated, unsupported child successful!

Dr Lloyd is aware that many parents don't believe her when she tells them that school makes very little difference to a child's GCSE results and knows of the dodges they employ to get their children into the school.

> I have never been bribed. What people do is move addresses and buy properties or they use grandparents' addresses. If those are found out about, a child loses a place. The downfall comes if you sell the property before the child starts the school.

THE NEW SCHOOL RULES

for getting your child into a school which sets its own admissions criteria

1. **Don't be a pest** Don't interrogate the secretarial staff at your favoured schools for inside information: they won't give you any. Ask them to send you the admissions criteria for the school and any other relevant literature and read it very carefully.

2. **Do your research early** Read the admissions criteria early. When your child is in Year 3 of primary school, scan the admissions criteria of your favoured schools carefully and check to see if they have particular facilities which might assist with your child's special needs, or if they specialise in a subject or area which your child is interested in. It can be to your advantage if your child is diagnosed as Special Educational Needs because most schools favour SEN pupils. This point is going to be more and more important in the coming years for all schools because the government wants to make all schools specialist in status. That means that their admissions criteria will probably favour children with the specialism the school espouses. Evidence of your child having expertise in that specialism could give you the edge. Find out whether you can hold on to multiple offers. For example, in London where you're not generally allowed to hold on to multiple offers, in 2006, parents were allowed to hold on to an offer of a specialist music place until one week after the 1 March deadline to allow the family to decide on their first choice school: so there are sometimes exceptions. Investigate them all. Don't forget to mention any special considerations that are relevant. Many schools will favour children

▶

who have struggled in one way or another: don't hide any important information with regard to this.

3. **Do the paperwork properly** Always put your first choice in first place on the form. Remember to apply through your LEA and the school if this is required – which it normally is – for voluntary-aided schools. Consider applying online. In London, this can be done by logging on to www.yourlondon.gov.uk/eadmissions/ (other boroughs are catching on). Currently, the best way of finding out which borough is doing this is by Googling 'school admissions applying online'.

4. **Appeal** As we saw with primary schools, you can appeal if your child is not successful in attaining a place. At the appeal hearing you must prove that you meet the admissions criteria. If you are rejected by the appeals panel, you may go to the ombudsman, who can look at your case.

Getting into a specialist school – one parent's story

Kate got her daughter into a top specialist school because she knew how to play the system. Despite not living in the catchment area of the school, she used her knowledge to attain a place.

❝ The change to secondary school is daunting for most parents, even if you are a fairly bright parent and can understand the admissions criteria for all the different types of schools. Some schools are doing something called "shadowing" which means that a Year 5 parent goes with a Year 6 parent to all the admissions open days. Our school did not encourage this. Therefore, most parents were in the dark about getting their child into a school which would suit them.

When Florence was in Year 4, I decided to have a look at the schools I liked the sound of. So I went to the most popular ones that everybody wants to get their child into, which were: a specialist Sports college school, and three faith schools, all of which placed a great emphasis on sports and music. I was really shocked when I visited them. I thought the schools would be much better than my old secondary school but they weren't: many were under-resourced; some of the buildings were in a poor state. The teaching seemed good in all of them. I'd heard about other schools outside our area which are known to be very good and which do seek to take students which fit their ethos, but the journey seemed too much. At the beginning of Year 5 parents have only got a three week time window in which to visit all of the schools and make your choice of 6 schools. And if you are panicker, it is terrible!

I know neighbours who have not spoken to each other in four years because one child was offered a place in a school which the second neighbour wanted for their own child, but didn't get.

In classrooms, parents become secretive in Year 5, not wanting to tell anyone else where they may apply. They thought if they told anyone else where they were applying that would harm their chances because there would be more competition for places.

To counteract this tendency, what I have done at the primary school where my son now goes is to offer any parent my experiences with my daughter, and to try and help people understand that they are not competing against my children, but against all the children who meet the set criteria. The idea is that we can help each other.

Parents get into rows over which school to put first on the application form. You see, it is vitally important to put your real first choice as first choice otherwise you won't have a hope in hell of getting a place if it is heavily over-subscribed. Never mind whether they ask you to put first place or not.

I took a big gamble with Florence and put a top specialist sports college school as first choice, even though it was outside the local catchment area. "No one gets in there," said the school secretary. Incredibly, Florence was offered a place. She met the criteria for each, although they are quite different. Both however sought church-attending all-round achievers, with a musical/artsy background. In other words, I had got very sharp and had filled in the application forms correctly, meeting the criteria precisely.

I jumped for joy when I heard we'd got in. One of the workmen inside the café where I having a cup of tea, said to his mate, "She's got the all-clear then!" **9**

Kate's story is exceptional but it is worth highlighting. I saw her application form: it was stuffed full of press cuttings and letters proving that her child was brilliant at swimming. Even though she was outside the catchment area, the school had the discretion to pick her because of this. Having interviewed many of parents, I have learnt that headteachers have more leeway than you think: if they like the look of you, they can easily sneak you in. Systems like the lottery and banding mean that it is more difficult than before for the Ombudsman to track why a pupil got into a school. Most savvy headteachers want to take on good pupils with supportive parents. A quick, friendly informal chat with them, a few impressive letters and press cuttings in the application form can make all the difference. Such approaches to headteachers need to be done very subtly and shouldn't be aggressive or demanding in tone – after all, you should expect that they may achieve nothing – but sometimes they do if done in the right way.

The truth about admissions for religious schools

Some schools are much more demanding about proof of religious commitment than others. In Harrogate I spoke to Tony Shepherd, the vicar of St Peter's Harrogate, governor of a Church of England High School, and chairman of governors at a Harrogate primary school. He has decades of experience of the admissions systems of both Church of England primary and secondary schools. He told me:

> The admissions criteria for C of E schools in Harrogate, in common with most in the country, are points scored. Typically it is nine points for a sibling, nine points for parent working in school, nine points for attending church, nine points for being in the Archdeaconry of Richmond, and six points for community and charity work. A parent usually needs between thirty and

forty points to get their child into a school. Every vicar is sent the parents' application. This is not just C of E vicars, any named vicar or minister writes comment on the parents. Parents attain high marks for being part of the PCC, the Parochial Church Council, being a Sunday school teacher, or ringing the bells. Parents are given nine points for attending church regularly for more than two years, and seven if they have attended regularly for less than two years. Fortunately, if you have attended for less than two years, you can gain extra points for doing extra jobs such as arranging the flowers or doing the church cleaning.

It is often claimed that parents have gone to church just to get their children into their favoured school. Parents, bitter at being rejected, often claim this at their appeals about other parents. But in my experience, this is not the case. The admissions panels of schools can tell the difference between the parents whose main focus is to get their child into school and committed parents by their willingness to initiate new bits of work in the church and to take new things on. I can count on the fingers of only one hand, the parents who are only interested in gaining admission to school.

As you can see, it is pretty hard to fake it in Harrogate. I am not sure that many dyed-in-the-wool atheists would clean their local church or do the flower arranging just to get their child into the best school in the area. Because competition for places is so strong – on average these schools deal with 40 appeals a year – the schools select on the basis not only of religiosity but intensity of religious faith by measuring the parents' 'good works' on a points system.

The Church of England has promised to simplify the process in future years but the fact remains that faith schools in general have much more power to set their own admissions criteria, and nearly always ask for a reference from a relevant religious figure, who may be a lot better disposed to you if you have worked hard for your church.

It appears that despite the government's best efforts, many religious schools have covert selection policies. One headmaster

I encountered a few years ago, before interviews were banned, was quite open about it. When he ushered the 11-year-old pupils into his study and asked them about their religious commitment, he graded them on the degree to which they gave articulate answers. He boasted that he could predict their GCSE grades based on the interview. When he showed me the correlations I was amazed: he was deadly accurate. While he drew back from explicitly stating that he was selecting the pupils based on their academic ability, this was the implication. This was something he was not allowed to do because he was running a religious school, not an academically selective one.

The government banned interviews a few years ago for this very reason. But as we have already seen, faith-based schools have introduced such stringent admissions criteria that disorganised, disadvantaged parents are clueless about how to get their children into them while articulate, middle-class, determined parents are able to charm their local vicar into writing them a good reference.

A parent from north London, where there is a growing social divide between the Church of England primary schools and the secular community schools, told me:

> Our local vicar knows that most of the parents at his church don't give a hoot about God, and are only there to get their children into a decent school. But he's very nice about it, and thinks that maybe he'll convert us if we listen to his sermons long enough. We try to persuade him he's doing a good job at it.

A 2006 study by the Institute for Research in Integrated Strategies (Iris) has found that, overall, church schools educate fewer children from poor backgrounds than community schools. The survey covered all primary schools in England, which number more than 17,000. 'The figures seem to indicate a strong correlation between Christianity and wealth,' says Chris Waterman, the author of the report, 'and yet that is not borne out by the population. The alternative explanation is that church schools are selecting or attracting better-off pupils.'[6]

THE NEW SCHOOL RULES
for state-funded religious schools

1. **Be realistic** Remember state-funded religious schools are very popular with parents and usually very over-subscribed and tend to pick only the most religious parents. Statistically such schools admit fewer children from deprived backgrounds than their secular counter-parts.

2. **Gather loads of evidence** If you want to get your child into such a school, you should keep in with your local vicar or priest. Check well ahead of time to see what proof of religious commitment your favoured school requires – two years at least. Don't think turning up to church a few times a year will be enough. Many church schools want a minimum of two years of 'weekly' attendance at a local church: which means three out of four weekends in a month. All Sunday schools take a register. This effectively means you should be going to church from the beginning of Year 4 in order to get your child into an over-subscribed secondary religious school. Some schools ask couples to offer proof of attending church from when they were first married! Check the admissions criteria for your preferred religious school very carefully before scrubbing church porches: it may be that you don't need to do this, and attendance once or twice a month at church may be enough.

3. **Don't become hysterical** Don't be too swayed by hysterical press reports about religious schools. The most influential people in your life are the admissions author-ity for your preferred religious school and your religious referee. Keep them happy and you'll be fine.

Working the system with your child's special needs – two contrasting stories

Oxana, having emigrated from Russia in the early 1990s, knew very little about the complexities of the English education system, and came unstuck as a result. She lives in Neasden, in north London, in a socially mixed area. She told me:

❝ When it came to filling in the form for the secondary school, I put down the Capital City Academy as first choice. It is a new school with nice facilities and the second choice was Queens Park Community School, which also is a big school with great facilities. I thought it would be quite straightforward because these schools are within the catchment area, but then I was sent a letter that said there was no place for Alice at either school. I was not aware of any of the bureaucratic procedures that are necessary to get Alice onto the SEN register. She has been diagnosed as having Asperger's syndrome by her doctor and psychiatrist, and is currently having therapy. However, I was told by her primary school that she couldn't go on the SEN register. I realise now that I should have been more forceful about this because there is no doubt in my mind that she has special needs. ❞

Oxana's case is typical of many parents throughout the country. I examined the admissions criteria for the Capital City Academy and saw that it explicitly would give preference to pupils with special needs. However, Oxana had been initially reluctant to highlight Alice's special needs because she felt that it might have prejudiced the school against her. Since having a special need and being within the local catchment area were the main criteria for the school, it seemed clear that she would have got in if she had filled in the form more fully. It is estimated that one in ten pupils have some kind of special need at some time or another during their school career and that most schools' admissions criteria favour pupils with special needs, and yet, like Oxana, many parents do not highlight this on their admissions forms.

Highlighting your child's special needs can be crucial if you want him or her to get into the best school in the area. In Northumberland, I spoke to Malcolm, a former head of PE, and his wife, a special needs teacher, about their struggle to get their daughter Laura into Marden High School. He told me:

> I had taught at Marden High School for 35 years and I knew everything about it. I knew that it was an over-subscribed school and it would be very difficult for us to get Laura into it because we didn't live in the catchment area. Many parents move house just to send their children to the primary schools which are the feeder schools for Marden.
>
> If you are not in those primary schools, which Laura wasn't, it is how far away you are from the school as measured by public road. Other aspects of the admissions criteria include special needs, which are taken into account. Marden is also a specialist Media and Arts school, and, as a consequence, the government allows up to 10 per cent of children to be selected from outside the catchment area based on their arts and media abilities. We stressed Laura's affinity for the arts and media on the form, and we also had her hearing assessed in Year 6. She does have hearing difficulties and Marden has a special unit to help students who are deaf. Once these factors were taken into account, Laura was admitted to the school even though we were not in the catchment area.

Malcolm's story is instructive because it shows how clued up he and his wife were about the system. They knew that highlighting Laura's special need would assist her because of the special needs facilities at the good school. They had her hearing formally assessed in order to assist with their application. They were also aware of the importance of the specialist status of the school and how important it was to stress her abilities in this regard too.

Most significantly, it helped a great deal that Malcolm knew the school so well and, as a result, was able to tailor their application to the school to fit the criteria.

Another 'insider' I spoke to was Donna Thomas in Ebbw Vale, Wales. She is a long-serving secretary at one of the best schools in the area – and indeed the country in my view – Glyncoed Comprehensive. She was shocked when she learned that her son had been allocated to go to Ebbw Vale Comprehensive and not the school where she worked and was able to use her knowledge of the system to change the situation. She told me:

> I knew that Glyncoed would be far and away the best school for him. It gets much better results than Ebbw Vale and is known in the local area as being the best school.
>
> My son has muscular dystrophy and, as a result, he has a statement of special needs. He has what is called Becker's Muscular Dystrophy, which is a mild form of the disease. He was discovered to have this in primary school. The LEA wanted him to go Ebbw Vale comp as it has a flatter floor plan and they felt that he would be able to move more easily, but I point-blank refused. I felt it would be detrimental for him to go there because his friends wouldn't be there and that it was the support of his peer group that was more important for him, not the physical layout of the school. The LEA accepted my case and we have been proved right. He has been helped so much with his disability in this school because the attitude of the children is very good. All his friends would go to this school, and they all knew his problems, and they were very sympathetic towards him.

THE NEW SCHOOL RULES
for getting your child into a school that caters for your child's special needs

1. **Get your child assessed by an expert** Make sure your child is assessed by a specialist or specialists if necessary and keep all documentation relating to your child's special need (see Chapter 4 Does Your Child Have Special Needs?).

▶

> **2. Slap it on the form in big bold letters** Don't be shy about your child's special needs. Under new legislation, any child with a serious learning difficulty should receive extra time and resources at school, and is entitled to study at the school which best will meet their needs. This means that if you feel a particular school would best meet your child's need and you can prove it, you have a right to send your child there.

The illusion of choice

Throughout the country I interviewed many parents, most of whom felt that they had some degree of choice about where they sent their children to secondary school. What I found was that for some parents there was a degree of choice but this was highly dependent upon a few things:

- The number of schools in the local area.

- The admissions criteria of those schools.

- The knowledge and know-how of the parents.

- The LEA's admissions policy.

There is no doubt that since the 1990s, when the Tory government stripped LEAs of much power by allowing schools to be in charge of their own budgets, LEAs are less influential than they used to be, but in many areas they still have tremendous clout. The LEA for Leeds, Education Leeds, is a case in point. Karen and Joe's disturbing story illustrates perfectly how a LEA can rule the lives of parents and pupils.

Looking stressed and worn-out from their struggle, Karen and Joe told me of their alarming encounter with the system. They lived near two secondary schools: one with an excellent reputation and another with an appalling one. The good school was well resourced, staffed by motivated teachers and had a good discipline record. The poor school had poor facilities, a horrendous turnover of staff and was notorious in the local area for the poor behaviour of the pupils. There had been times when the police had to be called there to quell the unrest. Karen and Joe told me:

❛ Everything seemed to be in our favour: the good school where we wanted our daughter to go to took the pupils from her primary school, we lived in the right area and she was the kind of bright pupil that our chosen school would want. However, it should be stressed that there were no set criteria for getting into the school; we simply filled in form with our choices. On the first application there was no room to say why we especially wanted our child to go to a particular school.

But we were given glossy brochures which proclaimed how flexible the system was to the needs and concerns of parents, when we learned later that actually it was all predetermined.

We had a friend who was deputy head at our favoured school, who gave us some advice about how to get in, so we were confident, which made it even worse when we heard the news that we'd been rejected. ❜

Karen paused here and sighed, clearly still traumatised by the memory of the tortuous process. She continued:

❛ We applied in November but heard about it in March, which is a very long wait to hear that you never had any choice at all. I cried for a week at my computer at work I was so wound up and depressed by it.

We decided to appeal. We had to put a case together as to why our child would benefit from going to the other school, and why the rotten school was detrimental. At the first appeal, the borough and school said they were full and that it wasn't the closest school to us. They rejected all our arguments as being invalid. Catchment area was everything, despite the fact that they had denied this in the brochures.

They stonewalled all our questions about how nonsensical the system appeared to be. We pointed out that there were local children who had been turned away from the good school, but at the same time, children were being bussed in by the borough from far away because schools had been closed in their area. We felt the bussing system was totally against local schools for local children. They had been bussed in from bloody miles away. The whole system was so bloody stupid that it seemed a complete waste of time. It completely messed up the summer for us.

It was agonising for us because we tried to hide our distress from our daughter as much as possible. We didn't want her to know that we disapproved so strongly of the school. The psychological effects of that sort of concealment are awful: snatched, whispered conversations behind closed doors, hiding your upset all the time.

A number of parents, who were aware that the school brochures and information from Education Leeds were misleading, took up bogus addresses in order to get into the better school on appeal. Once they realised the game and they could afford to do it, they set up these bogus addresses, parents swapped homes with friends, and children went to live with grandparents. I still cross the street when I see people who cheated and lied about their addresses. There is a lot of this in the neighbourhood. I won't say hello to any of them. It still cuts me up. Cheating seems to be rewarded.

Our worst fears were confirmed when our daughter Lottie joined the school. At the new school there is a permanent low level of violence. She doesn't tell us much but we receive some terrible reminders every now and then such as the parents' evening I attended when a pupil at the school shouted out at me, "I'd like to fuck your daughter!" and then laughed in my face. I was powerless; there was absolutely nothing I could do. But Lottie accepts the violence as a way of life in a way we can't.

THE NEW SCHOOL RULE

for dealing with the disappointment of not getting into your chosen school

Protect your child Try to hide any trauma you have about schools admissions from your child. Realise that sometimes there is nothing you can do: you have to accept the school your child is allocated. Remember, children are resilient and most can adapt. Give plenty of support and encouragement to your child at a difficult school. Study after study shows that it is parental support which plays a key role in a child's ultimate attainment.

No favours

While the majority of parents are either very confused or simply ignorant about England's Kafka-esque schools admissions system, some people are falsely confident that they know it all – when they don't. This particular folly usually afflicts parents who are teachers or have already had a few kids go through the system. But the crucial rule is: never be complacent. Take nothing for granted. The system is constantly changing and you need to be incredibly vigilant if you are going to play it and win.

The following two stories illustrate this point.

Denise had been a modern languages teacher for nearly 20 years in a top comprehensive in the suburbs of a city in the south-east of England and understandably wanted her child to go to the school she taught in. What she hadn't thought about carefully enough was meeting the criteria for the school, which in common with many over-subscribed, voluntary aided-schools are quite exhaustive: pupils have to have played a musical instrument for two years, been a member of a club for the same amount of time, shown an aptitude for sport, or have siblings at the school. She told me about the shock she and her husband got when they tried to get their son into the school:

❝ The school in our local catchment area is a notorious, failing school. Until quite recently, it was in special measures and there was a real issue as to whether it would close down. It's got a very poor reputation in the area. About a year or so ago, a boy committed suicide because he'd endured such bad bullying there.

We probably wouldn't have applied to our nearest voluntary-aided secondary school if I hadn't taught there. Being committed socialists, my husband and I wanted our son to go to a proper comprehensive school. We applied to the school where I taught expecting him to get in because every other teacher's child in the last 30 years has been offered a place. But he didn't get in because he didn't meet the criteria of doing sports and belonging to clubs.

When we were told in January that he hadn't got in I felt humiliated. I saw it as a reflection on me. It made me feel really undervalued. It was very upsetting. Then we had the worry of where our son was going to go.

We went through the appeal process, which was very nerve-wracking. We had spent hours and hours preparing what we were going to say. The panel, which consisted of two independent lay people and one expert in education, didn't respond to our case. My husband tried to say the school would be losing a valuable modern languages teacher if they didn't accept our son and therefore would be affecting the resources of the school. Tactically, this was a mistake. It was too much like blackmail and the school wasn't too keen on that. I was upset when I saw the rejection letter but not as much as before. ❞

Denise was a trifle complacent about getting into the school where she taught because she had seen every other member of staff get their children into the school. While she knew that her child did not exactly fit the criteria, she felt that the school would bend the rules for her in order to retain an important and long-standing member of staff. She has some justification in thinking this. In a recent survey, a quarter of head teachers admitted they don't adhere to their school's policy on admissions.[7]

But one thing is certain: no head teacher will bend the rules if they know the ombudsman is scrutinising them very closely. Denise's preferred school had been criticised by the ombudsman for having a 'hidden' selection process a few years before. He had even examined every single entry form for that academic year. The school was being watched and it knew it. It couldn't afford another slip-up.

Jane in Harrogate was similarly complacent and got a rude awakening when her third child was not sent to the best school in the area.

❛ My son was sent to the worst school in Harrogate because we naturally assumed that he would go to the same school as his siblings. They had all gone to St Aidans, which is one of the top schools in the area and is also a religious school. However, when it came to filling in the form for Henry, our third child, we neglected to mention our religious background, assuming that Henry would get in automatically because his brother and sister had gone there. How wrong we were!

It was such a trauma of going through the appeal because you have to be so well prepared with your statement. The whole thing was horrible – and we failed to get him in. ❜

THE NEW SCHOOL RULE
for those who think they know it all

Keep up to date Rules and regulations change every year. Even the most seasoned professionals get caught out. Check to see if your preferred school has been criticised by the ombudsman in recent years. If it has, then it is very, very unlikely that the admissions panel will bend the rules for your child.

Getting into a grammar school

Getting your child into an academically selective school can be even more time-consuming. Whereas there are not loads of criteria to meet, you do need to train up your child so that he or she can pass the relevant exams to get in. This involves preparation, planning at least two years ahead of the exam, assessing your child's abilities, buying past exam papers, coaching your child and being very patient. Even David Parry, a very experienced deputy head, found it traumatic jumping through all the hoops. He told me:

> I was very worried about how my daughter would perform in the eleven-plus just recently. I live in one of those areas where there are still grammar schools knocking around – there are more than you think. My daughter, Iris, is a well-behaved, aspirational child.
>
> We played the game well with the primary school because we got her into the middle-class one which has an excellent track record for getting children through the eleven-plus. But as an extra precaution, we got sucked into the tutoring as well. A year prior to the exam, Iris's mother paid for a tutor to come once a week. Being an English teacher, I tutored her for the verbal reasoning part of the exam.
>
> She was primed and ready to pass because that is what every middle-class parent in the area does. The standard of the English in the eleven-plus is in some ways more difficult than what you get at GCSE. There was an extract from *The Mill on the Floss*, which is an A level text for Literature. When I was going through the past papers with her, I found some of the old-fashioned comprehension questions quite difficult: they really put me on the spot!
>
> I was so relieved when she got in because I knew the alternative, having taught there for three years: it is a tough secondary modern. The teachers there are excellent but the prevailing student culture is very negative. Very few students want to learn.
>
> What you are buying into with a grammar school is a largely bully-free bubble to protect your child against the anti-learning culture that is prevalent even in some of the best

comprehensives. The teaching may well be sedentary: some of the most exciting teaching is now going on in failing schools. But at the grammar school, I know that my daughter will not be got at for regularly handing her homework in on time.

Getting your child into a grammar school is a costly business and you may not giving your child the best teachers in the world. Instead, you are buying your child a cocoon.

You can go overboard with the eleven-plus cramming though. A recent *Times Educational Supplement* investigation uncovered that children as young as eight are being tutored outside school for grammar school places. It appears that when these hothoused children eventually arrive at their grammar school they are not able to cope. One headmaster of a grammar school said, 'If a child is tutored above their natural level of capability for any exam then they could have a miserable time on joining the school.'[8]

The Grammar School Association estimates that 75,000 children annually sit the eleven-plus for only 20,000 places. This means that the vast majority of children don't get into grammar school. And it really isn't the end of the world if they don't. As we shall see in the following chapters, it is a parent's support of their child that is the number-one factor in their academic success, not the school a child goes to. We shall also see that grammar schools can be particularly unsuited to many different types of children: they are very pressurised places which try their best to chuck out children who look like they are not going to make the grade. (See pages 296–7 for more on Academically Selective Schools).

THE NEW SCHOOL RULES

for getting into a grammar school

1. **Train them early** Start training your child to take the eleven-plus in Year 4 of primary school. If necessary, pay

▶

for a tutor/tutors in English and maths. Use the Internet (www.11plusEnglish.com) and mock test papers to see how well your child is doing.

2. **Remember, grammar schools are not always the best** A grammar school may not have the best teaching, but it is generally a cocoon – a safe environment where children are not bullied for working hard or handing in homework. Don't assume that the worst teachers are in failing schools – sometimes the reverse is the case.

3. **Don't hothouse your child too much** It can be counter-productive in the long run. Your child may absolutely hate the grammar school if he or she is actually not up to it.

Getting your child into a private secondary school

Parents in the private sectors have different worries, but it appears that they are no less anxious. The contest to get your child into a fee-paying school in London is cut-throat, particularly in north London where there are a large number of very wealthy parents, quite a few state schools that are perceived to be war zones, and only a sprinkling of top public schools. If you can get your child into one of these private schools, you can get them in anywhere. Many parents who want their children to go to private schools are fiercely competitive and, as a result, the issue of getting your child into the best school is one of paramount importance. George, who had been through this ordeal, told me:

❝ It is a nightmare where we live to get your child into a good school, because it is so competitive. I had to think ahead because when your child is very young you don't know how well your child is going to perform. In London, there are four or five very good schools: Westminster, City of London, St Paul's, University College and Highgate. There is a pecking order with these schools, with Westminster and St Paul's at the top, then City of London and University College, and then Highgate. They are all very good schools.

If you don't get into one of those, you are finished. You are forced to go to schools which are perceived as second rate.

What happens is that games are played very early on with your children. You have to plan ahead for a secondary school more or less at birth, or at five at the very latest. If you are confident about your child you can leave him at a prep school like I did with my boy, who was at Northbridge House, and feel fairly sure that he will do well at his Common Entrance exam at 13, and will do well enough to get into one of those five schools.

But if you are not confident, you then angle to get him into one of the junior schools of one of these schools. There are special little schools who take children at the age of five, and train them to pass the entrance exams at the age of eight for the junior school, and then they have an easy ride because once they are in, they are almost certain to go on to the senior part of the school.

University College, St Paul's, Westminster all have junior schools that start at the age of eight. The problem with this is that you don't know whether your child is the right child for that school.

If you go, say, for Highgate at the age of eight, and you find that your child is too clever for the place then they are more or less stuck there until they go to university.

My son, Ian, went to Northbridge House preparatory school which encouraged him to stay until 13 and take the Common Entrance at 13. The danger there is that if he does badly at this very tough exam then he could fail to get into a good school altogether.

One or two parents with weaker children got nervous and withdrew them from Northbridge House having got them into Highgate Junior School, which gave those children an assured entry into the senior school. Some parents applied to University College. All the pupils that got in there were tutored to death.

The next hurdle to get through was the eleven-plus. Again University College opened their doors to pupils who passed this exam. So

Ian took it. He passed the exam and then there was an interview. They interviewed the child separately and then interviewed the parent. Ian got shut down at the interview. The school didn't explain why.

Three kids from Northbridge House passed the exam. The third boy who passed the exam was tutored like crazy, unlike Ian, who went on his energy and what he had learned in school. Ian had been reading 100 books a year since the age of nine. When he was 11 years old he read Umberto Eco, all of H.G. Wells, Orwell and Aldous Huxley. So he was no dunce! However, he wasn't tutored. The third boy was reprimanded for being disruptive and unruly, and also didn't do well in his lessons. He was bottom of the pile. When Ian was rejected, we figured that the disruptive boy must have been rejected as well. But he got in!

That hurt because all of a sudden this opened up our minds to something else. We realised that the selection was not a natural one; it was more connected with social status. This boy was being picked up at Northbridge House by a chauffeur-driven car. The boy was someone who blew his own horn: he talked up a storm. He was gregarious and talkative in a way that Ian was not. We felt that they were after children who had big mouths. With Ian they totally blew it.

Things were difficult at home after he failed to get into University College. My wife got into a real panic and had nightmares that Ian would have to go to the local comprehensive!

But he stayed at Northbridge House and made good progress. The story behind him getting into Westminster is a fascinating one. Since the age of nine, Ian has been addicted to computer games. He particularly enjoyed playing a game about Ancient Greece and Rome, called *Age of Empires*. At his interview for Westminster, he impressed the interviewer by knowing the meaning of the word 'aesthete', which he learned from playing the game. He also passed nearly ten exams in all the different subjects, including Latin and Greek.

Ian went through the tough route to Westminster. He didn't start there at eight and gain a more or less assured entry into the senior school. Instead he had to go through a very difficult, competitive exam at the age of 13, not knowing which school, if any, he would end up at. This has shaped him for the rest of his life: it has toughened him up. 〟

George's story illustrates some vital points about English public schools. First, you can't rely solely upon the prep-school system if you want your child to get into the very top public schools and secondly, the system is not primarily a meritocracy. It is as much a social network as a means for a child to gain a good all-round education. That's why parents who have done the social rounds, and befriended the right people, find that this has long-term pay-offs while other less gregarious parents can be bitterly disappointed.

Interviews are now banned in the state system but fee-paying schools still rely heavily on them; if your child is highly articulate and confident then he may have a much better chance than someone who is shy and retiring; or may not. It all depends upon the balance a particular school is looking for: most private schools don't want their classrooms stuffed to the gills with outrageously confident pupils. Private schools only interview pupils after they have taken the different exams that are required. While it will be your child's performance in the various exams – which normally follow the eleven-plus and Common Entrance format – which are the most important in deciding whether they are accepted or not, interviews do play a significant role. Schools are aware that those born between September and December always attain the best marks and they use the interview to spot the bright pupils who have not performed that well in the exams.

Public schools are desperate to have more of a social and ethnic range of pupils than they have done in the past. These days they are being watched very carefully by a government that is thinking of taking away their charitable status and, as a result, they are particularly anxious to take pupils from all social classes and ethnic backgrounds where and when they can.

To get a proper insight into pupils' social skills they will often seek two perspectives: usually a one-to-one interview and a classroom observation.

THE NEW SCHOOL RULES
for getting into a good private school

1. **Be prepared to spend, spend, spend** Make a bucket-load of money so you can pay the extortionate school fees! Shell out even more money, and hire a private tutor if you want your child to pass the rigorous entrance exams. They should do plenty of mock tests before taking the actual exam.

2. **Prepare them early** Carry out mock interviews and try to build your child's confidence. Don't try to turn them into someone they're not: they'll just come across as odd and false in the interview if you do.

3. **Expect snobbery** Don't assume that the top schools pick their pupils on academic merit alone: social status plays an important role. The parents are being tested as much as the pupils. Get to know your favoured private schools by going to their social functions such as fundraising events.

A few minutes on the Internet could save you a lot of time and pain. If you want to find out about the right school for your child, here's what you do:

1. Log onto the Ofsted website. Go onto the parents' page, choose which type of school you're interested in, and type in your postcode: all the recent reports for schools in your area will come up. Using the links at the bottom of the Ofsted web page for the school, go onto the DfEE website (http://www.dfes.gov.uk/performancetables/) and check out the school league table results. Look at the relevant reports and tables, and devise a shortlist of schools to look at.

2. Then look at your LEA's website and the website for your chosen schools. Check their admissions criteria (the entry requirements) carefully: are you living close enough to the school? Is there a banding system? Does the school favour pupils with special needs or an aptitude in a particular specialism? Is the school over-subscribed? From this information, you should be able to work out whether your child has a good chance of getting in or not.

3. Visit the schools and see if your Internet researches check out.

For a summary of all the rules in this chapter, please refer to 'A is for Admissions' in the A–Z of New School Rules in the Appendix C, as well as The New School Rules timetable for parents below.

THE NEW SCHOOL RULES
timetable for parents

0–1 years (approximate age of child)

Type of schooling offered
None

Learning
Welcome to the world.

Questions to ask yourselves, your child and your school
Private or state? Where do you live and how good are the schools in your area? Do you have a boy or a girl? How religious are you? What are your ambitions for your child?

Action
Investigate schools in your area. Move house if you are in an area where there are no good state schools. Go to church if you want your child to go to a religious school. Start saving for school fees.

2–4 years (approximate age of child)

Type of schooling offered
Nursery school, kindergarten

Learning
Play, socialising skills. No good nursery will force formal learning upon your child; the emphasis should be on their happiness and well-being.

Questions to ask yourselves, your child and your school
How is your child getting on at nursery? Does he/she thrive in big groups or does he need one-to-one attention? Have you noticed any problems with socialising, constant crying?

Action
Start making appointments and touring schools. Feel confident to ask anything that is nagging away at you. Use the DEATH analysis to make sure you go through the correct procedures. Usually with state schools you must fill in the LEA admissions form, and apply to the school as well.

---

4 years (approximate age of child)

Type of schooling offered
Pre-prep starts in private sector

Learning
Some formal learning begins. Learning of letter sounds, numbers.

---

5 years (approximate age of child)

Type of schooling offered
It is illegal for your child not to go to school. All children (except when parents choose to educate at home) must be admitted into full-time education by the beginning of the term following their fifth birthday. Year 1 is the year beginning in the September following the child's fifth birthday.

Learning
Formal learning begins in earnest. Literacy and numeracy hour in school.

Questions to ask yourselves, your child and your school
Is your child reading short, simple books by the end of the year?

Action
If you feel your child is finding it difficult to learn, you must get him/her assessed for special needs (see Chapter 4 Does Your Child Have Special Needs?).

6–7 years (approximate age of child)

Type of schooling offered
Year 2

Learning
January – May: Key Stage 1 SATS tests in all state primary schools. Entry exams in English and maths for pupils to prep schools.

Questions to ask yourselves, your child and your school
Are you happy with your child's current school? Are you considering switching to the private sector?

Action
Consider private coaching for your child if you want to switch to the private sector at seven.

7–8 years (approximate age of child)

Type of schooling offered
Year 3. Prep school starts in private sector.

Action
Check to see what the admissions criteria of the secondary schools in your area are. In particular, are there subject specialism, clubs, musical instruments that they should be taking up, etc.?

8–9 years (approximate age of child)

Type of schooling offered
Year 4

Action
Attend church, get your child to join clubs etc., learn a musical instrument if this is relevant for the admissions criteria of your favoured school. Begin private tutoring in English and maths for the eleven-plus exam for grammar and private schools.

9–10 years (approximate age of child)

Type of schooling offered
In Year 5 schools give parents a chance to observe secondary schools.

Questions to ask yourselves, your child and your school
Which school does your child's best teachers think he/she should go to? What do you think? What does he/she think?

Action
Visit prospective secondary state schools armed with your questions. As well as attending the open evenings, visit them while the pupils are being taught. Hire a private tutor for the bizarre eleven-plus verbal and non-verbal reasoning tests (see more at www.11plusEnglish.com) if you are considering sending your child to a private/grammar school at 11 or attaining a scholarship to a fee-paying school. Investigate the different scholarships and bursaries on offer (www.isc.co.uk/index.php).

10–11 years (approximate age of child)

Type of schooling offered
Year 6

Learning
Key Stage 2 SATS tests in all state primaries. Eleven-plus exams and entry exams to many private schools.

Questions to ask yourselves, your child and your school

Ask the teachers early on in the year about their Teaching Assessment Levels for your child – they are usually more accurate than the final test results, although often lower. If your child has not moved up a level from Key Stage 1, ask the school about what is going on. Do they need catch-up lessons in secondary school?

Action

September–October: make sure you fill in your admissions forms for state schools and you apply through the LEA. Check very, very carefully that you have met the criteria for the schools you are applying for. January–April: wait for your offers of places. If necessary, appeal.

11–12 years (approximate age of child)

Type of schooling offered

Year 7. State secondary schools and grammar schools usually start.

Questions to ask yourselves, your child and your school

What levels did he/she achieve in his/her SATS? What sort of school is best for him/her?

Action

Check homework diaries every week. Practise/tutor for Common Entrance if you are thinking of sending your child to a fee-paying school.

12–13 years (approximate age of child)

Type of schooling offered

Year 8

Questions to ask yourselves, your child and your school

Beware of the Year 8 drift: is your child being stretched at school or are they falling behind? This happens more often in Year 8.

Action

Practise/tutor for Common Entrance if you are thinking of sending your child to a fee-paying school.

12–13 years (approximate age of child)

Type of schooling offered
Year 9. Common Entrance exam. Most public schools (private boys and co-ed schools) test, interview and accept the majority of their pupils.

Learning
Key Stage 3 SATS tests in English, maths, and science.

Questions to ask yourselves, your child and your school
Has your child achieved a high Level 5 or above in their SATS? If they haven't, then you should be asking for extra help because it may be unlikely that they will get 5 A–C GCSEs.

14–15 years (approximate age of child)

Type of schooling offered
Year 10. Some modular GCSE exams are taken in Year 10.

Questions to ask yourselves, your child and your school
Is your child being entered for Higher or Foundation Tiers? Remember, it is usually impossible to get above a 'C' grade if entered for Foundation.

Action
Extra help/tuition for your child in the key GCSE subjects if they attained a low Level 5 in their SATS.

15–16 years (approximate age of child)

Type of schooling offered
Year 11. Preparation for GCSEs.

Questions to ask yourselves, your child and your school
What are your child's favourite subjects? What school should he/she go to in the sixth form? Does he/she want to go to university and what subjects should he/she study there? This will affect his/her A Level choices.

Action
Start visiting possible sixth forms. Look at the subjects offered and results carefully.

16–17 years (approximate age of child)

Type of schooling offered
Year 12. GCSE results are published and based on them, pupils may move to a variety of different schools. May study for International Baccalaureate or A levels. Entry at sixth form increasingly depends upon GCSEs.

Questions to ask yourselves, your child and your school
How well has your child done in his GCSEs? What are his strengths and weaknesses?

Action
Investigate crammers if your child has done badly.

17–18 years (approximate age of child)

Type of schooling offered
Year 13. AS results are published at the end of Year 12. UCAS statements are usually written over the summer before Year 13 begins. The best candidates usually send off their UCAS forms by mid-October of Year 13.

Questions to ask yourselves, your child and your school
What sort of university should your child go to?

CHAPTER 2

Getting the most out of your school

What do parents fear the most? Quite a few of them confessed to me that they really worry that they won't fit into their child's new school: they'll be labelled troublemakers if they complain, they'll be despised for their accent or clothes, the other parents and teachers will bitch about how terrible their child is and they'll be frozen out in the playground and their child will suffer as a result.

Perhaps what many parents don't realise is that at the root of all these anxieties is the problem of the way a school communicates with its parents. Let me explain: if a school is communicating well with the parents and laying out clear guidelines about what is expected of them and what is expected of the children, informing them reliably about all the different events and functions that are happening, then parents feel secure that they don't have to ask anybody else. Such parents feel secure because everything is clearly spelled out to them. However, if communication between school and parents is bad, if messages don't get through, then gossip occurs as parents desperately try to find out what's going on. Rumours arise, fears are fuelled by tittle-tattle, and the climate in the playground becomes fevered.

Unfortunately, research shows that many schools are poor at communicating with parents, which is a great shame because the way in which schools stay in touch with parents is vitally important. There is huge confusion over this issue. Successive governments have issued a great deal of legislation about what information schools should give to parents, but most parents still feel bemused by what they have a right to know and what they should know. All schools in England now obey the law and must report to parents at least once a year on their child's progress in the National Curriculum subjects. Schools must also supply information about the achievements of the school, which used to take the form of the governor's annual report but now will be published on the web as the school profile.

However, as we will see in this chapter, much of what schools are obliged to publish for parents totally bewilders them. Many school reports are written in a language that even the best educated of parents don't understand, statistics about a school's performance are difficult to interpret and home–school agreements seem baffling and arbitrary.

This chapter will unravel these mysteries of school. It will deal with all the aspects of home–school contact: the information the school tells you and how to communicate in the most fruitful way with your child's school. Among other things, it will show you how to get your child to settle into their new school, what the reports your child gets really mean, how to complain and how to change things that you know are not right. It will show you how to communicate with your school, what to expect from it, and how to sort out any problems you might encounter.

What parents want from new schools – primary and secondary

Rory, a large five-year-old in his Superman sweatshirt, just wouldn't stop crying as he stumbled in the crisp September air towards his new school. His mother, Edwina, clasped his hand tightly, trying to console him but it was no use. 'Mum, I don't wanna go! I don't wanna go! Don't make me go there!' he wailed. Edwina was nearly in tears as well. Later she confided to me that it broke her heart to be separated from him, having spent the majority of the last five years with him.

❧ It was different when he went to nursery school because I could stay as long as I wanted, and besides, it was all just playing and stuff, and there was a nice, cosy atmosphere. Also, he only stayed mornings; now he has to stay all day! ❧

Edwina found that Rory simply wouldn't let go of her in the playground and begged to come home. She was consoled to see that quite a few other parents were suffering from similar trauma, but she had to admit that Rory was the worst. This shocked her because he was normally a very confident boy. What was the school doing to him during the day? Was he being bullied? Was the teacher too frightening? She had spent a morning in the school with Rory on the first day and then a gradually diminishing amount of time in the succeeding days, and felt that everything seemed fine. His teacher, Miss Pennington, was nice, and the other children seemed very well into term?

Edwina found the school a bit inflexible now. They didn't want her to sit with Rory in classes any more and they didn't have any information about what he was doing in lessons and the rest of school time other than what was in the school prospectus. She told me:

❧ I could really do with a little booklet or letter that told me what he was learning in the lessons and what's happening around school generally. The teacher has told me in general terms but it is a bit much to take in. I want to know important things like is he allowed to go to the toilet during lessons? Can he get a drink of water whenever he wants? He likes colouring at home, is he allowed to do that anymore? What happens at break-time? Does he play with anyone? Does the teacher do activities that enable the children to become friends? Is he allowed to bring toys to school? Is there a locker where he can put his possessions? What happens at lunchtime? Does he sit with anyone? Does anyone check to see that he's eaten his meal? I don't know the answer to any of these questions except what Rory tells me in a distressed way. He's not a very good source of information really: he just bursts into tears when I talk about school. ❧

Edwina was experiencing, in an extreme form, what many parents experience when their children go to a new school: confusion and bewilderment about what actually goes on there.

Parents are crying out for more information about how to help their children settle into a new school. Too many parents have very little idea about the crucial practical issues that Edwina was asking about: information about food, toilets, drinking water, discipline policies, what goes on in lessons and school clubs – and they need to know. The best schools issue booklets to parents answering all these questions, but many do not, leaving parents distressed about the suffering they are seeing in their children.

The best primary schools I encountered were exceptionally welcoming places: parents felt free to drop in whenever they liked, sit with the child in lessons and breaks and could see for themselves what was going on. However, primary schools are under no obligation to do this and it is only the goodwill of the staff that means it happens. In schools where staff turnover has been high and where there have been problems, the barriers frequently go up, and parents are often 'locked' out, leaving them wondering what exactly is going on. Unfortunately, these are the very places that need to be scrutinised by parents.

With secondary schools, it is another matter entirely. Research shows that parents are often confused by what goes on when their child first joins at 11. Few primary schools prepare their pupils for their move to secondary school adequately, and written information about the transition is very patchy. Crucially, parents are crying out to know about four main areas: practical information, bullying policies and procedures, school facts and extracurricular activities, and special needs provision.[1]

A good head teacher should be responsive to these points and if you write to him or her asking for the information itemised in the New School Rules below, the head teacher should set the wheels in motion so that it is made freely available to every parent. Remember, exhaustive research for the DfES backs up your right to know this stuff: surveys show that huge numbers of parents want to know it as well.

THE NEW SCHOOL RULES
about what information to demand from your child's new school

1. **Get the nitty-gritty** Ask for practical information: a map of the school, access to drinking fountains, toilets, wash basins, medical facilities, the phone, procedures for break and lunchtimes. A particular concern for many parents I have spoken to is the toilet: they want to know how often the toilets are cleaned, what type of toilet paper there is, what kind of soap is in the basins. In many ways, the school's response to these questions will be an indicator of its attitude in general: if it is a nice place, it will have nice toilets. Ask for some up-to-date information about the extracurricular activities going on in the school and the social functions. You should receive a calendar or booklet with all the relevant dates of parents' evenings, concerts, and clubs and so on.

2. **Don't suffer in silence** If your child is being picked on or seems unhappy, ask for a copy of the school's discipline policy. These are the rules for behaviour that school insists upon – and shows how it deals with bullying (see Chapter 3 How to Tackle the Big Problems for more on bullying). If your child is finding the work difficult or seems to be making little progress, ask for a copy of the school's special needs procedures and talk to the special needs coordinator (see Chapter 4 Does Your Child Have Special Needs? for more on this). If your child is bored, you must ask to meet with your child's teachers and tell them about this. If the teacher tells you that there is nothing much they can do, you have a right to ask for your child to be 'given an Individual Action Plan (IAP) which sets out clearly a list of tasks that will stretch and

▶

engage them in your child's preferred learning style'. I know this sounds like terrible jargon but it's the way we teachers speak now. An IAP is, effectively, a list of specific targets or goals for your child to work towards that will motivate him or her. It should be drawn up with your child and have his or her consent so that he or she feels part of the programme. A 'learning style' is the way in which your child learns best: it might be that they learn 'visually' (drawings help them remember and understand things) or 'aurally' (they need to hear words read out to them in order to comprehend best) and so forth. To work out your child's learning style log on to: www.bbc.co.uk/keyskills/extra/module1/1.shtml. So, for example, after discussion with your child and teacher, an IAP might be drawn up so that they have a particular book to read, or a series of drawings to complete, and so forth by a particular date and then their attitudes and progress will be reviewed. For more on learning styles and IAPs see the Glossary.

Settling into a new primary school

It is generally agreed among child psychologists and educationalists that parents should be very involved with helping their children settle into school. Most reception and Year 1 classes encourage parents to come into school with their children and sit with them to help them acclimatise to the strange, new surroundings.

Sometimes, parents have to work very hard in order to help their child settle in. My mother-in-law, Ellen, told me this story about her daughter Erica, my wife.

6 We decided to send our child to an all girls' school. Erica was nearly five years old. She was very distressed because in her nursery

school there were boys and girls, and they were allowed to wear what clothing they wanted. She loved wearing her blue jeans like the boys did.

We spent six months gently advising her that this was a girls' school, and that it would be all girls. We did not discuss clothing. We thought that she had got the picture about all girls.

On the first day, I left feeling fairly contented like all the other mothers, but I got a call about noon. The school secretary said, "Don't be upset, but you are going to have to come back. Everyone has settled down except Erica, who is sobbing. But we think you can help us get over this difficult time."

I had to make the long trip from my workplace to go to the school. When I got there she was still sobbing. Everyone else was very happy. She said to me through her sobs, "They are all girls, I want to be with the boys like I used to be, and I want to wear my blue jeans, and I don't want to come back here tomorrow."

I explained that we had talked to her about it being all girls. She said that she just hated it. So I asked the teachers if she could go in her blue jeans. They said yes, and then they said, 'We will let you dictate how you can help her settle in.' I asked to spend some time at the school with her. First day: one hour. Next day: three-quarters of an hour. The day after that: half an hour. They agreed absolutely. In effect, I went to infants' school every day, until we got to the point where I didn't have to sit on those tiny chairs anymore.

On the first day when I hadn't sat with her at all, I met her at the school gates, and she proclaimed proudly, "I did it!"

Increasingly, teachers are finding that they are having to get parents more and more involved in their child's schooling in these early years. One reception teacher, Irene, told me:

The trouble is that many children come to school now not knowing how to go to the toilet properly, or knowing how to hold a knife and fork. Some children don't know how to hold a conversation or play because they've just been parked in front of the television for hours on end. Our school has decided to tackle this by running parent–child classes during the first few days of term where we go through all the things we expect the children to be able to do such as going to the toilet, holding a knife and fork, buttoning up a coat, saying please and thank you and so on. We also run through basics for the parents like getting them to put name tags on clothing and how to make a healthy packed lunch. It is all very patronising in a way but these induction days – as we call them – have been a success. The mothers are very grateful.

Surprisingly, Irene said that even the parents whose children knew how to wipe their own bottoms and so on, were grateful that the school spelled out so clearly what was expected of parents and children. It meant that they all knew where they stood. Most schools are not so confident – or bossy depending on which way you look at it. Most schools have no clear programme of expectations for parents and children, and take them as they come, often muddling through with the struggling children without contacting parents, except in cases of emergency.

The government is trying to change this situation by asking every school to produce a foundation stage profile, which is a booklet recording a child's achievements in reception – usually the first year in a primary school. There's a space for the child's photograph and, listed in brightly coloured boxes, all the things they might achieve by the end of the year.

During these early years, the best schools have an open-door policy for parents, which usually means that they can drop into the classroom before or after school and discuss any problems that may be troubling them, whether trivial or not. The parents I spoke to in Northumberland felt most at ease with their school in this respect. The primary school in the village of Embleton was praised by many parents because they felt the teachers were so approachable. There was a feeling that they could drop in at any time and talk through anything that was troubling them. Added to which, the school actively appeared to encourage parents to help out at the school with children's reading and writing.

THE NEW SCHOOL RULES

for helping your child to settle into primary school

1. **Get the nitty-gritty** As suggested in the previous chapter ask for vital information on the schools' policies and procedures. (See page 129 for The New School Rules about what information to demand from your child's new school.)

2. **Keep calm** Try not to let your emotions show, but keep calm and reassure your child that they will settle in eventually – even if you don't quite believe this yourself. Your school should have an 'open door' policy whereby you or a carer can sit with your child for a time at school and gradually wean them off your presence. Many schools have strategies in place that enable children to make friends, such as 'friendship benches' – places where children can sit and chat with a 'friend' if they feel left out. If it doesn't, suggest that it does take more active steps to encourage your child to make friends. Check to see that it isn't something like going to the toilet or the school dinners that are making your child anxious. Ask your child if he or she knows what to do if they want to go to the toilet or if they are hungry.

Settling into secondary school

Alice's personality change was very sudden and very dramatic. From being a smiley, happy girl who would skip along to school merrily, she became a surly, snarling monster who would never wake up in time, rarely talk in full sentences and appeared to have lost all interest in her work. Her father, Phil, said to me:

I knew it was moving to secondary school that did it. But the frustrating thing was she wouldn't tell me or my partner about what was going on. She'd loved her primary school where she'd been appointed the head girl, and had excelled at maths and science. That all seemed to change at secondary school. She got two teachers in maths and science who she didn't like, and she knew very few children in her new school. In a matter of a few weeks, she was becoming very aggressive at home: shouting at me that I was stupid, and telling her mother that she hated her. It was a nightmare.

Phil's story is not unusual. I spoke to many parents who found the transition from primary to secondary school very traumatic. Research shows that the school system is just not geared up properly for helping children settle into secondary school. Primary schools need to give detailed information packs to Year 6 pupils (the oldest year in primary school) about what goes on in secondary school. They should have Year 7 pupils from secondary school going into primary schools and telling the younger pupils what to expect, and group discussions about what to expect. Nearly all primary schools arrange visits to secondary schools, which can last a day or a couple of days, but this appears not to be enough. Just as importantly, the parents of primary school children need to receive standardised information packs about the new school, its bullying policies and special needs procedures. Moreover, the parents of children who are vulnerable in some way – such as having emotional problems – need to be given extra guidance about what to expect. Schools should also consider giving every new secondary pupil a 'mentor' in the year above to help the child settle in.[2] In most schools this is simply not happening, but it should be, and could considerably assist with making the whole transition from primary school to secondary much less of a nightmare than it is.

For many parents, schools quickly become sealed off. Karen told me:

After a day or two of being allowed into the classroom to settle our daughter in, then gradually weaning ourselves off that so we stayed in the playground, it was quite a shock that suddenly the door was closed. This feeling of being powerless, uninformed and totally removed from a school is increased enormously when your child goes to high school and you never set foot there except for parents' evenings and concerts.

In common with many parents, Karen didn't find that other parents were much solace. She said, 'I was totally unprepared for the cliques in the playground, and the snootiness from some non-working mothers about being a working mum.'

For Karen information about school life only came out in dribs and drabs from her children, such as the lack of proper water fountains in the school. She said, 'We were also unprepared for how little the kids get to drink during the day: the water fountains that never work!'

Apart from these odd snippets, she and many parents feel a little in the dark about what is going. Phil, the father of Alice, was only able to stop his daughter's tantrums when he made an appointment to see her year head and explained to him what was going on:

> The year head didn't have a clue that Alice was being like this. In fact, the year head didn't know who Alice was at that point because there are 180 pupils in the year and he didn't teach her. But he was the one in charge of her overall well-being so I did the right thing by contacting him.

Phil explained to me:

> After I told him what was going on, he carried out some investigations and found out that Alice was being very quiet in lessons – something she had never been in primary school – and that it appeared she was being bullied or made fun of by a couple of other girls in the form. He was able to speak to the girls who were mocking Alice and then speak to Alice. This made a big difference. The girls left Alice alone and she grew in confidence. It also helped for the science and maths teachers to know that Alice had

been very good at these subjects in primary school. They started paying more attention to her after that, and that helped her confidence. Alice made a few friends and she started becoming her 'normal' happy self after a couple more weeks. I am very glad I made the effort to speak to the school.

Phil's story is instructive in many ways because it shows that if you do contact the school, by and large, you will get a result. Most secondary schools do want to help but they are so big that it is very easy for children to 'get lost' and be ignored. It is only if you are pro-active that you will ensure your child gets the attention he or she deserves.

THE NEW SCHOOL RULES
for getting your child to settle into secondary school

1. **Get the nitty-gritty** Always demand to have the relevant information. (See page 129 for The New School Rules about what information to demand from your child's new school.)

2. **Don't suffer in silence** Contact the relevant person in charge of your child's welfare – this should be in the information supplied by the school, but it is usually your child's form tutor or year head.

3. **Keep calm** Try to do your best to let your child relax at home. Don't question them when they seem very tense or angry but wait until they are calmer and more relaxed then enquire gently about how they are getting on. Remember, moving to a secondary school can be just as traumatic as going to primary school, especially if your child is no longer with their friends from primary.

Home–school agreements

Azita, the mother of two sons at a secondary comprehensive school in the Midlands, shook her head in bewilderment and annoyance at the document, a home–school agreement that was in front of her. She said:

> Why is someone asking me to sign this? It seems a bit pointless and a little fascistic to me.
>
> I've got to promise to send my children to school in school uniform and attend parents' evenings which is well and good, but I've also got to encourage him to have a positive attitude to school, respond to letters promptly, and support the policies of the school and so on. Now, it may be that I actually think some of the policies are no good. What do I do then? I am being asked to sign this contract in the blind faith that I am going to agree with everything the school does. Sorry, but I am just not willing to do that!

I examined the agreement. It was a four-page document outlining everything the school promised to do, what the pupils should promise to do, what the parents should do, and what the governors were going to carry out. It seemed harmless enough on first sight, but on closer examination I could see Azita's point. Its demands on parents were high: they were essentially responsible for their children's behaviour in school and were expected to be propagandists for the school's policies.

It made me wonder what exactly the purpose of these home–school agreements was. My own research revealed that in an attempt to make schools much friendlier places the School Standards and Framework Act 1998 asked all schools to draw up a home–school agreement. Parents are usually asked to sign a document drawn up by the school. The agreement that parents sign should explain:

- The school's overall aims and what it believes in.

- What the school expects of its teachers and the standard of discipline it expects of its pupils.

- What support it expects from parents.

Parents do not have to sign this agreement and it was made clear in the legislation that no child or parent should be punished for their failure or refusal to sign the agreement. Schools are not allowed to force parents to sign the agreement before they send their child to the school.

The agreements were intended to get parents to reflect upon what the school required of them and their children, but in my experience they have become either another piece of paper, which is signed and then forgotten about, or a way of making parents more accountable for the behaviour and attitude of their children in schools. Whether this is a good or a bad thing remains to be seen. Many parents I interviewed felt alienated by the home–school agreements, seeing them as yet another imposition from an overbearing state. Azita said:

> I have tried my best to bring up my children well and I will try my best to see that they behave in school but I can't be held accountable for everything they do there. They are teenage boys now with minds of their own; to make me responsible for every little bit of misbehaviour is totally ridiculous and a bit scary. I think it might make parents be more confrontational with their children, which won't help in the long run.

THE NEW SCHOOL RULES
about the home–school agreement

1. **Read them carefully** They are much more than pieces of useless paper. Examine them carefully, looking particularly at the homework and discipline comments: it may

▶

well be that you have to talk to the school about both these issues. If the agreement makes promises about homework and behaviour, then it should be held accountable to them by you. Equally, if you sign up to support the school's ethos and policies, you need to do so, but perhaps you should find out what these are before you sign.

2. **Use them to your advantage** If your child is not behaving properly or is not doing his or her homework remind them of the home–school agreement. Don't be afraid of re-reading these important bits of paper with your child, they can really help.

3. **You do not have to sign it if you disagree with it.**

Letters home

Schools can be divided into two. Those which attempt to hold parents accountable for their children's work and behaviour – and those which don't. The main method of trying to hold a parent accountable is by sending a letter home. The realistic schools know that most letters never get read or reach their destination – and act accordingly. The schools which are hot on home–school contact generally believe that sending letters home helps: they send letters home about test scores, minor and major instances of misbehaviour and examples of good behaviour.

The more idealistic schools, of which there are an increasing number, believe passionately in letters home to parents as a means of boosting pupil performance and behaviour. These schools can be a nightmare as Shelley, the mother of a pupil at a comprehensive in Bristol, illustrated to me:

My son's school is very big on contact with parents and is always sending us letters home about punctuality, being late for registration, homework that is not done. I get more letters from the school than from my mother.

Recently, I got a letter from the head teacher. Apparently, Jack's behaviour had been so bad that the head had felt compelled to write to his parents. He explained that a supply teacher had called him into the classroom because the pupils were misbehaving. Judging from what my son said, there was talking across the classroom and missiles were being thrown. No matter what the hapless teacher said, she was ignored. The letter stated, 'Jack and a small number of other pupils were misbehaving.' It was very vague. However, I felt that this was not delinquent behaviour. This was naughty, bored 14-year-old kids behaving badly. But what Jack and his mates were doing was not a crime against humanity.

Under the guise of parental involvement, I feel the school is absolving itself of responsibility for the pupils' behaviour and their role in the education process. My son and the school should be dealing with it between themselves. The school is a bridge between the nurturing of home and the cruelty of the outside world. If mum is called in every five seconds when there is a problem, it makes a mockery of the whole educational process. I thought the head's letter was disgraceful – as well as devious. The responsibility for a child's misbehaviour is passed onto the parent.

As Shelley told me her story, I couldn't help feeling a degree of sympathy with the school. I too have been guilty of similar letters home to parents about 'lippy, middle-class kids' who have been running amok in my lessons. Such letters have nearly always backfired because the parents have been outraged that their child has been accused of such behaviour – and they react angrily as a result. Sometimes, the parents vent their annoyance on the child by grounding them for a few weeks or refusing to give them pocket money, or sometimes they have come into school and accused me of being devious and incompetent. Both approaches are counterproductive. The 'grounding' solution – which is favourite among many concerned, middle-class parents – leads to huge resentment against the teacher and parent. I am still reminded intermittently in the playground of the way a letter home about misbehaviour led to Dillip being grounded for a few weeks. He always sneers in a disgusted fashion at me, and we both know that the sneer is about that 'letter home' – which was sent over four years ago now!

The main thing is that parents shouldn't panic when they get a nasty letter from school and, rather than looking to punish either their child or the teacher, they should try to open up a discussion about what is really going on. This is where my letters home have been successful. I sent a letter home about a pupil who was constantly making farting noises in the classes and occasionally chucking bits of paper around. After the letter home, he miraculously improved and didn't do it again. At a parents' evening, I asked his mother what she had done to improve the situation. She seemed surprised he was much better.

'I didn't do anything really, I just had a quiet chat with him. I didn't even tell him off. I just asked what was going on, and what he thought of his behaviour,' she said, shrugging her shoulders meekly.

Crucially, she'd been able to get her child to reflect upon his actions: to think about the effect upon those around him, and to consider his overall education. He'd seen the light. This doesn't always work, but it is far better than clapping the teacher or child in metaphorical irons.

Lost letters

If I really want a letter to get home I never, ever tell the child that I have sent one because they are often intercepted and never reach their destination. I give vague warnings that letters may be sent, and then I send them unexpectedly, making sure that all evidence of the school's crest is hidden. Then they reach their target.

Most letters, though, that are given to pupils during the school day never make it. Some schools get around this problem by requiring parents to send back signed reply slips acknowledging that they have received the letter. This can be more trouble than it's worth both for the parent and teacher, who has to chase up every tardy reply slip. Margery in Chippenham told me this nightmarish story about what happened when she failed to do this.

I simply cannot deal with schools that have no common sense. One wretched institution sent a request for parents to give some money to the school fund. I did not make a donation and dispensed with the paperwork. It then became evident that you had to return the reply slip. My daughter was told that she would be punished with a detention if she failed to return with the envelope. As a very conscientious individual, she was very upset when she was punished. Every teacher spoke so highly of her, of the quality of her work, her attention in class and her contribution to the lessons that she was very alarmed if she got into the slightest bit of trouble.

I went to see the headmaster to complain. There was a great deal of obfuscation. He didn't seem to be able to get a grip on the logic of what he was saying. You suddenly find yourself in these surreal *1984* conversations which are about bits of paper and arcane regulations. 'Of what use to you is an empty envelope with no money in it?' I asked him. He explained that they asked for the return of empty envelopes because parents might put money in the envelope but their children might steal the money, or other children might take the money from them, and then the school would never know whether a donation was made or not. I expressed my horror that such criminality was assumed to be so widespread and then added that my daughter had been doing the school a favour and they had used her as a free messenger. I said, 'Have you ever heard the phrase, "Don't shoot the messenger"?' It was a ludicrous situation to be in. I was angry because my daughter had been so distressed about being punished for doing nothing wrong.

Perhaps these kinds of problems will be solved when most parents can be emailed with important letters, or perhaps not. Margery was angry with the school for a number of other reasons

– her child was being badly bullied – and the letter for her was the final straw. Some parents and some schools are never going to get on.

THE NEW SCHOOL RULES
about letters home

1. **Talk about them** Read the letters. Don't throw them in the bin. Discuss the contents of the letters with your children in a calm way. Don't get into a panic about them. If you find the contents of a letter objectionable, contact the person who sent the letter in the first place – do not run straight to the head teacher, who may know very little about it.

2. **Reply to them** Remember that schools do pay very close attention to parents' criticisms. They may appear to ignore your complaints in the first instance, but behind closed doors there will be a big discussion of the issue. Your voice will be heard.

Dealing with complaints from teachers

I didn't realise what it felt like until it happened to me. How many times had I called parents to school to account for their children's actions? Too many. Now it was happening to me. There was a note in James's reading record, 'Can you come to school to talk to us about James's focus in lessons?' Being a teacher I knew what this meant – or I thought I did. It was a euphemism for him not listening to anything that was being said, not following any of the instructions and perhaps mucking around instead. My first instinct was defensive: he's perfectly all right! How dare they say that my son is not concentrating! But then I thought about it for a little bit: he was a dreamer and it was quite possible that he was drifting off in the lessons. When I met his teachers, this turned out to be the case. He frequently needed to be reminded to keep his attention focused on his task. We agreed some strategies to help him with this: rewards for good concentration and easier tasks at strategic points to assist with his sense of accomplishment.

His problems were solved quickly enough because we all got our heads together to think of solutions for the situation. Unfortunately, I have had too many meetings with parents where nothing has been solved. I have phoned parents, or written to them, or asked them to come in and see me, and I have found that we have too easily slid into arguments about past actions. The parent is usually very defensive. Some variation on this type of comment often occurs:

> I know my son/daughter isn't like that. I know they are not mucking around in your lesson. They never lie and they told me that you're just picking on them. You're overreacting. No other teachers are complaining about them like you are. You know, I don't know why I sent them to this school. If you were teaching them properly they would be learning more.

As you can imagine, such meetings are not productive. The parent refuses to countenance that anything is wrong and, as a result, we can never move beyond stage one. They feel as though they've been sent down to the 'nick' to get their child out of jail. Crucially, they fail to see that most teachers are not trying to humiliate their child but to improve their chances of doing well in the subject.

The most productive meetings I've had have been where the parent and I have discussed the past, diagnosed what is going wrong and worked together to come up with some solutions, which have specific outcomes with specific deadlines. For this to happen, this requires that the parent isn't too aggressive but willing to concede that I may have a point, and is also interested in helping out at home with some aspect of their child's work.

THE NEW SCHOOL RULES

to help parents deal with teachers who complain

1. **Work out what's gone wrong** Don't be immediately defensive. Find out what has happened and trust the teacher is telling the truth. Diagnose the past. Find out what has been going wrong and ask whether this has been affecting your child's work and learning. Is your child working at the level expected for his age? Is he or she working at the level expected for their ability? What are they not learning that they should be? If your child is not working at the level expected for his or her age or ability, it may be that he or she has a learning difficulty. Don't be frightened or defensive if the teacher says this. He or she should be assessed by the special needs department, and could well receive extra funding and teacher time if put on an Individual Education Plan (IEP). (See Chapter 4 Does Your Child Have Special Needs?). It may be that your child's learning style is not being catered for. All schools now are supposed to cater for pupils' different learning styles: visual, auditory, kinaesthetic, and tactile. There is a belief that if a child is, for example, very 'visual' then the materials that they should be given to help them learn should be full of pictures and the exercises set should be focused upon drawing pictures and spider diagrams. Each child should be given a 'personalised' learning plan which enables them to learn the curriculum in their own preferred learning style. If your child has not been tested for his or her own particular learning style, request this test, and ask for the exercises set to be focused upon the result. IEPs are only given to children with special educational needs.

▶

2. **Set some targets** Above all, set specific targets with the teacher and your child. Ask the teacher to draw up an Individual Action Plan (IAP) with the pupil where specific tasks are set with definite deadlines on them. It is crucial that your child understands the action plan, so it should be done with him or her there and agreed by them and you. Every child is entitled to an IAP. It should be realistic though and not absurdly optimistic. It should be no more than a page and should have no more than five targets that your child will remember to carry out.

3. **Beware bribes and treats** As a general rule, avoid the carrot and stick approach unless absolutely nothing else is working. The problem with dangling the carrot too often is that it actually demotivates in the long run. Children become more interested and preoccupied with the reward in front of them than actually improving their work and attitude. Punishing children for the failure to do work often fails too because it makes them resentful and angry. By far the best way is to make it clear why the work is worth doing in itself. Your child should realise why it is worthwhile to do it without any rewards or punishments. If she doesn't know why she's doing it, and you don't either, maybe the work is actually pointless.

Setting and streaming

Her father pummelled the door with his fist. I leapt up, thinking it was a naughty kid trying to vandalise the door to my Portakabin classroom. I was just about to tell the miscreant off when I saw that it was Mr Ball, the father of a Year 10 pupil of mine. His face was red with rage. 'I am not having it, do you hear me, I am not having this!' he shouted.

I looked at him in bewilderment. What had I done? What was

he accusing me of? I couldn't think of anything. His daughter sat meekly and quietly in my lessons not saying very much but that seemed to be the worst of it.

'When I learnt today that Kerry was in the second set for English, I couldn't believe my ears. I mean, you've got to be kidding me, or what?'

I breathed in deeply and explained that Kerry had scored a low Level 6 in her Key Stage 3 English test and that meant that she had not been picked for the top set where nearly all of the pupils had Level 7s or high Level 6s. Mr Ball wasn't happy with this. 'You didn't tell us this last year. If we'd have known, we'd have got her to work harder for her tests. Now she's stuck in this set and all her friends are in the top set. She's totally demotivated. She couldn't care less about English now.'

I went to my then head of department who refused to let Kerry move. She knew that if she did, it could open the floodgates if word got round: all the pushy parents would want their children in the top set. However, Mr Ball didn't give up easily. He launched a guerrilla campaign against my teaching and the class that Kerry was in, writing in to complain about the behaviour of the group, her lack of motivation and his fears for her future for academic achievements. He just wouldn't stop complaining. It was pretty nerve-wracking for me, waiting to see what new missive he had sent to the head of department about the class. In the end, we were defeated by him because we had based our setting only on the final Key Stage 3 score in Year 9 and hadn't taken into account her superior scores in class that year. Kerry was moved to the top set because our procedure for setting the children was flawed.

Since those early days of my teaching career, I have encountered many parents like Mr Ball. This is the parent who refuses to accept that a child should be 'low' set – as he or she perceives it. The parent feels that it is a slur on a child's character and will potentially ruin any chances of attaining a high grade.

Even when a school is not putting children into sets of roughly the same ability, there can be problems because many parents think there is a hidden 'setting' agenda. I have had parents complaining because a child is not being taught by a particular teacher, who they think takes all the top sets. In every case, this has been false information.

Nearly all secondary schools and many primary schools put children into sets of comparable ability at some point or other; usually for subjects such as English and maths.

Some secondary schools 'band' pupils. This is can be quite awkward to get your head around. A year group of 240 children is split into broad bands of ability using performance data the school has gathered, for example, Key Stage test scores, reading, writing, maths test results and teachers' comments. This can then be used to create three bands, usually higher, middle and lower. Usually children in lower bands are put in smaller classes so that they get more support. As a result, generally, schools are keen to put fewer pupils in that band. So, for example, the split might be, 100 in the higher band, 80 in the middle and 60 in the lower band. These bands are then taught together for many of their subjects. This is only an example of the way a secondary school might do this. You need to make sure that the school explains their system very clearly to you.

Advantages of setting

1. It allows a teacher to cover more difficult topics and texts, and stretch the most able pupils.

2. A healthy competition between pupils fosters greater learning.

Disadvantages of setting

1. There is a tendency to confuse bad behaviour with lack of intelligence, and as a result truculent boys often get put into bottom sets where they don't belong.

2. Those in the bottom sets give up.

3. Parents are never happy unless their child is in the top set.

4. It's inaccurate.

5. Fosters unhealthy competition.

Keeping an eye on what set or band your child is in is very important though. It could affect the exams that he or she is entered for. In particular, it may affect whether your child is entered for a higher or lower tier in their Key Stage 3 and GCSE exams. If your child is entered for a lower tier GCSE, this usually means that he or she cannot attain above a grade C in their GCSE.

THE NEW SCHOOL RULES

for changing the set or stream your child is in

1. **Work out what's gone wrong** Ask to see all the relevant test data that the school has on your child. In particular, ask to see at the results of any IQ (Intelligence Quotient) tests which your child has. Many schools, feeling distrustful of the Key Stage test results, pay for companies to do multiple-choice IQ-style tests (the names vary according to the company carrying out the testing) and see what a pupil's IQ looks like. It may be that your child has scored poorly on these tests and has been put in a lower set or stream as a result of this. In which case, question the result. Most IQ tests are a little discredited now: they usually fail to take into account a child's creativity and social skills; instead they focus upon a narrow range of skills such as their mathematical ability, verbal knowledge, spatial knowledge and reasoning skills. The best schools will always look at a number of test scores and take into account the teacher assessment of a child. The most accurate assessment is usually the teacher's, if there has been no undue pressure for the teacher to inflate their scores in order to get a pay rise – which, in these days of performance-related pay, is always a problem. Examine the social, gender and ethnic mix of

▶

a particular group or set. Equal opportunities legislation these days means that all classes should reflect the ethnic, social and gender mix of the school as a whole. I have had to teach some disastrous bottom sets where there have been only white working-class and Afro-Caribbean boys, some of whom were pretty clever but who had been placed in the bottom set because of their atrocious behaviour. You are within your rights to ask that your child is moved to a class which properly reflects the social mix of the school.

2. **Don't slag off the class in front of your child** Don't entangle your child in all your enquiries by denigrating the set they are in. It may be that they will have to stay there. If you have done nothing but slag off the group to your child, or allowed your child to indulge in moaning endlessly about it, then you will not have done him or her any favours when they have to stay.

Complaining by phone and in person

There used to be a time when a teacher could phone a parent without much forethought: give him or her a quick call to say that little Johnny is being a bit naughty in class or hasn't done his homework and that was that. No more. Now, in a more bureaucratic world, many teachers are required to record the call, write a précis of it for a line manager and pass it onto him. This means that many teachers don't make informal phone calls to parents any more.

However, in some schools, where the head teacher is not that bothered about monitoring all the calls that staff make, the phone call is the main link between parent and teacher. Mr Wilson, head teacher of Newall Green School in Manchester (www.newallgreenhigh.manchester.sch.uk/), told me:

At Newall Green, we use mobile phone connectivity a lot. For instance, a parent will have the head of year or faculty's mobile phone numbers. We actually give out staff mobile phones, so parents are allowed to contact them at any time. We can be available 24/7 because I've got very good staff.

This is very unusual. Most teachers can only be contacted through the school and are usually teaching when parents want to talk to them and so the experience can be very frustrating. I know of many parents who have tried to contact me through my office phone and have spent days and weeks trying to get through; unknown to them and the office staff who passed them on to my extension number, my phone was broken. It was OK for me: I simply had no way of returning their calls because I knew nothing about them.

When I eventually spoke to the parents they weren't too happy. Their experience of trying to get hold of a teacher was typical of many throughout the country: of leaving messages that weren't answered or phoning when the teacher was busy.

Some parents just don't bother, but some do get through. Angela Sharpley, a parent with children at a rural comprehensive in Cheshire, told me this:

I am viewed as a parent who is concerned. If something hasn't gone well, then I will phone in. A few weeks ago, I rang in and said, 'I am a bit concerned that the science lessons are going wrong because the teacher had allowed two boys to lie on the floor of the room and flick elastic bands around the room.' I knew that phoning wouldn't be enough. If you want to get really serious, you have to come into school. I went to the teacher who was having problems, but she didn't have much to say for herself; the poor soul seemed to be a bit of a gibbering wreck and clearly unable to handle herself in the classroom. So I visited her colleague who then referred me to the science coordinator and informed him about what was going on in the lessons. He didn't want to deal with the situation so I was passed up the chain: I spoke to several other teachers in my hunt for a teacher who would say that they would do something about the problem.

Finally, a senior teacher had a serious chat with the teacher I think, but she still couldn't cope so I had to persist with my complaints. It was very sad that they didn't have the proper support for her because I think she was a good scientist but an appalling teacher. She's handed in her notice now. It can be challenging being a mum who wants the best for your child in a comp: you'll be passed from pillar to post, from one head of this and that, to the coordinator for this and that, but you have to persist.

What is typical of this story is the way Angela was passed from one teacher to another before she got any firm answers. In my view she followed the correct procedures. Many schools have policies for parents who have problems with the teaching their child is receiving, but if they don't, then follow these steps:

THE NEW SCHOOL RULES
for complaining about bad teaching

1. **Work out what's gone wrong** Contact the teacher you have a problem with first. Don't get aggressive. It may be that you haven't heard their side of the story: remember children are often not reliable sources of information. They often lie or deceive themselves. Have a quiet chat with the 'problem' teacher. In particular, you should focus upon what your child is learning in the lesson, not the misbehaviour of the other pupils – they aren't your concern.

2. **Set targets** You should ask for an Individual Action Plan (IAP) to be drawn up: a plan of action for your child in the area of difficulty. Specific tasks should be set with specific deadlines, and a definite review period to see if

▶

your child has met those targets. It is different from an Individual Education Plan which is given to pupils with special needs (See Chapter 4 Does Your Child Have Special Needs?). The IAP route is definitely the best for pupils who are working in a badly behaved class because it means that they can get on by themselves.

3. **Go up the chain** If the teaching doesn't get better, contact the teacher's line manager: this is the person directly in charge of that teacher. You don't need to ask the teacher himself who this is: the office staff should know who all the line managers are. Explain the problem to them, and if necessary go into the school. At this point, if you are seriously concerned that your child is not learning anything you are legally entitled to ask for an IAP for your child. The teacher should draw up these targets with the child in order to ensure that he or she learns the right material. If this fails, you should see the head teacher, and explain the situation. If that fails, you are entitled to take your complaint to the governing body, which is a monstrously bureaucratic procedure, but if you are dealing with a very severe problem, you may need to do this.

Parents' evenings

If you have a serious problem don't leave it until parents' evening to sort it out. Parents' evenings can be frenetic, emotional affairs where everyone is really uptight. The teachers can be terrified of the barrage of complaints they might receive from the parents, the parents can be petrified that their darling might be criticised, and they usually happen late in the day after everyone has slogged through a stressful day and no one is in the best of moods.

Teacher of the Year, Phil Beadle, offered this piece of advice about dealing with teachers at parents' evenings:

> The best way to speak to a teacher if you want them to do something for your child is nicely. If you bully me your child's book goes to the bottom of the pile. This is a joke. But there is a valid point here. I don't get up at five thirty in the morning to mark books and prepare lessons, to deliver with such energy and force that I am a wasted emotional shell at the end of term simply to be told I am not doing my job properly by a pushy parent.

He echoes the sentiments of many teachers here. The most sensible parents I spoke to were aware of this. Karen, a parent of children at a large, mixed comprehensive in Leeds, said:

> Show you are trying really hard to work out a problem with the teacher, rather than flouncing off down the corridor, after one conversation with them, in search of the boss! There are ways of saying things, too. You might want to say, 'You wanker, why can't you see that my child doesn't need to be told what reading level she is striving for and how you will accept nothing less.' Instead, you have to find a less pejorative and threatening route, such as, 'We know Caroline very well, and we've found that setting a particular target for her is not helpful, as she naturally does her best, and that is all we would ever expect. Giving her numbers to chase is causing sleepless nights, and none of us want that, do we?'
>
> One teacher moaned that she knew our daughter knew everything, yet she never stuck her hand up. Caroline was always very shy when younger, and the teacher knew that, yet she acted as though we'd reinvented the wheel when we suggested that she simply asked our daughter the odd direct question.

If parents want to get the best out of their child's teachers, they need to appear supportive, particularly if they sense that their teacher is a sensitive soul – as many are. Derek and Fiona told me the story of their child's primary school teacher who burst into tears when they suggested that their child wasn't learning much maths in the class.

'And I am trying so hard, and I get no appreciation for what I am doing,' the teacher sobbed. 'I have slaved night and day over those maths worksheets and this is the thanks I get.'

Derek realises now that a less direct approach may have evinced a more satisfactory answer, such as asking what was happening in the maths lessons. 'I could tell she was on the edge by the way her hands were trembling,' he said. 'In the end, we had to give her therapy and reassure her that everything was fine – even when it wasn't! It was very embarrassing.'

Some schools try to fit far too much into their parents' evenings. Nicola, who has a son and daughter at a comprehensive in a large town in Northumberland, explained to me why the parents' evenings at their school were terrible:

> At the beginning of the evening, you are given all your child's reports, with their baseline scores, their target scores and their actual scores. That leaves you with about three or four minutes to read at least eleven reports, digest all the statistical data on your child, and then talk to your child's teachers. It is impossible to feel informed about anything because you just can't absorb that amount of information in such a short space of time. The school do it I think because they don't trust the children to take the reports home, and they are too stingy to post them. Anyway, it leads to a most unsatisfactory evening where you basically listen to the teachers read the information that is on the report card in the few minutes that you talk to them.

Other schools leave big gaps between the issuing of reports and the parents' evening. This can be equally mystifying because everyone has forgotten what was on the original report and can't really remember whether anything has changed since then.

There are a number of different types of teacher that parents might encounter at parents' evening. It is worth bearing this in mind when taking into account what they say:

The zippety-do-da zebra Parents usually love this kind of teacher. The one who only sees the positive in pupils and talks about them in affectionate, cordial terms. Often they will say how wonderfully the child has got on regardless of whether they have or not, and will be relentlessly upbeat.

Good points: very caring.

Shortcomings: a tendency to bathe pupils in warm, generalised praise. Make sure that they offer specific advice.

The worry worm These teachers will always have the child's books to hand and will be remorseless about pointing out her shortcomings, illustrating everything with copious, scruffy evidence from the exercise book.

Good points: an eye for detail. The worry worm really knows what's wrong.

Shortcomings: can focus solely on the negative.

The power-point parakeet The full plumage is on display at parents' evening: the laptop is out and spreadsheets are shown that reveal the child's progress in tests over the year. The spreadsheets are then transformed into marvellous colour pie-charts and bar graphs.

Good points: terrific on test scores, the pupils' value-added results and other arcane statistical data.

Shortcomings: lessons can be ruled by the computer.

The lazy lion This teacher has no notes, no register, and generally provides the same spiel for each parent but has an answer for everything.

Good points: there is never a queue.

Shortcomings: doesn't know much about your child.

THE NEW SCHOOL RULES
for parents' evenings

1. **Be prepared** If there is a big problem, always flag it up before the parents' evening. Come ready, if you can, with your child's report. Bring a notebook and pen to jot down key comments.

2. **Find out the level your child is working at** Ask for their current National Curriculum level in the subject and find out whether this is in line with the national average: in Year 3, the state expects every pupil to be a good Level 2 which translates into teacher jargon as a 2b (a is top, b is middle, c is bottom of the level). Pupils should be moving up 'two parts' every year so, for example, in Year 4 pupils should be achieving a 3c in English and maths, in Year 5 a 3a, Year 6 a 4b, Year 7 a 5c, Year 8 a 5a, Year 9 a 6b. Ask for any other scores such as IQ tests that have given the school the raw data for their verbal and non-verbal reasoning skills.

3. **Get precise information** Try to pin down teachers when they make generalised comments such as 'he's doing very well' or 'he never listens': use the 5 Ws to work out: WHAT exactly is happening? WHEN is it occurring? WHERE is it occurring? WHO is involved? And WHY is it happening? Remember to focus upon the 3 Rs above all else: how good is your child's reading and writing and arithmetic?

4. **Be supportive** Always be the teacher's friend – even if you don't like him. Talk about the support you can offer, ask how you can help. That way the teacher will like your child more, and be more willing to go the extra mile to help. If it's been a bad night, don't return and hit the roof. Take time to reflect and review your notes. Follow up by

▶

talking to the teacher your child likes best: this may not be their form tutor. Most teachers want to help, the favourite teachers especially. Try to work out why your child is doing well in that teacher's lessons and not others.

5. **Set targets** From each teacher look for a specific piece of positive information and a specific target that your child can work towards.

Deciphering school reports

Every school in the country is legally obliged to report upon all their pupils' progress in all National Curriculum subjects at least once a year. Many parents do not understand these reports because they are often written in the jargon of the subject. As you will see later on, there is a definitive amount of content that every National Curriculum subject has to cover and report upon; this often leads to reports which are top heavy with information about what the child knows as opposed to how good he or she is at the subject. The emphasis in these reports is not upon comparing the child with other pupils in the class but with focusing upon their skills and establishing some targets they should work towards. Many schools use statement banks in order to write their reports. This means that teachers select the statement that best fits the child rather than writing an individualised comment. Even schools that don't do this inevitably produce reports which have a definite atmosphere of cut and paste about them. Burdened with writing exhaustive descriptions of what a child knows, many teachers opt to produce a 'stock report' which describes the content of the year and then fill in certain gaps where appropriate.

The net result is that school reports leave many parents mystified and angry. They are bemused by the detailed statements and jargon used to catalogue their child's progress, and angry because their child's report often looks very similar to many other reports that they have been sneaking a peek at.

However, with a little knowledge of the euphemisms that pepper such reports a surprising amount of personalised information can be gleaned from them. You just have to have a sharp eye. Most individual reports now run to 2,000 words because every school is obliged to report a child's knowledge, progress and targets in every National Curriculum subject. This is the length of a long feature article you might find in the *Sunday Times* magazine – the days of the three-word comment have well and truly gone!

Let's look at an edited set of reports given to a boy who is struggling with his work and not behaving very well in lessons, and examine the comments that are the most revealing:

Jago's reports

- Jago has made satisfactory [translate as 'unsatisfactory'] progress overall in this subject, although the quality of his work has been rather uneven [this is a loaded word, watch out for it in reports, it really means 'unreliable']. When concentrating on the task in hand Jago is able to apply his sound ['sound' means 'barely adequate'] knowledge and understanding of principles and procedures. A more consistent application would have resulted in his producing more successful work [translate as 'lazy'].

- Jago has continued to make adequate [translate again as 'barely adequate'] progress in Personal, Social and Health Education during the past year, displaying good knowledge of the topics covered in lessons [such as drugs and alcohol].

- He is starting to develop fair [translate as 'unsatisfactory'] skills of enquiry and makes articulate [translate as 'argumentative'] comments during discussions.

- Jago is a sociable boy [translate as 'has far too many friends of the wrong sort'], who has the potential to do well in the subject if he decides to. His concentration has improved, but

▶

he does need to continue working on this, especially when working on a group task. [i.e. 'He used to be an absolute pain in the neck, but now he's only a pain in the neck when he's chatting in a group with his mates.']

- Jago appears to require a high level of monitoring to remain busy and productive during lessons. [Translate as 'I have to watch him like a hawk.']

- His application in class could still be better, he finds it difficult to concentrate upon the work and is frequently distracted. He could also be reading more widely around the subject. ['He reads nothing and mucks around.']

- Jago is a lively ['lively' is one of my favourite euphemisms for someone who is far too boisterous for their own good], friendly boy ...

- I wish him well for the future. [i.e. 'I am very glad to be rid of him.']

What makes these comments so revealing to analyse is that they are trying to be constructive in their criticism. Teachers nowadays are not allowed to be overly negative in their reports and will be asked to rewrite them if the report is just a string of damning remarks. Increasingly, as Jago's reports show, teachers use a coded language to get around this problem.

THE NEW SCHOOL RULES
for reports

1. **Talk about reports with your child calmly** Always read through reports with your child after you have read them. Check to see if they understand. Look for specific

▶

praise. Generalised comments such as a pupil being 'good' or 'excellent' are not very revealing, but if the teacher writes about specific areas that a pupil is good at, this is far more useful. Praise your child for doing these things. Decode the jargon and euphemisms to get an idea of what your child is really like in the classroom, and then talk about WHAT is really happening in the classroom, WHEN it is happening, WHERE it is happening, WHO it is happening with, and WHY it is happening. Don't play the hard man, just get your facts straight.

2. **Set targets** Look for specific, comprehensible targets which your child understands. A number of pupils said to me that they found their reports very useful because I had pinpointed exactly what they needed to do to improve their grades. Rather than writing a generalised comment like, 'A pupil should improve his literary criticism', I had said in one case 'While she is able to quote from passages appropriately, she needs to use the 5Ws to analyse the quotes she uses in order to analyse her evidence in much more depth.' Now I think the parent had no idea what I was talking about here, but because we had covered these ideas in class, the pupil did know and was able to explain to her parent. The pupil was appreciative of the comment: I had written it before but because it was on a report she realised it was important.

Homework

Keith and Clare in Killay in Swansea, Wales, were angry about the amount of homework that their child was being given and told me:

The homework that Josh is coming home with is far, far too much. He gets given homework on Monday, Wednesday and Friday, and then on top of that, he is given extra English and maths homework. It is very stressful for him to deal with this great mountain of homework. He is in school for six hours a day; what is he doing in school if he is not doing work?

We feel we are doing the teachers' jobs for them at home. I have to sit down with him and help him quite a bit. I listen to him read the books and we check his maths homework.

Personally, I think the school has far too many trips out. They go to the wildlife centre, the church, the museums. Theatre groups come into work with them, but at the end of the day they should be doing their English and maths, and getting their reading right before they go on all of these trips which take up so much time. We feel that we are picking up the pieces for the fact that the school has not spent enough time on Josh's reading, writing and arithmetic.

We are now happy with Josh's reading and writing but we had to pay for a private tutor to get this up to scratch. She comes in once a week, and helps with his English, which is the main problem.

Keith and Clare's complaints contrast with the complaints I heard from many other parents that their children were not getting enough homework.

Homework is a subject beset by difficulties. It is perhaps the most emotional issue of school. In every school I have taught in, there have been significant problems with it. Either parents think that too much homework is being set or not enough. Teachers can never win.

Check your facts

Always check your facts first before complaining. Is your child really telling you the truth about the homework that is being set? I've had parents fuming at me because I had supposedly not been setting any homework, only to find that I had been indeed been setting homework but the child had not been writing it down in their diary. This is particularly a problem with reading homework which is difficult to monitor: many teachers have to assume, against their better judgement, that the reading has been done.

Now I make a point of not letting any pupil leave the class until I have seen their homework diary and that they have written the work down there. This has improved the problem of children pretending that no homework has been set, but hasn't solved the issue of the child who never has their homework diary. This chaotic child is, conveniently, forever losing their homework diary, and is then faced with the tragic possibility that they don't know what homework has been set at the end of the day.

The right conditions

Provide the right conditions in which homework can be done. Do this by assisting with your child's organisation: give her a clear and definite place to work, some files or drawers in which to store their work, and, if necessary, help her organise her bag for the next day. Many problems occur with children who are hurrying to get their stuff together in the morning and are always forgetting things in the rush.

Give encouragement

Encourage your child to do homework by designating a time when everyone does some work, including the parents. This could mean that you sit and read a book while your child does homework. This is far better than you slinking off to watch the television while your poor kid works. The children who really struggle with school are the ones who have parents whom they never see read or write at all. Homework time is the best time for a child to see a parent reading a book.

Communal work area

In this day and age of the Internet, having a communal work area is a brilliant idea. I don't think parents should let their children have televisions or computers in their own rooms. Too many children are distracted by MSN Messenger and the attractions of sites like MySpace (www.myspace.com/) while they are supposed to be doing their homework. If the computer is in a communal space, then the use of the Internet does not have to be banned because it can be monitored unobtrusively. Certainly all the parents I interviewed whose children were doing best at school had set aside communal areas and specific times when their children would work.

Parents should be aware that the Internet also gives children many chances too. I may be one of the most unpopular heads of English in the country for replacing GCSE English coursework with modular exams, but I did it because I was convinced that the temptations to cheat at coursework are far too great these days. Coursework can be tailor-made for a small fee, and stock essays can be copied and pasted for free. The pupils learn nothing except that cheating is the way to get on in life.

Deadlines

Unfortunately, too many schools are not able to enforce the proper meeting of deadlines because they have so few sanctions to hand. I know this to be the case from bitter experience. I have set many deadlines for coursework and homework only to find that quite a few pupils miss the deadline. If the work is important it is very difficult to refuse to mark it when it is handed in late, and so you set another deadline, or a detention, and that leads to a new set of problems: do you ask the pupils to do the work in the detention or not? If you don't, then often the work is not completed, and the next deadline is missed. If you do ask pupils to complete the work in the detention, you are sending the wrong signal: it's fine for you not to complete the work because you'll get the chance to finish it in detention.

Most teachers are left with muddling through as best they can. This means it can become very frustrating for everyone concerned. The good pupils who hand the work in on time are annoyed because they feel that they could have had more time to finish the work if they had been a bit lazier, while the poor pupils are rewarded for their tardiness with extra help.

What troubles me is that pupils are not getting a true picture of the real world here: in nearly every field of endeavour, missed deadlines mean serious consequences.

This is perhaps why pupils from the private sector are much higher achievers than their state counterparts. A private school can boot out a child who is failing to complete all the work on time, but a state school simply cannot. This means that a weary complacency creeps into the system whereby laziness is rewarded and promptness is punished.

Guidelines

Here are some rough guidelines about the amount of homework your child should get. Remember, these are only approximate timings. Many private schools give their pupils much more homework in primary school.

Primary

Years 1 and 2 — 1 hour a week (reading, spelling, other literacy work and number work).

Years 3 and 4 — 1.5 hours a week (literacy and numeracy work, occasional assignments in other subjects).

Years 5 and 6 — 30 minutes a day (regular weekly schedule with continued emphasis on literacy and numeracy, but also ranging widely over the curriculum).

Secondary

Years 7 and 8 — 45–90 minutes a day.

Year 9 — One hour a day.

Years 10 and 11 — 1.5–2.5 hours a day.[3]

THE NEW SCHOOL RULES
for homework

1. **Make doing homework feel easy and natural** Have a designated time and communal place for completing homework. Do some work while your child is working. Set a good example. Encourage the meeting of deadlines even if the school is struggling to do this. Remember things are different in the real world. Monitor the homework diary very carefully.

2. **Be suspicious** Don't trust the stock remark, such as, 'I don't have any homework' or 'I did it at lunchtime' or 'There was a supply teacher and none was set.' Even if there is nothing in the homework diary, check with the school if this is correct; don't wait until the parents' evening. Some schools have websites now where teachers post the homework on the web, so there's no escape.

3. **Don't hover** Don't do the homework for your child or hover around them too much. Let them have the freedom to make mistakes.

Coursework

Cheating

The suggestion that Prince Harry cheated at his A level coursework in 2004 did not surprise me. According to a tape recording produced by Sarah Forsyth, Prince Harry's art teacher at Eton, Harry says that he only wrote a 'tiny, tiny bit' of his art coursework: the rest was apparently written by Miss Forsyth. Any experienced teacher knows that cheating at coursework is rife. It is particularly bad in the so-called 'posh' schools such as

Eton, where the pressure to get amazing results out of indolent, arrogant pupils is intense.

I can still see the sly grin on my former deputy head's face when I asked him why the school's English results were so good. I had been teaching at his comprehensive in a leafy suburb of London for a few weeks, and while I had been impressed by some of the children's abilities, I was puzzled how the department had gained 100 per cent A–C grades at GCSE; there were clearly children who were getting marks way below these levels. The deputy head leant close to me and whispered, 'We cheat! But everyone does, so it doesn't matter.'

This was back in the days when English was assessed entirely by coursework. All the struggling children were placed in Mrs McCracken's class. She was a large lady with a motherly manner and she would sit next to them, day after day, 'marking' their work. Her marking was very specialised: she would insist they wrote their essays double-spaced so that she could write the correct answers above their shoddy prose. The pupils would then 'redraft' their work – copying her sentences.

When the 100 per cent coursework scheme was disbanded, surprise, surprise, the department's results nose-dived. However, it did not stop the cheating. With English GCSE, 40 per cent of the final grade is assessed by coursework, and roughly a third of the English A level grade can be assessed by coursework. The same is more or less true for most other GCSEs and A levels.

Nowadays, cheating usually happens when there is a stressed head of department who is being driven to get amazing results by the school's head. Such managers feel the need to check pupils' coursework obsessively, and then bully teachers to get it improved. They never ever say, 'Write it yourself', but if the teacher says that there is no way a pupil is going to improve his or her work, the answer will come, 'I am worried that you are just not teaching these children very well. You're not up to it, are you? This coursework is terrible!' Stinging from such rebukes, I have – on the odd occasion – done a 'Mrs McCracken' and received lavish praise and smiles when I have resubmitted work. Now that I am a head of department, I have made a decision to eradicate cheating. I don't care if the department gets rotten results in the end; I feel that pupils should learn to think for themselves. I have changed GCSE courses so that we now do a syllabus which offers exams instead of coursework. However, when we decide we would like to submit coursework, the department has agreed to some important rules: pupils can do one rough draft in class, have that marked but not proofread by the teacher, and then they submit their final copy. No endless re-drafting, no endless teacher annotations.

This said, cheating still goes on. The Internet means that coursework can be written by an expert for less than £50, and many literate, harassed parents do end up writing important pieces for their darling offspring. What can a teacher do about this? Not a lot. It is almost impossible to prove plagiarism, particularly if a pupil has had an essay tailor-made from their first draft.

Government changes

The government is proposing to change this situation by introducing what is known as 'controlled conditions' coursework. Pupils will be asked to do their research at home, but then will complete their coursework under the supervision of a teacher. Whether this improves anything remains to be seen. The 'Mrs McCrackens' of this world will be supervising the coursework and may well want to give it their special personal touch.

In a climate where teachers are paid by the results of their pupils, cheating will always flourish. I have spoken to many teachers who have confessed in private that their line managers have demanded 100 per cent pass rates and they've then felt compelled to write the coursework for their pupils. This is particularly the case for younger members of staff, many of whom are on short-term contracts and need to achieve fully qualified status by pleasing their bosses.

So where does this leave parents? I think sensible parents should be the voices of sanity amidst all this madness. They should be insisting that their children do their own work and should be complaining if they feel a teacher is completing the coursework for their child. After all, all this cheating may boost a child's results in the short term but in the long term it gives a child a totally false picture of their abilities: sooner or later they are going to come a cropper when they have to do some work of their own.

THE NEW SCHOOL RULE

about coursework

Let them make their own mistakes Insist that your child does his or her own work. By all means show them how to research a topic, but don't do the research for them. Do not make your child frightened of failure. Encourage them to have a go. Complain if you think your child's teacher is doing the coursework for them. You can easily find this out by picking up some coursework and questioning your child about some difficult passage that they probably haven't written. Remember, in the end, cheating is totally counter-productive. Your child is not learning anything except that being a cheat is the way to get on in life. Sooner or later, cheats in a law-abiding society land up in serious trouble.

Home-schooling

An increasing number of parents are becoming so fed up with the schools in England that they are educating their children themselves. The organisation, Education Otherwise (EO), which assists families with educating their children at home, has over 4,000 member families and its helpline receives 700 calls a month. The DfES estimates that up to 150,000 children in England may be home-educated. Research indicates that children who are home-educated significantly outperform their school-educated peers in various tests and exams, although this is usually not the real reason why parents home-educate.[3] More often than not, the rigid structure of the school timetable, bullying, lack of a good quality school in the area are the reasons why parents opt out.

I am not surprised that children do much better in the one-to-one environment of the home: a parent is able to pay proper attention to the different ways in which their child learns. Parents have the flexibility and time to focus upon topics that interest their child and to relate the main school subjects to their child's enthusiasms. In educational jargon, this is called 'personalised learning' – something which the DfES is desperate to introduce into many schools, but is struggling to do so.

The best home-educators are amazing at making learning 'personalised'. I interviewed a mother of four who home-educated all of her children for ten years; every child achieved incredible GCSE and A level results and attended a top university. She devised personalised learning programmes for each of the children, making sure that they covered all the National Curriculum subjects. Most importantly, she bought books that were tailored to her children's interests: biographies of sportsmen, travel journals, collections of great journalism, the diaries of important scientists and philosophers. She also was able to visit many museums, galleries and wildlife areas in order to stimulate her children's interests. 'It was great,' she told me. 'For some of our science lessons, I was able to take them to the science museum where they learnt about engineering and Newton's laws and so on. To do music, we'd go to the Wigmore Hall. Living in London, this fantastic capital city was our classroom. I wasn't tied up in red tape, I could go anywhere and everywhere.'

Another home-educator Peter Cox, a literary agent, told me:

6 My partner and I started investigating home education because the schools in the area where we lived at the time were so dire. We were dismayed by the primary schools run by Camden, our local council, and we felt in many ways the private schools we saw were just as bad. They were producing children who were very bright and

polite, but to us, they seemed like they were machines. We felt very uncomfortable with the rigid products that such establishments produce.

But we decided to take the plunge properly when we came across some parents who were home-educating themselves. They had three children and they were educating them beautifully. We had been scratching our heads and wondering how we could mug up eight subjects and carry on a job at the same, but we saw, with this family, that it could be done.

My partner, Peggy, stayed at home and carried out nearly 80 per cent of the teaching, while I worked as a literary agent and organised my time so that I could go out on trips and suchlike.

We took a topic-based approach to educating. When the children were young we started with dinosaurs because they were so enthusiastic about them, and we found that we could cover so much by doing so. Then history, geography, Latin, English, science and so on. We quickly established a routine, which more or less mirrored a typical school day, with our 'school hours' running from 8.30 a.m. to lunch, and then finishing at 4.00 p.m.

We used two great resources as the days loomed when our boys had to take their exams. The National Extension College (NEC), a sort of junior version of the Open University, enables anyone to take GCSEs from their home, and sit them at an approved centre. We entered our eldest, Louis, a year early for three GCSEs and found that he did rather well. He then went on to take a full complement of GCSEs, averaging B grades in most, but achieving As in English.

Education Otherwise, the home-education charity, helped us immensely as did keeping in touch with other parents who were home-educating. We were able to club together to arrange things like science lessons with top scientists in a fully equipped laboratory, and so on.

Now my eldest son is going to sixth-form college in Islington and is finding it a bit of a culture shock. However, contrary to the stereotype, he is no social misfit: he is an articulate, confident boy who can hold his own in any company, even the rather tough inner-city environment of the college.

Even if I lived next door to the best school in the world, I would still home-educate my children. The way in which it helps bring a family together is amazing. We really are a true family. I think that the government should be much more supportive of home education because most values are learnt at home, and clearly, if you look at our evolution, that's how we have learnt to survive and flourish as a species for hundreds of thousands of years. Parents are "hard-wired" by their biology to educate their child, and it's a crying shame that society does everything it can to stop it happening. 9

Advantages of Home Education	Disadvantages
1. Parents have time to personalise learning.	1. Parents lack genuine subject knowledge.
2. It is much more flexible and less rigid in structure.	2. A school timetable gives a much needed routine.
3. It is more stimulating. The world at home and outside your door becomes your classroom.	3. Schools contain a wide mix of people and assist with the development of vital social skills.
4. It is a more productive use of time. It is estimated children at school spend half their time waiting. Bearing this in mind, at home you could have completed all your lessons by 11.00 a.m.	4. That waiting time in schools is important preparation for life.
5. It is a safer, homelier environment.	5. School is a much needed change from home.

► **CHECK OUT**
www.nec.ac.uk/info/ (The National Extension College)
www.education-otherwise.org/ (Education Otherwise)
www.home-education-centre.co.uk/
www.witsendcs.com/
www.selfmanagedlearning.org/

CHAPTER 3

How to tackle the big problems

There are many beasts lurking in the school jungle which parents can really help their children fight. These are often psychological beasts which leap out at children from school cupboards and exam halls, gripping them with intense fear and making them feel inadequate and defenceless.

Equally, parents themselves have their own fears, quite different from their child's. A recent survey concluded that parents worry more about bullying, drink and drugs than academic achievement when their 11-year-olds start secondary school. More than half (53 per cent) fear that their child will be bullied while one in five worry about the influence of alcohol, drugs and tobacco. Only 11 per cent are concerned about a child's academic achievement.[1]

This chapter looks at the reality of these parental concerns in schools today, and offers a number of remedies.

Dealing with disappointment

Every year, I have to deal with pupils who have not done well in exams. The ones whose children have done well never bother me except, on the odd occasion, to say thank you. But the parents of the pupils that have failed: they come knocking on my door, their lips trembling, pointing at the printout of their son or daughter's test score and saying, 'What is this, what is going on here?'

I teach a particularly tricky subject: English. It is not mathematics or one of the more factual subjects where you can have some degree of objectivity in marking it. Once a pupil has shown the basics of writing sentences, spelling and punctuating correctly, the marking schemes leave a great deal to the discretion of the examiner, even though the exam boards will deny this furiously. Some years the results are amazing, full of As and Bs, and in other years with more or less the same pupils and exactly the same teachers, the results are, well, not very good. I used to panic about this, but now I realise that a poor result in today's climate of resits can be a great opportunity to get things right. Often, I have seen pupils who have done atrociously in one set of exams go on to get great grades in their resits and their final exams, because the poor result had motivated them to go on and revise very thoroughly for the next exams coming up.

Parents need to learn that the best way of helping a child is not to panic, but to calmly work out what the best thing is to do.

THE NEW SCHOOL RULES
if your child has done badly in an exam

1. **Work out what's gone wrong** Was this result expected? Is it the same as the teacher's predicted grade? If it isn't, ask the school's exams secretary or administrator to request a re-mark. You could, alternatively, ask the school to request a photocopy of the script so that your child's teachers can examine the marking on it. If it is not good marking, they could then request a re-mark if there is time. However, remember that exam boards do not like re-marks. They do everything in their power to make it

▶

difficult to get a script re-marked. Also, re-marks are often expensive and the deadlines are very tight.

2. **Set targets** See if the exam can be retaken. Most exams can be retaken nowadays. However, do bear in mind that some exams such as Key Stage tests cannot be retaken except in exceptional circumstances. Make sure your child's teacher draws up a detailed action plan about how, when and where they will learn the relevant skills to help them with the next test. The action plan should be understandable for your child and should have clear deadlines set on it.

3. **Keep calm** While he or she should be working for the exam, exams should also be put in perspective. They are not the be-all and end-all of life. This is probably just as important as working for the exam, and your child needs to have the right balance between work and life.

Slob culture

He was a big, tubby boy who wasn't doing well in lessons. He had a penchant for pulling out his shirt during lessons, rubbing his belly, yelling out inanities, and not doing any work. He knew he was going to fail all his GCSEs but he didn't appear to care: a wry smile and chuckle was never very far from his lips. He was by no means a nasty boy: he would frequently shout out across the classroom, 'Love ya, Mr G!' in a humorous and genuinely affectionate fashion. As part of an exercise for GCSE, he wrote a descriptive letter informing me about his life.

Dear sir,

As you know I am a slob. I don't do any work I don't care about the work I couldn't give a toss about the work. I no I am going to fail I have known that for ages now. You see, my parents divorced when I was ten. Dad went to live miles away and so I only see him at weekends.

I used to like my parents cos they let me do whatever I wanted when I came home from school I didn't have to do any work or nothing and I loved that while lots of kids were swotting away I was just sitting watching TV eating Nachos and seeing my mates.

So I just got into the habit of doing nothing just sitting around doing nothing I see my dad at weekends and he just lets me watch TV or play computer games and my mum only pays attention to my younger sister she says I am a lost cause.

Now GCSEs are coming along and I haven't done any work and it looks like I am going to fail them all and I don't want to fail them but that's what's going to happen. I tried to ask my mum to help me with my work but she said that she's busy she's always busy and so's my dad everyone is busy working or not working busy watching TV on the computer something like that.

Sometimes when I am sitting on the sofa watching TV I see my reflection in the glass and see how fat I am and I know that I should be doing something else but I don't know what and I feel tight in my throat like I am going to cry but I don't and I know I am drowning but I am still on the sofa so I have another Nacho and watch the TV.

Yours truly,

Reece

What struck me most about the letter was the way in which Reece's parents had allowed him to slip into a routine of not doing any work. When he wanted to snap out of this lethargic routine, he was unable to do so because he was so used to the old routine of not doing anything except lounging around and watching TV.

For me, the greatest moral philosopher remains the ancient Greek Aristotle because he saw more than any other modern philosopher that being 'virtuous' is a matter of habit. Every parent

I spoke to who was successfully guiding their child through the school jungle had established good routines with their children.

Laura Tennant, whose daughter is thriving at a local state primary school in London, said:

> I think Artemis is loving her school partly because she has the security of a good routine. She has a proper supper time, a bath at seven, a story after that and her bedroom door shut by half-past eight. It's these little things that make all the difference to a child's education. I am staggered by the number of parents who are late for school. They park on the zig-zag yellow lines and are often late. What a terrible start to the day!

Sharon in Embleton, Northumberland, explained to me why her children are doing so much better at school than she did. She said:

> When my children come home I tell them that they have to do their homework. I am not always home. They come in themselves and they get on and do their homework. They know it's got to be done. But we all have tea together. I never allow the TV to be on. Me and my husband and the children make conversation but it's not important talk. We talk about anything. It is just family time.
>
> This kind of routine wasn't something I had with my own parents. I came from a large, chaotic family where there were no proper routines: you just did whatever you felt like. I did badly at school because I didn't really have a work ethic. But I realised that if my children were going to have a happier time than I did, they needed to get into good habits.

Another parent, Karen, whose children are now at a comprehensive in Leeds, told me: 'At primary school, homework was, as far as possible, done before the evening meal, so there was a relaxing period between eating and bed. Library time was important on Saturdays, so that our techno kids could enjoy browsing and hear stories read aloud in a group.'

The most fascinating case of a successful routine I came across was in rural Cheshire. Angela told me how her daughters managed growing up on a working farm in this modern age.

❛ Because we are a working farm and it is a one-man band, the children have to get involved, and there is no reward for them other than they know that it helps their dad to finish the day earlier.

There is a very clear routine. My husband is up at half four in the morning, seven days a week to milk. By the time he has done the milking it is half seven, and he is ready for breakfast. I would expect that my children are up by then. Even during the holidays. Frances always makes him porridge. They have to be up and ready. There is no checking their school bags though. They have to organise themselves. When dad has had his breakfast, he and the children go out and clean up around the farm, check and replenish the stock, clean the pigs, feed the hens. It is a fun time. They're always chatting about the farm and school and life in general. It is my husband's time with them when I am not there. Then he takes them to school.

They could be picked up by a coach but we have never done that because we cherish that time for meeting them. We pick them up. It's either my husband or myself, depending on my hours of work. And as we drive them home, we chat about the day and what's been going on.

When they get home, their dad starts the milking and they sit and do their homework in the kitchen while I make the dinner. There are open bookshelves. There is access to resources. The homework is always done on the kitchen table. It is a living kitchen. It has no TV in it. They sit there doing their work on their laptops while I am chopping and cooking. I used to sign off their homework in their homework diaries. I have never had a complaint that they haven't done it. Over time, you trust that they've done it. There is nothing to fret about because routine has become second nature to them. This overflows into the house. I expect that their bedroom is their own. They strip their bed and make their beds. They clean and choose their own clothes. They hoover their rooms. We expect the children to do their bit to make our lives bearable. We have enough to do ourselves. ❜

It was intriguing to hear Angela describe her daughters' lives and their set routines. She explained to me that money is very tight. The daughters all bought their computers by doing part-time jobs, and rarely have spare cash to spend. However, the household appeared to be one of the happiest I came across because it was so disciplined. All the daughters had done remarkably well at school and were either at top universities or destined to go there.

It struck me that far from being hampered by their relative poverty, they had benefited from having to work for what they wanted. The winner of the hit TV series *The Apprentice*, Jim Campbell spoke about the importance of work at the 2006 Jack Petchey Speak Out Challenge in east London. He explained to the audience of secondary school pupils and teachers that, growing up as he did in East Ham in a poor household, his mother had been very strict and didn't have the money to buy the trendy trainers which were the big thing at school, so he went out cleaning cookers for his aunt, to earn some money. The other kids laughed at him and said he was a slave, but he won in the end when he could afford some great trainers. 'You have to learn to get rich slow,' he told the rapt audience.

Many studies into the psychology of happiness have shown again and again that winning the lottery or receiving a windfall of money doesn't make people any happier in the long run if it disrupts the routines that made those people happy in the first place. In fact, some people become a great deal more miserable if what made them feel fulfilled in life is removed by the sudden arrival of millions. Effectively, this has happened to many people in the developed world. We are a much wealthier society than we used to be 50 years ago. The old routines such as washing our own clothes, doing the dishes, making our own food, walking to the shops, amusing ourselves in the evenings have been swept away and replaced by machines which do all those things for us. There isn't the same necessity for a routine, and many of us appear to be much more unhappy as a result: mental illness among all ages has sky-rocketed.

> **THE NEW SCHOOL RULE**
>
> for stopping your child becoming a slob
>
> **Get into the groove** Establish a good routine with your children. Establish clear times and places when and where work is done. Make your child see the intrinsic value of work, but also help them see that some work is just boring but it has to be done. That's reality! Pay attention to them by having family meals together, reading stories to them before they go to bed. Ration TV and computer use.

School dinners

Her words were enough to make Jamie Oliver tear his hair out. Joanne, 14, a pupil at a large comprehensive in London, was sucking her Triple Power Push Pop as she explained to me why she insisted on stuffing her mouth with such sweets. She said:

> I don't buy any of the stuff in the canteen, it's disgusting. The drinks are vile – there's no sugar in them. And as for the food, well, it's all salads and vegetables and stuff and I don't like that. So I stock up before school on crisps and lollipops and chews, then at lunchtime I go and eat them where none of them nosy teachers is looking.

Joanne's friends laughed and agreed. They said that since the school had got 'sick-bag food' they never went to the canteen. They much preferred to munch their sticky, fatty snacks in secret where no 'health police' could find them.

It's not quite what the government intended when it set up the Healthy Food Initiative. New legislation, which came into effect in September 2006, demands that school caterers ensure pupils are provided with 'high-quality meat, poultry or oily fish on a regular basis' and that a minimum of two portions of fruit and vegetables accompany every meal.

Prompted by the wrath of celebrity chef Jamie Oliver, who highlighted the horrors of junk-food school meals in his *School Dinners* television programmes on Channel 4, the government has pumped hundreds of millions of pounds into providing healthy school meals.

I am staggered by the change I have seen in my own secondary school canteen. I have always quite liked the food there, but this term I have found it to be of a much higher quality: the pasta and rice dishes, in particular, are delicious.

In common with all other state schools, sweets, chocolates and crisps have been taken out of the vending machines and off the meal counters. Bowls of fresh fruit have replaced racks of doughnuts with jugs of water and sugar-free drinks served in place of bottles of fizzy pop.

But the government overlooked one crucial point when it instituted these changes – and that is that changing the law doesn't change children's minds. Any teacher will tell you that children don't learn much when they're being taught by fascists. While children's food intake is very heavily policed in school, outside the gates they are free to do what they want.

One school caterer I know called Jane, said, 'It's a real disaster for us. We're losing £70 a day compared with last year.' Explaining that the new guidelines mean food preparation is much more labour intensive than before, she added, 'I've had to hire more staff to make the food but the kids are just not coming along. The canteen is half full at lunchtimes. I feel in a state of despair.'

In many other schools, where head teachers have taken the hard-line decision to ban pupils from bringing sweets and chocolates onto the premises, the rebellion against healthy eating is much more secretive. I have heard about a number of pupils who are buying junk food before they come to school, and, like Joanne and her friends, consuming it where they cannot be seen by the teachers.

Some 16-year-old pupils I have heard about are even running

a thriving black market in mini-cans of fizzy drinks at their school in Surrey. 'The drinks are crap and expensive in school so you can make quite a killing if you buy a batch of pop wholesale and flog it at 30p a shot,' one budding entrepreneur told me.

The problem is that the whole initiative was started by Jamie Oliver, who gave the government a very big kick up the back-side when his Channel 4 programmes highlighted how school kitchens had been neglected for decades. But whereas Oliver may know how to cook, he certainly doesn't know how to educate.

His yobbish approach has influenced many politicians, edu-cators and bureaucrats throughout the country, and his abrasive imperatives have been adopted by the food police in our schools and our government.

While these people stop short of calling parents 'tossers' and effing and blinding at anyone who disagrees with them – as Oliver does – their sanctimonious injunctions are eerily similar to his.

As any good teacher will tell you, knee-jerk reactions, rigid rules and blind dogma are not good educational tools. Issuing orders is not the way to win over reluctant children. Such pupils

---

THE NEW SCHOOL RULES
for healthy eating

1. **Talk it through** If your child is eating a lot of junk food, don't immediately ban it. Discuss the issue, and find out what he knows about the content of the junk food they are eating. Agree to phase it out slowly, replacing the junk food items a little bit at a time.

2. **Get into the groove** Get your child into the groove of eating healthily. Don't ban junk food entirely. Have it as a treat. Cook fresh food and eat it yourself.

need to be coaxed into eating healthily in a careful, caring fashion. They should be introduced to eating vegetables and fruit gradually.[2]

Friends and enemies

A major worry that many parents have is that their child might not make any friends or might feel left out. Most good schools have thought about this; the parent of a daughter at primary school, Laura Tennant told me:

> In the playground world, children's relationships are quite complicated. There might be somebody who wants to play with Artemis but she doesn't want to. When I was at school negotiating those playground things, I couldn't tell any adults about the feelings of loneliness and shyness I suffered from. I think teachers are much more approachable now and children are encouraged to discuss their feelings with them.
>
> Artemis's school has a friendship bench where you can sit if you've got no one to talk to. Schools are much more aware that for a young child the whole world of the playground is a scary jungle. Schools have now built in structures that enable children to be properly policed and stop them being mean to each other. At Artemis's school there are older children who are appointed monitors and will help children if they are lonely.

Unfortunately, there are no such friendship benches for parents themselves. Another parent, Valerie, in Newcastle, told me about a nasty squabble she became involved in because her daughter, Alison, didn't want to invite June, the daughter of Valerie's best friend, to her birthday party:

> The thing was June is borderline autistic and can be violent at times, and Alison just didn't want her ruining her party. I was quite embarrassed but felt I should go along with my daughter's wishes. But things got very heated in the playground when

June's mother confronted me and started shouting in my face that I was such a cow for not inviting her daughter to the party. Well, I wasn't having that, and shouted back that I was only doing what Alison wanted. After that, there was a lot of cold-shouldering where quite a few people were wary of talking to us because of the slanging match they'd seen. We could both have done with a friendship bench then.

THE NEW SCHOOL RULES

for helping your lonely child

1. **Join in** school events with your child. Get them to help out at the school fete. Show your child that you are a joiner, and do your bit to help the school as well. Invite one or two children of your child's choice to play at your house.

2. **Talk it through** with your child's teachers about what the school does for pupils who are lonely. Is there a friendship bench? Are there monitors who talk to younger pupils?

Battling the bully

The most frightening beast in the school jungle must be the bully. Despite the government's efforts to eradicate the problem of bullying, it appears to be growing. ChildLine (www.childline.org.uk/), an anti-bullying charity, has said that year on year calls to their helpline have been growing in the thousands.

Bullying can be fairly horrific even in primary school. One of my pupils, James Cooper, told me about the terrible bullying he was subjected to when he first arrived at school.

❝ I remember being taken into a toilet cubicle and being beaten up by a seven- or eight-year-old. I was only five years old. I remember going into the toilet, and someone else coming in behind me and locking the door. These two boys said that they were going to be my bodyguard. One stood outside watching for teachers, and the other took me into the cubicle. He hit me around the head, and then when I fell to the ground, he kicked me as I curled myself around the toilet.

My parents only found out about this when I refused to go to school. My teacher said it was all a fabrication. They didn't believe I was being beaten up because they insisted that there was no real bullying in the school. After the toilet incident I did not want to go to school ever again. In the morning, when my mum took me to the gates and left me there crying, I would stay with the Year 5s who were playing football because they would leave me alone. However, one day a football was kicked at me and when I picked it up, a boy came over and said, 'That's my ball, it's got my name on it,' and he threw the ball into my face and my nose started bleeding.

I felt completely isolated from everyone else. The teachers again thought I had fallen over and was fabricating a tale. I was seen as an outsider and troublemaker by the pupils and teachers.

My parents really knew that something had to be done when I explained to them that the teachers were wrong and I had been attacked. So they moved me to another school. This time I felt safe. The teachers there were much fairer. They were democratic and not autocratic. The teachers at the new school conducted proper investigations into any bullying that was going on, they didn't make snap judgements like the teachers in the other school. ❞

James's story is instructive in many ways. Most importantly, it highlights in perhaps an extreme way the context in which bad bullying goes on. The bullies were allowed to thrive at James's first school because the staff were in denial about the problem and had no procedures to deal with it. Their insistence that James had made up the bullying is shocking in this day and age and it shouldn't have happened, but it does go on. Parents should be aware that any school that says there is little bullying going on in a school probably means there is quite a bad 'underground' problem with it.

James was a victim of bullying because he was a visible outsider; he was better at reading than the other children, he had arrived halfway through the year and he was argumentative with the teachers. This set him apart in a school where there was an intolerance of outsiders generally.

The problems that Marjory's children suffered were also because they were visible outsiders. She told me her own harrowing story.

❛ We live in the south-west of England in a large, rural town. Initially, I was keen for all my children to attend local schools and develop friendship groups within the community. The problem was though, we just didn't fit in. The fact that we didn't have a television and we read books all caused problems for the other children.

It is difficult to know when the bullying started. I knew something was wrong just because my children were behaving in a disturbed manner. One of my children, Josh, came home from primary school, took off all his clothes, rolled himself up in the duvet and went to bed at four o'clock immediately on his return from school. He would get up for supper, but then return to bed. This continued for months.

We tried to find out what the problem was, but he just wouldn't talk to us about it. But one day, my husband and I felt that enough was enough. Josh's collarbone had been broken in the playground. Obviously, I wasn't there so I don't know what happened but he told me that he had been pushed and he had fallen against a concrete upright bench. There was a big thing at school then about children being told not to hit each other. This led to a lot of confusion in the children's minds about how they could be treated: some of the children felt that it was OK to push each other as long as they didn't hit each other. The victims of this pushing – which was endemic in the school apparently – were then admonished if they hit back.

Josh's personal situation improved after his father told him that no one was allowed to hit him and that if anybody attempted to attack him, he should defend himself. Almost immediately another situation arose in the playground. Again he was confronted with violence, but this time he said that he would defend himself. And it soon became necessary for him to defend himself. But he was challenged by the supervisory help, who threatened to report him to the head, and he said that his dad had told him he could defend himself.

He came home from school in his usual state, with buttons off, looking thoroughly distressed and said, 'Mum, I think you are going to hear from Mrs Jackson because I defended myself against a boy who hit me. I explained to the dinner lady that my father said I could defend myself.' We never heard any more about that incident.

The general level of unhappiness continued. At nine, he still couldn't read. I think the constant bullying really knocked his confidence. As a household we were having some difficulty with the local children who went to the school. They were stealing the children's toys from the garden. Two of them broke into the house during our absence and vandalised the boys' bikes with paint and also scribbled a rude message on the blackboard in the kitchen. Meanwhile I had a little nine-year-old boy taking his clothes off and going to bed every day after school. He was a really angry person. Full of rage.

A few months after Josh's collarbone was broken, there was a terrible crash in our house one evening. One of the local children had thrown a brick through my oldest boy's window.

Finally, Josh admitted what was going on: he said that the aggression happened every day and had done for weeks and months. He was pouring over with anger, like a volcano vomiting lava. It was the first time I had heard him talk about this. Before then, he had absorbed it all. I formed the view that the situation was irrecoverable. He never returned to school from that day. It was three weeks into the autumn term. I considered that he was so disturbed that he wouldn't be able to integrate into another school.

He stayed at home and I educated him myself. In September, he could barely read Roger Red-Hat, but by January he was reading a sophisticated historical novel. It made me feel very angry with the system, and still does. 9

All of Marjory's children suffered from bullying because they were perceived as outsiders, but Josh was their most significant victim.

Every aspect of his life was blighted by the bullying; all he wanted to do was curl up into a ball and stay under the duvet.

He was, in many ways, a classic victim. His tormentors were wilfully aggressive towards him, knowing that there was little chance of ever being caught or reprimanded. He suffered from the whole gamut of bullying: constant taunts, being routinely ignored, being excluded from playground games, having missiles thrown at him and being pushed around.

As we saw with James's case, the ethos of the school is very important. In a school where bullying was taken seriously, in all likelihood, Josh's collarbone would not have been broken because the bullying would have been reported. However, since there were no procedures for reporting bullying and no proper discussion of the issue, Josh felt isolated and reluctant to admit to himself that the bullying was going on, and even more unwilling to report it.

The five stages of bullying

Keith Sullivan in his excellent *Anti-Bullying Handbook* shows how most instances of bullying follow five distinct stages. Here are my summaries of the stages:

1. The bully or bullies watch and wait for who might be good victims to pick on. At this point, usually at the beginning of the year, instances of bullying occur the most as the bullies pick on a number of people to see who might be the 'best' victim for them. The number of people picked on decreases as the year progresses as the bullies home in on their victim.

2. The bully picks on his victim by committing a minor offence such as knocking his or her pencil off the table. The bully scrutinises the victim's response and if he or she fails to respond – or overreacts – he or she know they have their victim.

3. The bully maybe hits the victim or 'toy-fights' him or her, and claims that it is all a bit of fun.

4. If nothing is done about it by the victim, the bullying escalates into a proper fight, name-calling and threats.

5. The fifth and final stage is when the bullying becomes the status quo and the victim is constantly physically and psychologically threatened and intimidated.

All along in the process, it is the ethos and atmosphere of the school which can play a decisive factor in whether bullying escalates or not. If a victim at stages 1–3 is aware about what is appropriate and not appropriate behaviour, if there is a general culture of reporting behaviour which makes children feel uneasy, then the bullying may not be allowed to move on to stages 4–5. Perhaps more importantly, if other children who are seeing the bullying going on feel empowered to report the bullying to the school, then it rarely occurs.

Whatever the atmosphere of the school though, victims, for numerous psychological and social reasons, are very reluctant to admit to being bullied. As a teacher, I know this to be true myself. On a few occasions in various comprehensives, I have found that psychologically disturbed pupils have thrown missiles at me at school or have, essentially, bullied me by the threatening tone of their voices or the aggressive way they have demanded things from me. On each occasion, I have been reluctant to tell the relevant person about it because I have felt ashamed. Something in me thinks that maybe I deserved that treatment. Perhaps I am a bit of an idiot who deserves to be treated with contempt.

However, I am an adult, and I know why I feel ashamed. I know that I was essentially bullied by my mother from a young age, and that my feelings of shame are ones that go right back into my past. Now I am able to put aside these feelings and go and talk to the relevant person about the problem. But knowing that I feel this way, I realise that many children must feel far worse and not have my adult's confidence and self-knowledge. Far from it, many children who are bullied very badly may be suffering from some sort of bullying at home, and have an innate distrust of adult authority which means that they never report what is really going on.

It is estimated that about eight out of ten instances of bullying go unreported.[3] This means that concerned parents and teachers need to be aware of the effects and symptoms of bullying.

One of the biggest problems is knowing whether your child is being bullied or not. Only 20 per cent of bullying is discovered; the vast majority of bullying is concealed for years. To a certain extent you may well have to play the 'bully detective' if you are really going to find out what is going on. In order to do this, you not only should be aware of the clues that tell you your child is being bullied, but you should also be conscious of the types of children who bully.

Types of bullies

Stephenson and Smith (1989) identified three types of bully:

1. The first and perhaps the scariest of the lot are the confident bullies who are strong, feel quite secure about themselves and are usually quite popular. They are not immediately recognisable 'bully' types and their bullying may well be done under the guise of 'joking' around in a group of pupils at school. They tend to cement their predominance in a group by picking on a target whom they think will not fight back. This kind of bully may well be your child's 'friend' in their eyes and your child will probably be very reluctant for you to talk to the school about the problem.

2. The second type of bully is the anxious child who is not doing well at school, can't really concentrate on anything and is not that well liked. He or she is an angry child and will be easier to spot than the confident bully because they will frequently be seen and heard mocking or deriding other people.

3. Finally, there are the victims of bullying who are bullied constantly and learn to bully in return. They are very unpopular and your child will probably be willing to identify him or her because they won't be incurring the opprobrium of the rest of the group by picking them out.

Clues that your child is being bullied might be:

- Your child is worried about going to school.

- He or she appears to feel ill in the morning a great deal, has broken nights' sleep where they have bad dreams or wet the bed.

- He or she comes home in a distressed state, with books missing or torn, or seems injured either psychologically or physically.

- He or she receives phone calls/emails/messages which make them unhappy, silent or snappy.

- His or her school work starts to deteriorate.

- He or she behaves in an unusual way.

If you suspect something is wrong, don't just leap in and ask whether your child is being bullied. You could enquire about the following things:

- Gently ask your child about his friends and the sorts of games he or she plays with them during the school breaks. Often this is very revealing. A child who is being bullied is usually: a) not participating in any games, b) regularly being left out, c) being asked to do humiliating things during these so-called games

- Ask him or her about who they sit next to at lunch and the sort of things they talk about.

- Ask him or her about who they sit next to in class, and the kind of help they get in class to do their work. Most teachers now ask that children work together on various projects. Bullied children are often sidelined in such groups or have their work damaged or destroyed.

A parent should be satisfied that a school has clear rules and regulations about dealing with bullying: rules for pupils, information for what parents need to know and clear guidelines for teachers.

School approaches to bullying

Many schools take very different approaches to dealing with bullying. The most notorious of these is the 'No Blame Approach to Bullying'. This approach has supposedly worked in many schools throughout the world. However, I have yet to find a school that is wholly satisfied with it, and have heard numerous complaints from parents that it doesn't solve the problem.

Particularly sinister is 'circle time': this is a time when the class gathers around in a circle, with the bully and the victim both present, and discusses the bullying that is going on. If bullying is rife within the school, 'circle time' becomes yet another excuse for pupils to intimidate their victim with veiled threats and smirks. The teacher may not even notice what is going on because the bullying might be subtle and references may be obscure.

At the heart of this approach is the notion that if the children can work out solutions for themselves then that is the best for all. As a result, this method of tackling bullying involves a lot of meetings where the victim and the bully talk about their feelings and how unhappy they are. A larger group is often involved, for example, members of a class who had been passively observing or encouraging the bullying. They too are involved in meetings with the bully and the victim. The group are asked to accept responsibility for the bullying, but are not blamed for it and discuss ways of stopping it. Meetings are held every week until bullying stops.

The flaws in the approach are obvious: too much responsibility is left to the bullies to sort out the problem. In my view, a teacher should always be the ultimate judge. However, the best teachers will always investigate the issue thoroughly, interview the main people involved, and arrive at a solution which takes into account what the other children have said.

The police

Many parents complain that schools don't do enough about the bullying but they should remember they can go to the police in the last resort. This is what the parents of a pupil in my borough had to do.

In 2005, Calli-Jo Hicks, 14, was removed from George Green's School on the Isle of Dogs after her life was ruined by bullies. Calli-Jo had been bullied for three years but the start of term in September 2005 marked a new low when a series of threats were made. Girls told her she would be 'cut up', killed and thrown into the Thames – all because she was too pretty. Stalkers followed her home and malicious phone calls were made during the early hours, forcing the family to place a trace on their landline. An ad was post in *East London Advertiser* congratulating Calli-Jo on her pregnancy. Her parents complained bitterly to the school and governors, but when the trouble continued, they went to the police. Officers issued harassment orders to two girls at George Green's that September.

Mr Hicks, a 44-year-old musician, said, 'We feel totally let down by the school. They should be ashamed of themselves. My daughter is a bubbly, outgoing girl, but she has been robbed of her social life at school.'[4]

THE NEW SCHOOL RULES
for doing something about bullying

1. **Tell the school** Your child may beg you not to contact the school after they have confessed that they are being bullied. Ignore their pleas. Contact the school immediately. If there is no one obvious to speak to, speak to the head teacher who will normally pass the enquiry down to the relevant person.

2. **Reassure your child** Remember to tell your child that it is not his fault.

3. **Investigate** Read the school's anti-bullying policy – all schools should have one. Follow the procedures on this

▶

in the first instance. A good school will carry out a thorough investigation into any allegations of bullying, and report to parents about what they have discovered. It will take parents' concerns seriously and try its best to solve the problem.

4. **Go up the chain** If you are not satisfied with the school's response take your complaint to the governors of the school. If the governors are not able to stop the bullying, go to the police.

Cyber-bullying

There it was: a direct threat to kill me. It was posted on the discussion board on my website. Since I 'moderate' all the postings on the discussion board, I was able to delete this threat and numerous other unpleasant personal comments written by the same person before it got into the public domain. I was never able to trace the source of the threats satisfactorily, but it appeared that they were posted from out of the country. However, the Internet is an unbelievably vast and shadowy domain and you can never be sure about anything.

I was badly shaken by the comments and felt, first hand, what it was like to be the victim of cyber-bullying. A recent survey of 500 teenagers suggested that one in ten had been bullied online. Liz Carnell, head of the charity Bullying Online, blames the growth of websites such as MySpace and Bebo (www.bebo.com/) where anyone can post their own comments and pictures in the public domain at the click of a mouse, 'The bigger they get, the worse cyber-bullying will become. It is not a problem that will go away.'[5]

One of the great attractions of cyber-bullying is that it allows a bully to conceal his identity and yet publicly humiliate someone. Bright, middle-class children who in the past may have channelled their frustrations and anger into writing a diary or gossiping with friends, now are able to air their grievances without being caught, particularly if they invent 'ghost' ISP addresses whereby their websites and emails can't be traced.

My head teacher, Dr Lloyd, felt that this was going to be an increasing problem for schools:

> The thing about verbal or physical bullying is that you can always find the bully or bullies, and deal with them accordingly. However, with cyber-bullying, it is extremely difficult to get to the bottom of who is doing it. That's why I always say to parents, keep a child's computer in a communal room so that you can see what's going on.

Sometimes, children are very reluctant to admit that they have been bullied online – even though they know who their bullies are – because they know they will be banned from using the Internet if they do. Alice, now 17 years old, told me about how she was the victim of cyber-bullying but didn't tell her parents because of this:

> When I was fifteen, my friends told me that I should sign up with this website called *face-pic*. You search through people by looking at their faces. Even though I saw that there was an adult section to the site, I still thought it would be a laugh, and my friends had posted pics there so I wasn't worried. Anyway, I contacted this boy who was a couple of years older than me, who looked nice, through the site. I just wanted to be his friend, to get to know him. But he wanted more. He started messaging me about how he wanted to do all these things to me. Then he said he wanted to meet so we could do all this scary stuff. I said no, and blocked him off the messaging board. But he got all of his friends to send me all these abusive messages saying that if I had signed up in the first place, I was blatantly up for it. I didn't tell my parents because they would have banned me from using the Internet altogether. They don't understand about this kind of thing. I had to change my email in the end to stop the barrage of horrible messages.

Other pupils told me that a lot of bullying can go on with instant messaging services, such as MSN, because kids can hide behind made-up or false identities and post all sorts of malicious gossip about people without the fear of any reprisals. Seeing defamatory comments in print is far more upsetting than hearing about third-hand gossip that has been bandied around in the playground.

THE NEW SCHOOL RULES
for avoiding cyber-bullying

1. **Keep an eye on that computer** Always insist that the computer is used in a communal area where you can regularly monitor what is going on.

2. **Talk it through** Tell your child about the dangers of cyber-bullying. Remember again to tell her that it is not her fault. Help her develop a thick skin: it is probably going to happen at some point in their life.

3. **Investigate** If you think that the cyber-bullies are at your child's school, inform the school, saving the relevant messages, emails, and Internet addresses. Make sure you get the ISP address where the abusive message was sent from. Report instances of cyber-bullying to the ISP which is usually the name of the ISP plus the word 'abuse', for example, abuse@hotmail.com or abuse@btinternet.com.

▶ **CHECK OUT**
www.dfes.gov.uk/bullying/
Kevin Brown, *Bullying – What Can Parents Do*, Monarch Publications, 1998.
Keith Sullivan, *The Anti-Bullying Handbook*, OUP, 2000.

When your child is a bully

Mr Ball was furious when I complained that his son, Nick, had been bullying some children in his class. 'Look, he's only twelve years old, surely you guys can sort him out?' I asked Mr Ball what he meant. He winked at me menacingly. 'The trouble is everyone is soft at school,' he explained:

> At home Nick never causes any problems because he knows that he's going to get punished if he steps out of line. What you need to do is take him to a dark room and give him a good beating. You've got my permission. I won't say anything because I know that's what Nick needs: a good beating.

Somewhat taken aback, I said that I didn't think that would do any good. At this Mr Ball became angry, 'The thing is you don't really care, do you? You're not willing to do what is necessary to get him in line. You're just going to leave him to his own devices and let him bully kids and muck around in class, and you're not going to do anything, are you?'

I explained that as Nick's form tutor, I had a duty to do something but that didn't include hitting the boy or trying to frighten him. I said that may solve things in the short term, but it wouldn't solve the long-term problem of Nick's lack of empathy for his victims. 'If we're really going to get him to stop what he's doing, we've got to make him see the misery he's causing the other people in the class,' I said.

A few days later, I spoke to Nick privately and told him about the sleepless nights he'd been causing one of the pupils in the class. Nick grinned. 'Serves him right, he's a tosser,' Nick said. His whole attitude made my heart sink. I was talking to Nick in a very calm, almost friendly fashion, without emotion, without anger. I was not attempting to frighten him into stopping his behaviour. Nick didn't appear to be respecting me particularly for this: his attitude was cocky and arrogant. Interestingly though, the bullying did stop for the next couple of weeks. As a result, I started to be much more friendly to Nick. On the odd occasion I would give Nick a 'high five' in the corridor when Nick requested it. This boosted Nick's standing with his mates: he dared to ask a teacher for a 'high five' and had got one. I felt a little uneasy about the whole thing, but sensed that by keeping Nick on my side I was winning the battle with the bullying.

A couple of months later, I got an irate call from his father. Nick's grades had been poor in his most recent report, although he was congratulated upon the improvement in his behaviour. 'These reports are rubbish!' his father fumed. 'He's getting D grades in English and maths. He's rubbish. I've tried to get him to see sense but he's getting this attitude at home and he's starting to backchat me. He never used to do that. To be honest, I think he's a bit of a prat. He's not listening to what I say.'

I explained that I thought Nick should be congratulated on stopping bullying and that we needed to get Nick on our side. I said that I had given him the occasional 'high five' and that he seemed much happier in school.

Mr Ball was disgusted. 'The next time he tries to give you a high five, you need to totally humiliate him in front of his mates. I want you to tell him he's a complete prat and that you'll never do it again.' He was furious with me for daring to be friendly to Nick. I tried to explain that this sort of attitude was probably making Nick feel frightened and demotivated, but Mr Ball wasn't having any of it. 'I give up! I give up!' he said. 'I've done my best for the boy and you've done nothing but mess it up for me.'

The phone call ended shortly after that. I spoke to Nick after this and said that I was pleased that he wasn't bullying the pupils anymore but he needed to improve his work. Nick started crying and said that he hated his dad because he was always threatening him.

I referred the matter to the Child Protection Officer in school – as all teachers are supposed to do if they suspect physical abuse – but Mr Ball wasn't doing anything perceived as serious. No allegations of beatings were proven. But one thing became clear to me: Nick had been bullying and would probably continue bullying for the rest of his life because he learned that frightening people was the way to get results. I don't think Mr Ball was a very bad bully; my mother treated me in much the same way when I was a child. Nick was certainly better off at home than in care.

What helped Nick the most were the calm discussions about his feelings and why he bullied. He'd already begun to see that he was bullying children because he was bullied himself at home, and this realisation, to a certain extent, mitigated his behaviour.

THE NEW SCHOOL RULES

for stopping your child being a bully

1. **Be honest with yourself** Examine your own behaviour very carefully. Do you get angry with your child a lot? Do you attempt to effect a change in behaviour with fear? Learn to avoid threats as much as possible. The child who is threatened a lot at home is a child who then threatens others at school.

2. **Talk it through** Learn to talk to your child in a calm way. Talk about your own feelings and try to give them the tools to talk about their own emotions. The first step to changing behaviour is by talking. Teach your child to empathise by telling stories. Psychologists have shown that telling stories about bullies and victims can help children learn to empathise with victims more. Roald Dahl and J.K. Rowling's stories are particularly good for this; they have shown time and again what it's like to be on the wrong end of bullying behaviour.

School trips

Khaled was one of the most difficult children I have ever taught, and that, considering some of the schools in which I have worked, is saying something. I am reminded of him when I go on a school trip with one of my classes. Khaled was in the very first 'form group' I was in charge of as a fully qualified teacher, which was over 15 years ago now. I remember being terrified, when I learnt that I would be taking my tutor group to Wales on a week-long trip to a residential course, because Khaled was such a bully.

At the time I was working in a mixed-sex comprehensive in east London, teaching English to Bengali and Somali children. As Khaled's form tutor I was responsible for monitoring his progress and teaching personal and social skills. It was not a success. Although he was only 11 and knew very little English, he did manage to say 'Fuck you' to most of the form and become involved in frequent fights. He spent a lot of his time scowling outside classrooms, kicking at doors with pathetically dilapidated trainers. The approach of the annual school trip to a rural studies centre in Wales filled me with dread. As a form tutor I was expected to supervise my pupils for a week while they learnt about geography and science. The train journey was long and difficult, and Khaled got himself into a fight with a boy wearing a fake gold ring who punched him in the face. Khaled sat with me for the rest of the journey as the blood congealed on his wounds.

Once we got to the centre a lot of the children were terrified: they had never ventured beyond Stepney in their lives, and the mountains and the forests intimidated them. Khaled seemed the most afraid and, while most of the children soon began to explore their surroundings, he remained indoors, sitting on a windowsill with his back to the landscape. Fortunately, the enthusiasm of George, the teacher in charge of the place, turned nature into a wonderful adventure playground. He constantly challenged the children to do daring things: to climb steep hills, ford tricky streams, climb trees.

This was before the outcry about the 'dangers' of school outings. George was a lot more cautious than the teacher, Paul Ellis, who, on a fatal Lake District expedition a few years ago, encouraged his charges to jump into a swollen stream, and who was convicted in 2003 of the manslaughter of 10-year-old Max Palmer. But George wasn't afraid to encourage the children to take risks then – as he certainly would be now.

This policy paid rich dividends with many of the children, but was particularly rewarding with Khaled. The boy began to scamper over hillsides with abandon, to climb trees, to splash around in the icy streams. At one point, George told Khaled to run down a steep mountain with his arms up and shout, 'Geronimo!' He duly raced down the incline and then suddenly came to a precipice, about eight feet high – at which point he flapped his arms and leapt off it. It was a scary moment; I fleetingly thought that he would break every bone in his body and was extremely relieved to see him pick himself up without a scratch, glowing with delight. It was the first time I had seen him smile.

This small incident was a sort of rite of passage for Khaled. From that moment, he seemed much happier; he started joining in lessons, talking to the other children and avoiding fights.

For me, this incident epitomises the reasons why every parent should encourage their children to go on school trips: they can be really liberating for everyone. Most teachers are very careful, but the best ones do allow children to take some risks; without giving them the chance to take some risks, children will never learn.

THE NEW SCHOOL RULES
for school trips

1. **Talk it through** Make sure that your child is prepared mentally and physically for the trip. Encourage him to think what he might do if there is a problem: if, for example, he is bullied, is homesick or gets separated from the group.

2. **Investigate** Read the school's literature about the trip very carefully.

3. **Don't panic** Remember that allowing children to take risks can be a very valuable learning experience.

Sex, drugs and rock 'n' roll

Underage drinking

It was the kind of story that would make any parent shudder with horror. A couple of years ago, while I was researching my book *Yob Nation*, James, 15, told me what really goes on on Friday and Saturday nights when he and his mates have got some money. 'We go down to Romford and hang around the bars,' he said, with his smirk on his face.

'How much do you drink?'

'Not that much because the beer's so expensive,' he said.

I didn't believe him at the time because he and his friends looked so young. What kind of bar would let such fresh-faced innocents into their establishment? However, I decided to check for myself one Saturday night. I caught the train to Romford and walked out into a scene which astonished me at the time: the centre of Romford was heaving with kids staggering around pissed out of their heads, lurching from bar to bar. There were bouncers on nearly every door, but they didn't seem to be checking any of the children for ID.

There was an intimidating atmosphere. I saw one fight kicking off near a nightclub, and felt as though I should be prepared to run as fast as possible if one of the groups decided to approach me: many of the children were shouting and yelling at the top of their voices in a threatening fashion.

I was tapped on the shoulder. I whirled around in fright. I breathed a sigh of relief when I saw it was James and his mates. They laughed at seeing me there. They were dressed in designer jeans and T-shirts, and looked a little older than they did in their school uniforms. 'Hey, sir, what are you doing here?'

'I came to see if what you said is true,' I said.

They laughed. As I chatted to them I saw a number of pupils and ex-pupils of mine wandering up and down the thoroughfare in various states of disrepair. Some were from a girls' school I had taught in a year before, and when they saw me they looked horrified. I knew that they really weren't supposed to be here.

'But how can you afford it?' I asked, pointing to the extortionate prices on the boards near the bar door.

They explained that most kids sneaked in bottles of vodka that they'd bought from the offy, and perhaps bought one round, fortifying their drinks with the spirit. 'That's why all these lot are pissed as newts,' James said, pointing at the sloshed teenagers slopping around the street. 'They maybe buy one round of drinks, and top them up. Otherwise, it would be too expensive. Mind you, you've got to realise that a lot of kids here do part-time jobs so they get quite a bit of pocket money that way.'

As I headed home on a vandalised train, I reflected that this was a depressing state of affairs. I subsequently travelled around the whole of England visiting city centres, schools and estates, interviewing people about the drinking culture in the country, and saw that what happened in Romford was not the exception – it was the rule.

Some exhaustive research carried out by the Prime Minister's favourite think tank, the Institute of Public Policy Research (IPPR, www.ippr.org.uk), has shown that British 15-year-olds are more likely to become intoxicated, act aggressively and have underage sex than their counterparts in Europe.

There is an epidemic of underage drinking in Britain. In recent years, convictions of teenagers for being drunk and disorderly have risen by nearly 200 per cent in sedate, well-heeled counties such as Cambridgeshire, Lincolnshire, and Surrey.[6] The IPPR study found that nearly three out of ten teenagers in Britain regularly binge drink.

Many children buy their drink from off-licences and wander the streets getting drunk. In areas of high social deprivation, this problem is undoubtedly worse but it would be a mistake to think it is confined to the 'lower classes'. As we have seen in the area where I teach, like numerous others in the country, there is a significant problem with youths from middle-class homes getting drunk in large groups. In truth, they have been victims of a poorly regulated alcohol industry which has targeted young people with the sale of 'alcopops' and the setting up of 'vertical drinking establishments' or pubs where there are no seats but lots of loud clubby music and an atmosphere of louche restraint.

Some academics estimate the industry is expanding by 10 per cent year on year in Britain and accounts for 3 per cent of the GDP but looks set to further increase its market share with the introduction of round-the-clock drinking in bars and pubs. Many studies show that anti-social behaviour is most concentrated in areas where alcohol is most readily available.[7]

The same isn't the case in Europe. The reason for this is cultural. On the Continent, parents teach their children to drink sensibly, at meal times. Alcohol is there to complement food and to be savoured for its taste. In Britain, the IPPR found that over a third of children do not eat with their parents compared with 93 per cent of children in Italy. The IPPR quite rightly pointed out that it is this lack of quality time with adults that is fuelling much of the disorder on the streets.

Underage sex and drug taking

Part and parcel with the 'risk-taking' drinking culture that is prevalent among young people today are other types of 'risk taking', such as unprotected sex and drug taking. Young people get together at school and plan out parties where drinking, drug taking and sex take place: it's part of the package of 'having a good time', 'having a laugh'. Undoubtedly this has always been the case to a certain extent: my father has told me tales of similar parties going on the 1950s when he was a school boy, and I can remember some fairly risqué parties when I was at school in the 1980s. However, what is striking now is that communication by mobile phone and the Internet has made them a great deal easier to arrange, and a lot bigger. Many schools have entire year groups or even schools in the same MSN chatroom – this could amount to thousands of children – which can mean that parties with huge numbers of people can be arranged very quickly.

I have interviewed many teenagers, some of whom have told me about some fairly hair-raising parties where they have witnessed unprotected sex and drug taking – although they assured me that they hadn't participated in anything like that. I took them at their word and believed them, and was interested to note how they 'resisted' the lure of getting too involved. One boy, J, told me:

> The thing is, it's really the insecure ones that do the stupid stuff. It's like they've got to prove themselves in front of everyone. So let's take Ingrid – not her real name – she encouraged a couple of boys to have sex with her in full view of everyone at this party. But I know her. She's got this bad situation at home, her mum wants to kick her out, and her dad's nowhere around, and I can't help thinking that that's got something to do with it. I mean, I hang around that circle a little bit, but my mum and dad talked to me about all this stuff. And they showed me that you can have a bottle of lager and be part of the crew without getting pissed out of your head when you start to do stupid things. It's like I don't need to be pissed to chat up a girl. I don't need to smoke weed to feel like I am someone. But the weed thing is difficult. I just tend not to be around when it's offered.

J was a confident boy who had been informed of the risks, and his parents had sat down with him and spelled out what can happen with all these things. Ultimately, they trusted him to make his own choices and he felt confident enough not to get lured into anything too stupid.

There is no doubt that if your child wants to get drunk, have sex, and take drugs it's a hell of a lot easier than it used to be. This means that the 'prohibition' route that many parents take – banning them from attending certain social functions or seeing certain people – won't be that effective if they've got their own email account or mobile phone.

It is more important than ever that parents teach their children personal responsibility with drink, drugs and sex. That's very easy to say, but how is it done?

THE NEW SCHOOL RULES
about sex, drugs and rock 'n' roll

1. **Talk it through** When you think the time is right, talk to your child about your fears. It is important to explain that you are concerned for them, and that you care, but try not to ban things – all the evidence suggests that this approach backfires. Keep your child informed. Tell the truth.

2. **Investigate** Use the web to keep up to date with the latest news on these subjects. The best place to start is the Parentlineplus website (www.parentlineplus.org.uk/) which provides links to all the best websites dealing with these concerns. An organisation called DARE (Drugs Awareness Resistance Education) has been particularly effective in dealing with these problems. Its website (www.dare.uk.com/) is very good and provides much up-to-date information about various drugs.

Yob culture

While bullying is focused on the individual and tends to be localised, the effects of yob culture can be felt by everyone in the school whether they are being bullied or not. One 17-year-old pupil, Taj, who is at a secondary school in a socially deprived area told me that drugs cause all sorts of problems:

> For me school has a lot of problems. This is due to the fact school is where a lot of the drug dealing takes place and scores are settled. In my school anyway, soft drugs are sold in the school because it's mostly young people who buy them and the hard stuff is kept on the streets. This causes problems when people don't pay. Because of this there are fights and attacks. Just a few

weeks ago a boy got beat up with a shovel due to a drug deal that had gone wrong.

The police are often at the school because pupils have been caught with knives and other weapons in school. The police are often called to fights between other schools. Many pupils also take drugs during school and even drink alcohol. Several offenders have been excluded but the majority don't get caught.

The kids who want to work will get it done. However, distractions are easy as misbehaviour is common. In particular, teachers are victimised and the same goes for pupils. So it's up to yourself if you get involved with the pupils who are not doing the work.

I tend to work well in the classroom regardless of what I've been up to in the yard. However, most pupils who are dealing drugs don't do well in class and intentionally disrupt lessons whether it's to impress or to look hard.

Taj's main point is that the buying, selling, and taking of drugs lead to a great many fights between rival gangs. Many children find that in large secondary schools where there is not much discipline being part of a gang is the only way to be socially accepted.

In Wales, I spoke to Gareth, who told me about his experiences growing up in a tough senior school in Ebbw Vale:

I got tangled up in gang culture in order to survive. I can remember how I was lining up for the bus for school in the morning, and somebody tried to take my money off me. I was 11 years old. They ripped my shirt and took the buttons off my shirt. Unfortunately, I started doing that to other kids so I wouldn't get picked on. I got involved with a gang. We was the 'Cwm' boys – which is the name of the village where we all came from. We went together at school and out of school.

In school, we had our own room. We took over this room, Room 22, at break times and nobody else could go into the room other than Cwm people. No else dared to go in there. Initially, the fights all went on in school.

In schools where gangs are prevalent, it takes a year to find your rank, and your room, and your personal territory, and then things settle down, but until then it is chaos, because it is dog eat dog. The teachers can't really control it. A lot goes on that the teachers know nothing about or if they do, they just ignore it.

As we have seen with bullying, unless schools address the issue of gang culture head-on, violence can flare up at any time. At the secondary school nearest to where I live in Bethnal Green, the head teacher advised some parents to keep their children away from school for their own safety because of violence supposedly sparked by the cartoons of the prophet Mohammed that were published in Denmark. Parents with children at Bethnal Green Technology College in London said fighting in the playground and outside the school gates had escalated in February 2006 when the cartoons were published. Linda David, a learning mentor, said her 15-year-old son had not worried about his safety until that month but that she had since caught him carrying a knife for self-defence. She claimed that the rows over the Danish cartoons of the prophet Mohammed were being used as an excuse by some pupils for the fighting. Most tellingly, the school had significant behavioural problems: it was in special measures and had recently taken in 50 Turkish pupils from a closing school.[8]

Violence and weapons

While in Taj's school drugs were a significant problem, and in Gareth's school territory was the issue, in Bethnal Green Technology College, it was clashes between different ethnic groups which were the underlying causes of the fights. In all of the schools, there was a deep-rooted contempt for authority and a culture where violence and misbehaviour were the cool things to do. At the 2006 Jack Petchey Speak Out Challenge in Stratford, London, 15-year-old Poppy Noor spoke of knife crime at her school in Newham. She won runner-up in the competition for her eloquent speech which detailed the general school culture that allowed knife crime to thrive. In her school, knives were seen as a fashion accessory. 'Being hostile and aggressive is seen as being cool,' she said. She explained that the moment there was a fight in the playground, the children were shouting out, 'Eh, there's beef oh!' Beef is rap slang for a violent fight, usually involving guns or knives.

Unfortunately, gangs are a feature of life throughout the country – as I detailed in my book *Yob Nation*. A Home Office study estimates that six per cent of young people aged 10–19 are members of 'delinquent youth groups'; this is probably a conservative estimate since no one knows the real number. Gang members are much more likely than non-members to be involved in crime, take drugs or carry a weapon. The perceived glamour and rewards of the 'gangsta' lifestyle act as a magnet for some disaffected pupils: not one of the gang members in one Manchester study had completed formal education. Others join for their own protection.

'They look out for you. You don't want to be there all the time, but it's better than home,' one 15-year-old told researchers on the Manchester study. Groups usually take their name from a street or area, usually with an added epithet such as 'Boyz', 'Mob' or 'Posse'. Territory is marked with graffiti, with proxy battles played out through gang members' tags.[9] At the heart of gang culture is a deep-rooted materialism: an almost reverential worship for certain violent rap stars, football players and teams, certain designer clothes and trainers, and jewellery.

Security

Not surprisingly, given this sort of street culture in many of our British cities, one top concern of parents is security. In Manchester, I was shocked to see that one of the city's top schools – a state-funded Jewish school – was very heavily guarded. I spoke to one of the security guards at the school gates and he told me:

We guard this school very carefully indeed. I suppose it was 7/7 that really triggered if off when everyone realised that these nutters didn't care who they attacked, be it themselves, or the general public. And we know now that they would think of nothing about killing school children. So we are here, at the gates, watching very carefully what is going on.

But funnily enough, it hasn't been the terrorist threat that has been the biggest headache. It's the drug dealers, you see. The kids are wealthy and they want to buy drugs from the local dealers around here, of whom there are plenty.

Anti-Semitism is always a problem, you have to keep an eye out, and you have to also keep the parents calm about everything. I had a couple of parents complaining about the radio's traffic plane, the Eye as it is known, which checks the city's traffic, a week ago, saying that it was circling the school too much. I told them I'd get some Stinger rockets to take it out.

One parent I spoke to who was very much against the kind of segregation I saw in Manchester was the author, Labour Party activist and TV personality John O'Farrell. His novel *May Contain Nuts* satirises the paranoia that some parents feel about the state sector. He told me:

> We live in such gated communities where different social groups just don't mix that I felt it was very important that my children went to a school where they knew their local community properly. I am very against this helicopter parenting where you helicopter your children into schools which are far away from where you live just because you are frightened that they might mix with the local poor children. I know of parents who hire a private bus just so that they can take their children miles away from the Lambeth area and be educated in the leafier, nicer suburbs at a private school. Likewise, children of these parents are always being whisked off to extra classes: music lessons, dance classes, Latin lessons, yoga exercise sessions. It is ridiculous.
>
> To get the most out of your school, you should respect your local community, and let your children mix with them. It is more important that they know their neighbours than they learn Mandarin at the age of eight. This helicopter parenting causes children to be pale-faced and it is counterproductive. You are

storing up social problems if you do this. The most important thing a school can assist you with is to make your child confident and independent. I take pride in seeing my son hanging around with a bunch of his 13-year-old friends and chatting happily. I am not too worried that he is not learning French or the trombone because he is gaining the social skills that are most important in life. Just the other day, he went off by himself on his bike down the Queenstown Road. My heart was in my mouth. I was worried that something that might happen to him because there he was going off with his mates on a trip with them, without me watching his every move. When he came back beaming and happy, I could see he was ten times bigger.

That's what a good school can really give your child: true independence and the ability to mix with a whole range of different people from all sorts of backgrounds and cultures.

O'Farrell's central point is that parents' fears about local state schools being breeding grounds for yobbery and criminality are not justified, and that it is your child's ability to mix with a wide variety of people which is his most important education. But equally he did not deny that his children were likely to encounter difficult personalities and social groups. He felt that it was the child's ability to deal with these groups that was the central issue, and that with good parenting and a supportive environment at school, any child should be able to cope.

Ways around the problem

Some people I spoke to saw religion as the answer. In particular, some Islamic youth groups are trying to counter the trend of gang culture by hitting the streets and promoting a different set of values. My former pupil, Hassan, who himself was caught up in gang culture, told me:

Gangs are still visible in Tower Hamlets, though it has somewhat changed. Ten years ago, gangs were not just criminal – everyone was in one. It was a sense of belonging, something to pass the time, a sub-culture in which everyone partook. But in recent years, as second generation Bengalis like me have grown up, we've been able to advise the younger kids because, more often than not, most of us were in gangs and know how to relate to the kids. Gang members from 10 to 15 years ago had no one to educate them, the elders were first generation immigrants, too busy earning a buck and no time to run after the kids – nor did they know how to deal with the issue.

Older generation Bangladeshis and Muslims have a higher level of respect and reverence for elders, so they could not relate to or comprehend the insolence of us kids back then. I also think there has been somewhat of a religious renaissance – not just in Tower Hamlets but the UK in general. This has seen things become polarised. Whereas before you could be 'religious' on a Friday and a 'rude boy' all other times, now there is no space for hypocrisy. Things are black and white, there are no shades of grey – you are in one of two camps; either religious or not. There are less gangs because of that but of the gangs remaining some are more brutal than before – because they feel the religious people have washed their hands of them.

For many other parents though religion isn't the answer. First and foremost, as with bullying, it was the concern of knowing exactly what is going on. Karen, whose daughters are at a rough comprehensive in Leeds, offered this advice:

Eavesdropping in cars is essential. Children learn subtly to protect parents from what's really going in school, so this is the only way to find out. We heard years later about awful things that had happened in school. These came out during idle chat over lunch on holiday, so we had a laugh. Had we known at the time, we'd have had apoplexy. You should get involved in school in whatever way you can. For some, it's easy to go in and listen to reading once a week, for others maybe just a yearly day out on a school trip. Having lots of children round to play is also a good source of inside info, as is the pre-Ofsted meeting for parents: lots of people jump up and down and let off steam at these meetings.

Anya Rosenberg's story of how she managed to achieve at a very tough comprehensive in Southend shows how seeking extra help from the teachers pays dividends. She told me:

❦ Although I definitely wasn't a model student at school and I did my fair share of messing around and not paying attention I still knew that I wanted to get a decent education and go on to study A levels and hopefully go to university. I didn't learn anything in classes – all the kids had absolutely no interest in listening to the teachers and the teachers had little enthusiasm or authority. My maths teacher always stunk of booze and was clearly having troubles at home. I remember once, when nobody was listening to him, he completely lost it and shouted out that his wife was leaving him and the last thing he needed was us lot playing up. My French teacher had absolutely no control – everyone used to laugh at him and because he was shy and quiet and everyone used to talk over him, I could never hear a word he was saying. It was a real shame because I liked French and despite trying quite hard out of school classes I still only managed to get a D grade. Going to school was more about hanging out with my friends and trying not to get caught smoking cigarettes at break-time. However, when it came to studying for my GCSEs I knew I had to change things. I knew that in order to get into the girls grammar school to do A levels (the school I was in didn't offer A levels) I had to get at least five grade A–Cs.

I had a genuine interest in English and History. My history teacher was great. He knew that I got drawn into messing around during class but he was one of the few teachers who could see that with a bit of encouragement I could do well. He agreed to stay late after class once a week and help me learn what I needed in order to pass. We literally went through the syllabus and pretty much started from scratch. I got a grade 'B' of which I felt very proud; as did my teacher. When he heard that I had been accepted at Southend High School for Girls he wrote me such a lovely letter congratulating me.

I found Maths really difficult. I definitely needed extra help there and so my dad agreed to pay for me to get a Maths tutor. I needed to get a grade C and there was no way I was going to get that if I didn't take the situation into my own hands. Unfortunately, I wasn't interested enough in Science to pursue it outside of school time which is the only thing that would've made me pass so I only got Ds but all of the subjects that I liked I made the effort to pass.

It was a shame because there were definitely subjects that had I been encouraged and pushed a little I know I could've done better. I would've liked to have been inspired to get into other areas and learn about things that didn't naturally intrigue me. I'm always quite jealous of people that are suddenly reminded of something they learned in Physics or Geography because I literally don't remember being taught anything in these classes.

When I arrived at Southend High for Girls I worked so hard. I couldn't believe the difference — the teachers were brilliant and all showed an interest in me. I turned into a real geek! I wasn't interested in making any friends and I just spent all my time working. I was so pleased to be in an environment where I could work — I took on an extra three GCSEs at the same time as doing my A levels and did a typing and word processing course too. I couldn't get enough of it. For the first time ever I started getting As and Bs.

I was so upset when I failed my eleven-plus and didn't get into a grammar school but luckily I was driven enough to turn things around. When applying for jobs after I left university I felt really embarrassed at how bad my GCSE grades were. I remember looking through the CVs of the people who had applied for the publicity assistant job that I got at Bloomsbury Publishing and they all had 10 As. it made me feel a bit inadequate but I do always feel proud that I had to really work for what I achieved and luckily I had such a strong interest and passion for books that I knew exactly where I wanted to end up. 9

Anya's story is instructive in many ways: it shows how difficult it is to battle against a prevailing culture of yobbery, but it illustrates that it can be done.

THE NEW SCHOOL RULES
for battling against yob culture

1. **Investigate** But be subtle with your spying. Don't go stomping into a situation demanding to know what is going on. Try to figure it out with some gentle questions, by observation and discussion with any other people involved or in the know. Find out what is really going on. Talk to your child, talk to other parents. Invite other children around to your house.

2. **Talk it through** Educate your child from an early age about society: how it is made up of different social groups, how some people behave differently, discuss drugs and alcohol, and gang culture. Don't make them frightened, but tell them the truth.

3. **Show them how to avoid trouble** Give them strategies for avoiding trouble. Lead by example: don't get drawn into vitriolic arguments in front of them, show them that you can laugh things off and walk away from sources of conflict you encounter on the street and at home. Help develop a constructive social activity such as a sport or recreation which involves their friends, football, music and so forth.

4. **Be jokey** Help them develop a sense of humour. Making jokes that are not personalised and vicious is an excellent way of avoiding real trouble. Buy them a joke book suitable for their age and go through it with them.

5. **Don't panic** Finally, try not to worry too much. Karen told me: 'It is very, very easy to obsess and feel cheated by the state school system. We really did not want our daughters to go to the school they're in and appealed twice against our older daughter's school allocation. Yes,

▶

> I think they might well have had a more pleasant experience in the school up the road which people in our street traditionally went to, but they are bright kids and are taking the best from where they are. Academically they'll do OK because they are able, they tend to go around with other bright kids, and they have positive influences at home. Organisationally, discipline-wise and environmentally, the school is really awful. Socially, they have made friends from many backgrounds, races, creeds which is always a good thing.'

Improving your own child's behaviour

Up and down the country, I spoke to parents who were finding their children's behaviour impossible to deal with. Phyllis was by no means alone in being a parent who had spent huge sums of money on trying to keep her daughter happy but had failed. She told me with tears in her eyes:

> My daughter is rebelling against everything and everyone. She's 15 and out on the streets doing whatever and whenever. I think we have spoilt her. She has a horse which she doesn't really deserve. I find it quite terrible that my child can say 'f off' to me. She slams doors, she drinks, takes drugs, goes off with boys. I am quite frightened of her.

Addressing emotional problems

The best schools are now trying to address the emotional problems that children like this have. The best teaching scheme I have ever come across that genuinely improves children's behaviour is currently being taught in a number of Wiltshire schools. It is worth examining in some detail because if you understand the principles behind it, it could significantly help you improve your own child's behaviour. Janet Grant, a year learning manager at Corsham School in Chippenham, and two other teacher trainers – Suzanne Corrywright and Sue Allen – have devised a wonderful set of lessons called 'VisionWorks: Empowering Pupils Through Emotional Intelligence' (www.vision-works.net/education/index.php). The programme is based on the ideas of Daniel Goleman, the American author of the book *Emotional Intelligence*.

I first came across the Wiltshire scheme in a mailing a few years ago. I was a form tutor, struggling to deal with some serious behavioural problems with my Year 8 group. I had a disturbed girl in my form who stirred up all kinds of trouble between other members of the group. Spotting some of the exercises suggested in the mailing – and being the 'magpie' teacher that I am, forever thieving other people's ideas – I tried them out, in a diluted form, with my class. My school at the time wouldn't pay for the full programme (PSHE budgets are minuscule) so I had to make do with the activities on offer through the mailing.

One idea was to ask the pupils to describe their feelings at different moments in the school day: feelings of fear, excitement, nervousness, elation. This simple exercise was surprisingly successful and I never forgot its effectiveness in calming children.

When, some years later, I was still teaching these basic rudiments to my form group – and I was researching yob culture for my book *Yob Nation* – I contacted the writers of the programme to ask them about the ways in which they tackled anti-social behaviour in schools. The scheme they showed me made me think they could really assist with stopping mindless thuggery in schools and society in general: my book concludes that it is only genuine education that can solve Britain's current problems with yobbery.

Suzanne Corrywright of VisionWorks believes that decent EQ (Emotional Quotient) programmes not only help curtail anti-social behaviour but they can also assist with improving results. 'Daniel Goleman always spoke of how he hoped his work would be used in schools,' she says.

Ironically, it was picked up by American business schools, who, seeing that the ability to relate with others was the most significant key to success, used his principles to make an EQ test, which is a more reliable predictor of success than IQ tests. Only now, many years after the book was written, are his ideas being picked up by schools for dealing with issues such as bullying and anti-social behaviour.

In Goleman's view, emotional intelligence is the ability to recognise, understand and express your feelings – and then understand those of others.

Janet Grant cites the example of one Corsham pupil to illustrate how the programme works. When she first encountered Shana in Year 7, she was having a rough time. Her parents were divorced but still at war with each other, her work was deteriorating, and she was bullying other children. However, like all Year 7 pupils at Corsham, she took part every week in twenty-minute tutor sessions aimed at improving the pupils' emotional intelligence. She was assigned a buddy, which she was initially very resentful about. The buddy system is central to the emotional literacy sessions. Pupils take a name randomly out of the tutor bowl and have to work with that pupil for half the term. The idea is that pupils learn to work with someone outside their friendship group. Shana wouldn't talk to her buddy to begin with, but during one lesson she was invited to make a mask of the symbolic 'face' that she presents to the outside world. 'She made this amazing mask, which was coloured black and red and encased in barbed wire,' says Janet Grant. 'Some of the other pupils didn't understand the concept of the mask and so Shana went around the class explaining it to them. She told them the barbed wire was how she looked to the outside world: that she was prickly to ward them off.'

Towards the end of Year 7, Janet Grant happened to take a message to Shana's class. She found the pupils without their tutor, sitting in a circle, listening to each other in silence, as they arranged an old person's tea party entirely of their own free will. 'The programme has meant that pupils know everyone in the tutor group, and are much less inclined to argue with each other,' says Janet Grant. 'There is much more of a spirit of co-operation.'

What makes the programme so appealing for me – as a teacher who has endured his fair share of bad behaviour – is that it implicitly recognises that the individual teacher is not to blame for poorly disciplined pupils. It realises that improving the way children behave must be a whole school effort. Children must be given a language with which to analyse their emotions before they can alter the way they respond to those emotions.

The warning signs have proliferated for a long time. A Teachers' TV survey earlier this year discovered that nearly seven out of ten teachers think that there is a discipline crisis in our schools. On the streets, the incidence of violent crime and yobbish behaviour is rising at an alarming rate. Last year Ofsted – in a publication called *Managing Challenging Behaviour* – confirmed what teachers already know: pupils with emotional and behavioural difficulties are the most difficult for schools to manage. Between 2001 and 2003, there was a 25 per cent increase in the number of children sent to Pupil Referral Units. 'The most common form of poor behaviour is persistent, low level disruption of lessons that wears down staff and interrupts learning,' comment the authors of the Ofsted report. A significant number of these pupils, they acknowledge, face disadvantage and disturbance in their family lives.

Teaching materials like the ones proving effective at Corsham School were never more needed.

THE NEW SCHOOL RULES
for improving your own child's behaviour

1. **Talk it through** Give your child a language to describe their emotions, get them used to talking about their feelings. ▶

2. Praise them Pay attention to your child when he or she is behaving well. Try to ignore misbehaviour. Reward good behaviour, not bad. Be specific with your praise. Say precisely what you like about your child's work or attitude. People always feel better when they know precisely what it is that they have done well. That way they can repeat that behaviour more easily.

3. Keep calm Try to keep calm most of the time. Avoid shouting and appearing angry. Show that you have control over your own emotions. Never give in to panic. Panicking inhibits the mind's ability to make rational and good decisions. Walk away from confrontations. Emotionally intelligent parents always buy themselves time to think about how best to deal with a situation. Don't tell your child off when he or she behaves badly, but talk about feelings, explore the reasons for misbehaviour with them, and raise awareness of the effect this behaviour has on others.

CHAPTER 4

Does your child have special needs?

Many parents are ashamed to admit that their child might have special needs. The word has come to have a pejorative ring to it, with many people thinking that it is a euphemism for 'a bit thick' or 'very stupid'. In fact, the phrase has a legal definition: 'Children have special educational needs (SEN) if they have a learning difficulty which calls for special education provision to be made for them.'[1]

Children are viewed as having a learning difficulty if either they have a significantly greater difficulty in learning than the majority of children of the same age, or have a disability which prevents them from accessing the average school. Children are not viewed as having SEN if they have learning difficulty because English is not their first language.

As you can see, the definition is very wide-ranging: it covers all children who may need extra support and help with their studies because they are struggling to progress at a similar rate to most pupils. It is estimated that two out of every ten pupils will need extra support at some point during their school career.

The sharpest parents use the 'special needs' label to get what they want for their child. The most egregious example of this is the way the former Education Secretary Ruth Kelly removed her son from a good state primary school in Tower Hamlets and placed him in a £15,000 a year boarding school which caters for pupils with SEN. Most interestingly, she could have received state funding to send him there, but turned it down – on her wage she doesn't need the money. Clearly she was unhappy about the education he was getting at the primary school and used her knowledge of 'special needs' to wangle him a place at a top-of-the-line private school.

But she is not alone. A trend in recent years is for canny parents to use SEN as a way to get their child into their preferred choice of secondary school because most secondary schools favour pupils with SEN on their admissions codes – as we have already seen. This has meant that certain primary schools with lots of bright middle-class children have suddenly become overwhelmed with SEN action: in some cases over half the pupils are on some kind of SEN action. This makes it difficult if your child genuinely has a problem: in which case you'll need to read this chapter very carefully.

Don't be shy or ashamed

It was only when Denise had failed to get a decent grade in her English GCSE mock examination that she finally admitted that she might have a few problems. 'But I'm not special needs,' she pleaded with me. 'Everyone will make fun of me if I am special needs.'

We looked carefully at her examination papers together and saw that her comprehension and even expression was not the problem, but her spelling and her tendency to miss out important words was. 'The thing is I don't have enough time to go over my work in the exam,' she said. I explained to her that if she was 'diagnosed as special needs' by an educational psychologist she would be entitled to extra time in the real examination. Reluctantly, she agreed and was diagnosed a few weeks later as being 'mildly dyslexic and dyspraxic' by the educational psychologist. She'd gone through the system for 11 years thinking that she was rubbish at English instead of knowing the truth. Now she was entitled to extra time in her examination and was given one-to-one coaching by a special needs teacher, all of which assisted her considerably.

Luckily, we caught her in time and she achieved a C grade in English as a result; but many, many more pupils are never diagnosed, largely because they are ashamed of being labelled SEN.

If you are worried that your child has a learning difficulty, do not remain silent. Your LEA is legally bound to give your child extra help if he or she needs it, and you are perfectly entitled to ask for an assessment of your child if you are concerned. Also, remember in today's climate, children with SEN are given preferential treatment, often with admissions to secondary school and with extra funding.

Diagnosis

It is very important to work out whether your child has a learning difficulty or not. This is particularly important when your child is at primary school. If your child is struggling to make progress in one or more of the following six areas set down in the SEN Code of Practice, then you should have cause for concern:

1. **Their personal, social and emotional development** Do they have difficulty making friends? Is their behaviour hampering their progress? Do they seem very unhappy? Are there any other behavioural or emotional problems that are stopping them learning properly?

2. **Communication, language and literacy** By the age of five, your child should be speaking fluently and clearly, and be able to listen for extended periods of time. If your child can't read basic words by the end of Year 1, you should make urgent enquiries. Look carefully at the pages devoted to English in this book (see pages 334–6) and see whether he meets the required standards of the National Curriculum.

3. **Mathematical development** Look carefully at the requirements for the mathematics National Curriculum and see

whether your child is meeting the required standards for his or her age. If they aren't, make urgent enquiries.

4. **Knowledge and understanding of the world** Is your child able to absorb information easily? Is she organised? Apart from literacy and numeracy, are there subjects she struggles with in school because of some learning difficulty?

5. **Physical development** Does your child have sight or hearing problems? Is he having difficulty holding a pen properly? Are motor skills not controlled enough to enable legible writing? Is he physically mobile? Are there any other physical or sensory needs that affect development? Is your child not able to use specialist equipment because physical problems get in the way?

6. **Creative development** Is your child able to empathise with other people? Is he insensitive to other people's feelings? Is he able to play games and role play?

Gifted and talented

I have come across a number of parents who have not liked the school that their child is attending because he or she is not being stretched enough, and are often becoming very bored and disruptive in lessons as a result. More often than not, the parents' response is to try to take the child out of the school. However, I would advise that they try to go down the SEN route first before encountering the massive disruption of moving a child out of a school. If you think that your child is particularly gifted in one particular area – all the categories above are relevant – then you should contact the school and ask for an assesment for being gifted and talented. Although being gifted and talented is not a special need, it is possible that your child may have a special need because of a gifted and talented nature. For example, she may be easily bored and distracted because they are picking up concepts too quickly.

It is worth fighting for this, because there is a lot of extra funding for gifted and talented children. If it is felt that they have learning difficulties because of their gifted and talented nature, they will be entitled to an Individual Education Plan (IEP), which, as we will see, brings extra funding and attention for your children.

THE NEW SCHOOL RULES
about gifted and talented pupils

1. **Don't be ashamed** You must not feel ashamed if your child has a learning difficulty, and therefore a special need. Do not feel it is a stigma. Precisely the opposite is the case; it may well be that your child is actually gifted and talented but has interlinked special needs.

2. **Learn the lingo** If your child is gifted and talented in a particular area this does not mean he or she has a special need, but often the special needs coordinator (SENCO) will deal with gifted and talented pupils as well or will work closely with the gifted and talented coordinator. Therefore it is worth contacting the SENCO, in the first instance, if you feel your child is gifted and talented. Try to use the correct language for the school. Say, 'My child has learning difficulties because he/she is a particularly talented reader/artist/sports person, etc. As a result of this, he/she wants everything to be related to his/her topics of interest.' Or you could say, 'He/she is becoming easily distracted because he/she is becoming bored with the work; he/she is clearly gifted and talented in such and such an area.' Using this language will help the school tap into the relevant funding.

2. **Set targets** Make sure that a detailed IEP is drawn up for your child so that he or she receives help which is 'additional to and/or different from' the ordinary work. See below for more on IEPs.

▶ **CHECK OUT**
The National Academy for Gifted & Talented Youth
provides details of all the courses and events gifted and
talented pupils can get involved in. www.nagtv.ac.uk

The graduated approach – what schools are supposed to do about special needs children

If you think that your child has problems or 'learning difficulties' in any of these areas then you should contact the school immediately. Barry Dixon in his excellent *Education – A Carer's Handbook* (www.ntas.org.uk) recommends this and much else besides: the following pages on the graduated approach, school action and statemented provision are based on his clear, essential recommendations. The first port of call should be your child's teacher or the SENCO in the school. In the first instance, she may try to address the need by adapting existing learning materials so that your child finds them easier to use. For example, if your child is having difficulty with reading, she might give her some more engaging books to read and see if this brings them on.

If, however, adapting or rejigging existing resources doesn't work and an assessment has been carried out, your child will be put on the special needs register and 'School Action' or 'Early Years Action' – if you have a young child – will be required. Don't be alarmed by this! This is simply a way for the school and the LEA to monitor the progress (or not) of your child and do something about it. The school must write out an IEP for your child. It is very important that you understand that an IEP should include 'interventions that are additional to or different from'[2] the normal curriculum. In plain English, this means extra time and/or money should be spent on your child. This could mean:

- Funky new textbooks – or tired old boring ones that haven't been used before.

- Great new sparkling equipment such as computers or a different kind of pen.

- Working in specialised groups: that is, groups which are not usually seen in lessons. They may be part of a larger lesson or be withdrawn from the normal lesson.

- A great new teacher who motivates and enthuses or the same old boring teacher in a different setting or context.

- Fabulous new training tricks for staff.

- A super-duper boffin from the LEA or a clueless bureaucrat.

- A whole load of exercises for you to do with your kid at home instead of watching *The Simpsons*.

The watchword for all special needs provision is: review, review, review! You and the school need to check that your child is benefiting from all the wonderful things you are doing. If he or she has a big smile on their face and is sailing through their lessons, then they can be taken off the register. If not, then his or her name should remain there, and you should all progress to the next level which is:

School action plus

If you and the school are still scratching your heads and thinking that your child is really not getting anywhere, then you and the school may decide more help is needed. At this point, you should really ask that a specialist looks at your child: either an expert from the school, or LEA, or an educational psychologist who specialises in the learning difficulty your child appears to have. The school does not have to comply with your wishes, but it is probably in its own interests that it does.

Make sure that you don't get sidelined in all of the discussions – and refuse to be bamboozled by all the jargon. Yet more targets should come out of these meetings but hopefully they will work. These targets might include:

- Special multi-sensory ways of captivating your child into learning – or handwriting exercises.

- A brand new teacher to enrapture your child with the wonder of maths – or a different group to work in class.

- A fantastic, interactive computer programme to work through – or watching a relevant video.

- A spanking new laptop, a natty little spell-checker – or a new biro.

- A therapeutic chat with a psychiatrist – or anger management lessons.

Statemented provision

So it feels like you are banging your head against a brick wall. Your child still hasn't learnt to read or write, is still behaving like the Terminator, is still drawing pictures instead of concentrating on anything that is being said, or still has a disability which means that he or she just can't appreciate much of what is going on in school. Now it is time to call in the big guns! Your school should call a meeting where all the people involved in your child's education should discuss whether it's a good idea for the LEA to carry out a detailed assessment of your child's educational needs. If you feel really let down by what has happened so far, you should request that a formal assessment takes place. This is not always granted but usually is.

Only about three per cent of all children are formally statemented so it is probably unlikely that your child will be given a statement unless they have an extreme learning difficulty. Statementing is a Byzantine and bureaucratic process which involves thousands of bits of paper and usually takes about six months, but can be longer if there are complications. Once it's done, it is a weighty document which carries the full weight of the law. It should say, in exhaustive detail, how your child's educational needs will be met in the coming 12 months, with a review after that.

You can appeal to the Special Educational Needs tribunal if you feel that you have been unfairly treated, but as with everything in education, appeals are not usually successful.

> ▶ **CHECK OUT**
> www.parentscentre.gov.uk/educationandlearning/special needs/

Inclusion

Inextricably tied up with special needs is the thorny issue of inclusion. It used to be the case that many pupils who had emotional and behavioural problems were segregated from other pupils, supposedly for their own benefit. They were consciously 'excluded' from the mainstream and put into 'special schools' – not to be confused with specialist schools. However, in January 2002, new legislation came into effect which strengthened the right of a child with a statement of special needs to be educated with everyone else.

Perhaps my most striking encounter with the issue of 'inclusion' came when I taught or attempted to teach Lancel Hendricks. Let me explain. For a few months I had been teaching a Year 9 English class with reasonable success in an average London comprehensive – not dissimilar to thousands of schools throughout the country in terms of intake and results – when Lancel arrived.

Lancel had been permanently excluded from his previous school for pulling a knife on another pupil and systematic bad behaviour.

The school I was teaching in was obliged to take him because the LEA had a policy of 'inclusion': that is, it didn't have any 'special schools' where it could send emotionally and psychologically damaged children.

It was clear from the start that Lancel was in severe psychological distress: his eyes exuded anger. He sat hunched up as I told the class to read the beginning of a Roald Dahl short story in pairs, then he snatched his partner's book before he could even start reading, flung it on the floor, and let out a throaty laugh as his partner – a perfectly affable 13-year-old boy – protested.

It soon became clear that Lancel did not have the reading skills to cope with the text, nor the concentration.

Since I was one teacher dealing with 30 children, I asked a particularly patient girl to read to him. While my back was turned, he told her to get lost. Then he began to walk around kicking the backs of the pupils' chairs and shouting loudly that he had done nothing when they complained to me about his behaviour.

Over the year that I taught Lancel, his behaviour – of which the first lesson was typical – made it very difficult to carry out the tasks that the class had been accustomed to doing because the other pupils were constantly on the look-out for Lancel.

He soon found a contingent of pupils who revelled in his antics and that made the whole class's behaviour deteriorate over the year as pupils came to the lesson prepared to watch my quiet battle with the boy.

I had been told that on no account should I annoy him, simply note down his behaviour and report it on a detailed and complex form, which was then circulated to numerous agencies.

By now, Lancel was expert at knowing how to handle schools, so he never did enough to get himself permanently excluded – he didn't 'deliberately' hit pupils or swear at staff – but he was always disruptive, wandering around the class, flinging books on the floor, making loud protestations of innocence, cursing under his breath, 'accidentally' knocking into pupils, arguing with staff.

By the end of the year, the school had enough documentary evidence to exclude him permanently and he went on to another institution, where no doubt he did exactly the same.

He was, in a way, unscathed by the experience: he had hated the school when he arrived and he hated it when he left, but he'd managed to hamper the progress of a lot of children in my class because I had had to spend so much time supervising him.

The truth is that Lancel would have been much better off in

a 'special school'. These are schools that are set up to deal with challenging pupils.

Professionals who are trained to deal with pupils with all sorts of disabilities teach at these schools and often achieve remarkable results. There are usually two teachers to about four or five children and the curriculum is designed to cater for pupils who struggle. They are very expensive to run, which probably explains why more than 400 such schools have been closed in the past two decades. The government pretends that this new initiative is for the good of the pupils, but the real reason for it is that it will save the Exchequer billions of pounds: there are more than 1,000 special schools that could close.

While this is happening, the government will continue mouthing the mantra that 'including' challenging children in the mainstream system is beneficial, as thousands of pupils, parents and teachers mourn the loss of their special schools.

My feeling is that the government needs to let teachers in mainstream schools teach their subjects and deliver the curriculum. They also need to fund properly a decent system of special schools that caters for pupils who cannot cope.[3]

My feelings about inclusion are backed up by many teachers, parents and pupils. In particular, Jane, an experienced special needs teacher of severely disabled pupils in Leeds who has taught at a special school for over 20 years. She told me:

> We have found over the years that many parents really value the extra care and attention that they get from the special school. Apart from anything else, the parents need the support. If you have a child with a severe disability you haven't got the time to fill in all the correct forms or even know about what's available educationally because you are so busy looking after the child. Our school really helps parents with that side of things.
>
> The school can do some very special things. I used to take children out for trips in the minibus and sometimes overnight. Some parents told me that this was the first time that they'd ever spent a night away from their child. One child called Connor

came with us twice. The nurses were very unhappy that he was going because he was so poorly. He died suddenly this year in October. We had a special service at the school for three children who had died. All the children were crying. We brought them down to the classroom with the parents.

On my interactive whiteboard, I showed them the slides of the things he had done on his trip away with us. When his mother saw the photos of him enjoying himself, she said, 'I'm so glad that he was having a good time.' Other parents have said that they are pleased that the children have the same sorts of trips and experiences that their able-bodied brothers and sisters get in the mainstream schools. The special school is actually giving the children a 'mainstream' experience by virtue of being a special school which can cater properly for their needs.

Now our school doesn't have a nursery or primary department because they've been 'included' in the mainstream. In the past, there were many more pupils in the primary and nursery school, and less in the secondary because the children had gone to mainstream schools. We were always very satisfied when they went to mainstream school.

Now it is the other way round. We are getting more and more who come into the secondary school. What I am finding with the children coming from the mainstream is that they are not independent. They don't know how to put their coat on or find their own way to their place, or put their things in their own tray. They've had an assistant in the mainstream who has done this all for them because the assistant has wanted to help the mainstream teacher get on with the lesson, or has felt that the child needs to keep up with the other children. I've found that the children's self-esteem is very low because someone has always done the work for them. I can see them transforming before my eyes as they grow in confidence at the special school. They are so proud of learning to be independent. Things like the wheelchair dancing, the drama, the sports all build their self-esteem. These are things that they wouldn't do much of in the mainstream.

But let's not be misunderstood here. No one wants to go back to the days when children were put in special school because their handwriting or spelling was terrible, or because they were rather withdrawn or eccentric, or had mild behavioural problems or physical disabilities. Clearly, this was very unsatisfactory and resulted in the unfair treatment of many pupils. However, in extreme cases like the one encountered with Lancel or with the severely disabled pupils Jane teaches, it seems clear that inclusion just isn't working.

Even the expert who espoused the cause of inclusion in the 1970s, Mary Warnock, is now beginning to have her doubts about its use across the board. She has called for more schools to use 'nurture groups' – small classes of up to 12 children – in mainstream nurseries and primaries. She said, 'Nurture groups are useful for children who are emotionally and behaviourally incompetent.' A visit to a group in Birmingham convinced her of the need. 'The children at the group could not really speak or communicate. One girl asked whether I liked her. I said yes.'

She said, 'Mummy doesn't.' She was just astonished that an adult was actually talking to her.

Clearly, Mary Warnock is advocating these sorts of 'segregated' classes because they are better at nurturing disturbed children than mainstream classes. Recent evidence is also suggesting that one in five comprehensives is offering only vocational courses to children with SEN. John Brown, an adviser for inclusion, noted in March 2006, 'Some schools are only offering vocational provision at Key Stage 4 to pupils with learning difficulties.'[4]

If you feel 'inclusion' is not working for your child, you should be aware of their rights. Part 1 of the Special Educational Needs and Disability Act 2001 states that all children with a statement must be educated in mainstream school unless this would 'be detrimental to the efficient education of other children or against parental wishes'.

Parents can protest if their child's education is being impeded by someone like Lancel, and have the right to ask for their own child to be educated in a special school if they have a statement.

THE NEW SCHOOL RULES
about SEN

1. **Don't be ashamed** If you think your child has a learning difficulty talk to your child's teacher or the school's SENCO.

2. **Investigate** Find out any relevant test scores such as IQ tests, Key Stage test results, internal assessments and see whether you child is under-achieving. Ask for a breakdown of the results if necessary: your school will not only have the overall level for your child in English but will have scores for reading, writing and speaking and listening. Survey the general atmosphere of the school: how seriously does the head take SEN? Does the SENCO have an important position on the senior management team or do they have lots of other duties which mean they won't have much time to devote to SEN?

3. **Demand your due** Remember, you are entitled to ask for your child to be assessed by a properly trained educational psychologist if you and the school feel there are significant problems. If your school appears to be hazy about this, contact the SEN department at your LEA. Your LEA is obliged to give you details of reputable educational psychologists who could test your child but, except in certain circumstances, they may not be obliged to pay for the testing. Always use an educational psychologist recommended by your LEA in the first instance. If you have the money you could get your child tested yourself, particularly for dyslexia issues. Look up the relevant contact details on: www.dyslexiaaction.org.uk/. If necessary ask for concessions in public examinations. This has become a bit of scam which is much abused, but if your child has a genuine need then it is worth asking for extra time in

▶

public examinations. Potentially, children can receive extra time – up to 25 per cent in some cases – if they have a special need such as dyslexia or they are a slow reader or writer. If motor skills or physical disabilities are the problem, such is the case with dyspraxic, children then they may use a laptop or an amanuensis (a person to write for a child).

4. **Be patient** Be prepared to go through a laborious process of assessment and target setting if you want your child to get extra help and resources. The procedure now is: school action, IEP, review of IEP, school action plus, IEP, review of IEP and if necessary statement. Remember, acquiring a statement of SEN can take months, even years.

5. **Talk it through** Talk to other parents who have children with similar special needs. Talk to other children with SEN. Listen to their stories.

For more on key SEN terms such as dyslexia, dyspraxia, please see the Glossary at the end of the book.

▶ **CHECK OUT**
inclusion.ngfl.gov.uk

CHAPTER 5

Getting involved with your child's education

The greatest motivation is praise

Teacher of the year 2004 and TV star of Channel Four's *The Unteachables*, Phil Beadle, helped me to realise the importance of enthusiasm. In the TV show, he was able to enthuse the most disaffected teenagers by getting them to pronounce Shakespeare to the cows, and learn to punctuate by practising kung fu exercises. He was a master at motivating. He offered this crucial advice:

> The greatest motivation is praise. Praise regularly, accurately and specifically. Don't make broad brushstrokes such as, 'this is very good Nigel.' Home in on the specifics. For instance, as an English teacher, I might make comments like 'I really like the way you have described that character's dress' or 'I think your use of adverbs is very good in this sentence.' We all like praise. It makes us feel good about ourselves, and when we feel good about ourselves, we work harder.
>
> All parents should have relationships with their kids' books. Make a point of reading your kids' work. If you don't do that, then you are not interested in your kid's education.
>
> The key to motivation is not external. Kids have to be motivated within themselves. The educationalist Ian Gilbert talks of

the notion of KITA motivation, or Kick-In-The-Arse-motivation and how it does not work. KITA motivation relies on making people scared. But when you are scared you are stressed, and when you are stressed, you are not open to learning.

The other common form of motivation is PULL motivation. This is the notion that if you work harder, there will be some external reward. This is also bollocks. Research shows that although dangling a carrot before a child might produce short-term results, in the long run, it can be demotivating. The happiest people and highest achievers work because the reward is the PROCESS of doing the work, not what they might get at the end of it.

The only motivation which works is the one which is generated by the self, or intrinsic motivation. The key for a parent to motivate the child is simply to get them to see how important and valuable their work is in itself.

Some of the most significant educational research in recent years for the DfES has shown that the children who do best at school talk regularly and positively with their parents.[1] This seminal research showed that if a child had his or her parents' support then no matter what school the child went to, no matter what ethnic or social class he came from, they should do well at school. In other words, if you learn nothing else from this book, you should see that it is your influence which is the most important.

Praising a child is the best way to get her talking. It is much better than arid interrogations about their progress in this or that subject.

THE NEW SCHOOL RULES
for helping your child learn properly

1. **Talk it through** Engage your child in pleasant, non-confrontational conversation every day. The research shows that no matter what you're talking about –

▶

whether it's the weather, what your child had for lunch, stories about your life – every little bit counts and helps your child do well at school.

2. **Praise them** Praise specifically and regularly.

3. **Don't threaten** Avoid Kick-In-The-Arse and PULL motivation.

The number games I played with granny

The sun blazed down on the glossy lawn, overhead the clouds scudded through a blue sky and a labrador lay in the shadow of the yew tree as my grandparents, and my brother and I played croquet. My brother and I always loved playing: positioning the balls, working out our tactics and angles, calculating who was best to hit and how to get through the hoops. My grandmother would talk about the different angles you could hit the balls from, and how this was the key to the game. Everything was about angles.

My brother and I would often arrive at my grandparents' large, rickety, rat-infested farmhouse feeling dispirited and unhappy. Later on when I was grown up, my grandmother would tell me that it would always take us a day or two to settle in. Our 'home' – if one could term it that – was a miserable place. We moved silently through our days, trying to avoid annoying my mother and stepfather, keeping our heads down at school and doing our best not to get told off – which we frequently were for some minor misdemeanour or other.

My mother was a KITA motivator. We knew we had to work because we'd get punished if we didn't. In a way, I am grateful that she did, at least, urge us to work.

My grandmother was the opposite. Although she could be very cutting in her remarks about people – she was a highly intelligent woman who didn't suffer fools gladly – she didn't get her children or grandchildren to do things by KITA. She knew the importance of motivating us by playing games.

She would often play games with a mathematical slant. When I was a little child she would get out a set of bricks and a die, and we would roll the die. When a particular number was rolled, I had to pick up that number of bricks and build the tower. It was a very simple game but it got me counting properly – something I had not done until then.

When I was older, she would get me to do this game: think of a number, double it, add 4, multiply by 3, divide by 6, subtract 2. I would find out, to my astonishment, that each time I was back where I started.

Otherwise, she would play Yahtzee, gin rummy, checkers, chess, Monopoly, snap, Scrabble, dominoes and even darts and archery with us; whatever game was around, we would play it. These are obviously games that many parents play with their children but my contrasting experience of having a mother who didn't play anything with us and a grandmother who did has made me realise the importance of these games in motivating children to be good at counting and simple mathematics, at interacting with people, at calculating and formulating plans, at articulating desires and disappointments.

My grandmother was a maths teacher and realised the importance of playing maths games in getting children motivated about numbers. Japan is generally considered to be the most numerate country in the world, largely because there is such a strong tradition of children playing number games. Sudoku may be about logic rather than arithmetic, but it gets children using numbers and problem-solving. Kakuro, which is called the mathematical equivalent of crosswords, is even better at honing children's numeracy skills (see www.kakuro.net/).

There is a tradition of number games in this country as well. Some of the most recently invented games are the best. Mathematical versions of Scrabble, where children use a mixture of symbols and numbers to build equations, are brilliant at encouraging good numeracy skills; while everything from darts, dominoes, blackjack and bridge make use of maths skills.

There is no doubt that playing these games with children at an early age pays huge dividends later on. Crucially, they make children enthusiastic about maths, and that enthusiasm, once generated, can motivate them to love numbers for the rest of their lives. Recent surveys have shown that children's numeracy skills are declining in this country. One survey shockingly revealed that children's ability to solve 'real life' numeracy problems has fallen by 11 per cent.[2]

When you consider that extra maths lessons account for more than all private tuition outside school hours, playing a few games could save you a lot of money.

THE NEW SCHOOL RULE

for helping your child learn properly

Have fun Play games with your child if you want them to become good learners.

▶ **CHECK OUT**
www.playkidsgames.com/mathGames.htm

Reading and word games

It is exactly a year after I had been called in by James's teachers to discuss his reading. He is sitting at the kitchen table, drawing a picture of Doctor Who on a piece of scrap paper I had given him. On the other side of the paper is a rough version of my last book, *Yob Nation*. Suddenly, James realises that there is writing on the other side of the paper. He turns it over and starts reading with ease and fluency:

The plump girl still had her black bikini top on, but her skirt was floating on the water. The blond young man had a shirt on but no trousers. She didn't have her arms around him but was clearly attached by other means: she was riding her 'pull', bobbing up and down slowly, as he lunged drunkenly into her.

I stopped him there. 'Err, very good reading, very good reading. Excellent!' I said, taking the page from him.

'Daddy, what was the boy doing to her?'

I didn't know what to say to this, but muttered something about them behaving yobbishly, adding, 'But the main thing, you are getting very good at reading.'

Part of me wanted to say, too good. His reading had suddenly taken off. He could read most pieces of writing now. I could scarcely believe it. Only a few months before, he had struggled to read the simplest words, but now he was racing away. And, more importantly, he was intrigued by all sorts of reading material: posters in the swimming baths ('Daddy, what are vandals?'), labels in shops ('Daddy, what are sanitary towels?'), and books on our shelves ('Daddy, what is a yob?') and billboards at various festivals ('Daddy, what does LBTG stand for?').

Sometimes there was a temptation to ask him to stop asking the questions, particularly when I had just come home from work and was feeling very tired, but I stopped myself. I can still remember being hit by my mother when I made an origami game at school with some other children and then played it with her. I asked her to say a number and lifted the flap with that number on. Underneath, it said, 'Fuck off!' I had no idea what these words meant at the time, being five years old. I got a clip on the back of my head for my pains. That was the last time I ever tried to play a game with my mother.

Later on, when I was several years older and really struggling to read, I read proudly in the newspaper that Graham Chapman of *Monty Python* was gay. I didn't know what the word meant but I knew she liked *Monty Python*. Reading the passage to her was an attempt to prove to her that I was interested in serious adult things like newspapers and that I could also read. I was told fiercely to stop wittering.

I can see now that I was very slow to read because I was frightened of annoying my mother.

My happiest memories of reading as a child are with my grandmother, who would read to us every night during the holidays. She would make a ritual of the whole occasion. As the evening drew on, she would make real cocoa in a broken pan with no proper handle, and ask us what book we would like to have as our bedtime story. My favourites were *King Arthur*, *Robin Hood* and *Just William*. We would carry our steaming mugs of cocoa up the stairs, change into our pyjamas and sit up in our beds, sipping our cocoa and listening to Granny taking us into the magical world of Excalibur, of Sherwood Forest and William's barn. The twilight would gather at the window. In the distance, I remember seeing swallows duck and dive amidst the great trees that stood on a hill near the house. The house would creak like a ship setting off on a long voyage. The sweet taste of chocolate would mingle with the words, and I realised that there was something magical about words that Granny read.

THE NEW SCHOOL RULES
for helping your child learn properly

1. **Be enthusiastic** Read to your child with enthusiasm. Read in front of your child and show them that you enjoy reading.

2. **Try different approaches** Story tapes can work wonders for slow or poor readers. When the tape finishes they often try to read the next book. Make sure their room has lots of reference and non-fiction books as well as fiction suitable for their age/reading group. Charity shops, church fairs, and libraries are wonderful resources for these.

The importance of parental enthusiasm

While I remained a very reluctant reader until I was much older, those stories had an important long-term effect upon me. The most enlightened parents are aware that much of what they do may not have an immediate effect, but do pay dividends in the long run. Mary, a journalist and parent of two children at an urban comprehensive in the north of England, told me:

> We are enthusiastic about learning, and have loads of books strewn around the house. That is a silent but strong influence. Biggest lesson: nagging doesn't work; offering a carrot of playing outside, or an extra story at bedtime does. One daughter doesn't need to be cajoled into homework, but the other does. She finds it boring and leaves things late, but does them brilliantly.
>
> At 16, we can't try to manipulate her into doing anything. She either wants to do it for herself or she doesn't. Usually she does but we have to say the high school habit of allowing massive extensions on coursework is outrageous! Deadlines for different subjects are deliberately separated by teachers, so the burden is spread for both delivery by pupils and marking by teachers. Extensions then come into play, and it all comes crashing down. One week before Easter, six pieces of work had to be completed by the same Friday!
>
> Once your kids get close to Key Stage tests or big exams, everything they do is so serious, and counts towards something big. Learning never goes off at a tangent, just for fun. This last two years of their GCSE course has been silly, and coursework is so prescriptive, with so much teacher intervention, that imaginative thought is actively discouraged! Awful.

Mary's observations show how important it is for parents to be enthusiastic about reading and learning generally. Parents have to face facts: much of what their child learns at school may well be quite boring, prescriptive and reductive. The one thing that may keep them enthused and motivated may well be their parents' enthusiasm.

Tony Shepherd, the vicar of St Peter's, Harrogate, and governor of a Church of England high school, chairman of governors at a primary school, warned parents against actively seeking boring work for their children to do, especially at primary school. He said:

> Parents' enthusiasm for life in general is very important. It is important to have as much interaction as you can with your child and the school. In an area like Harrogate which is a privileged community, parents contribute a lot to school life.
>
> I do think that parents can be overly enthusiastic about the wrong things though. Parents are quite keen that there should be a lot of worthy homework for their children. Generally though, schools want the children to be children. When I make pastoral visits, I feel a little anxious about seeing parents towering over their small children, making them do their homework. A child has a solid working day and needs time to relax and be a child. There needs to be more sense of play and games. It is sad that children can't play more, particularly from the ages of five to 11. Ultimately, you make children enthusiastic about learning if you make them enthusiastic about life. My experience is that children don't do things like riding through woods on bikes any more and this is a great shame.

The dreaded PTA

Is there anything more scary for a parent than seeing a bullish member from the PTA (Parent Teacher Association) lumbering over to you outside the school gates? We all know the type of person who runs the PTA: the bossy, nosy housewife who has nothing better to do than emotionally blackmail over-worked parents into being the victim at the throw-the-sponge stall at the Summer Fayre. They are scary, scary people, but they are very necessary ones. If we didn't have them, then our schools would definitely be bereft of many resources that PTAs fund: new buildings, computers, DVD players, interactive whiteboards, books and so on. The PTA essentially helps raise money for the school by running such staples as the summer fete, the Christmas Fayre, jumble sales and so on.

The PTA is often stereotyped as being peopled by domineering women who boss other parents into standing behind cake stalls at the various fêtes and fairs that go on. Most of the PTA members I interviewed agreed that there was an element of truth in the stereotype. Kim Gallagher, a businesswoman and PTA member of a primary and secondary school in Northumberland, told me: 'Other parents do tend to run a mile when they see members of the PTA committee approaching them at the school gates. Some of them shout out, "No, no, no!" They think you are going to ask them to do a job – and they are probably right!'
She went on to tell me:

I think most mothers join PTAs because their children are quite small and they want to get involved with their children's education. Mothers also sign up because they've just moved into the area and they need a new circle of friends. Being in a PTA is an excellent way of becoming part of the community.

Every active PTA has to have a strong leader who is able to drive things forward. Basically, you've got to be quite gobby! You've got to be able to pick up the phone and persuade people to get involved. You've got to be able to run a committee and make sure that everyone is doing their job properly.

Nowadays you have to be quite inventive about the way you raise money. I'm afraid the days when you could hold bingo competitions in draughty school halls have gone. Most parents don't want to sit in a bleak school hall on Friday nights. So we have done things a bit differently, like holding fundraising quizzes and meals in the local Indian restaurant. We also have got parents and children to do 'bag packing' at the local supermarket for the customers and asked for contributions.

I think the reason why a lot of parents want to run a mile when they see me coming is that they think they will get roped into a major enterprise, when in actual fact usually I am just asking for a small thing like doing an hour on a plant or cake stall.

Linda Humphrey, a leading member of the PTA at the school where I teach, explained to me that there is a big difference between being in a primary school PTA and a secondary one. She told me:

> With primary PTAs it is very hands-on. When you do a summer fayre in the primary school, the kids come, the families join in, and there is a great family atmosphere. At secondary school the children don't want to be seen with mum and dad, and it is very difficult to get anyone involved. Here, we are reliant on sending letters home and the kids giving the letters to parents. Seventy per cent of the letters never get home. The parents don't pick their kids up from school, and they don't know what's going on.
>
> The cliché of a PTA being full of housewives who want tea and biscuits is totally wrong. It is myth. The head teacher now comes into the meetings or a representative from SLT [Senior Leadership Team] and you learn things about the school – and contribute to it. For the major projects, we are guided by the head teacher, who has suggested to us in the past that we should pay for minibuses, and help fund the building of the new pavilion and the music block.

The PTA's fundraising has significantly contributed towards a total transformation of the school. The music block is a marvellous creation with a concert-sized hall on its top floor, and state-of-the-art music and practice rooms rigged up with all sorts of amazing new technology and instruments on the bottom floor, while the pavilion has a plethora of changing rooms and a marvellous meeting area and balcony. The PTA has also been very helpful to all the different departments in the school, giving money to help them buy add-on extras which can't be afforded out of capitation. Most recently, they donated a £1,000 to my department so that we could buy some decent display cabinets. This relatively small amount of money has changed the lower school block: four imposing, cinema-screen-sized display cabinets are now housed in the stairwells of the block, full of children's work.

Trouble at the PTA

Sometimes some parents can be a little too enthusiastic for some schools' tastes. Author and parent Francis Beckett told me about the traumatic time he had when he tried to do more than sell raffle tickets. He told me:

> Being keen, new parents, having had our first child at an early age, my partner and I immediately wanted to get involved with the school he was going to. We were very enthusiastic about doing more than standing behind jumble sale stalls; we wanted to teach the children, to enrich their lives with extracurricular activities and so on. Unfortunately, the school where our son went was one of those sorts of schools that didn't like that kind of enthusiasm.
>
> So in order to fob us off, we were implored to sell raffle tickets, we were told to run the school fête, we were instructed to assist with jumble sales and so on. But all the time what we really fancied doing was getting involved. But all the school said was, 'Yes, yes, that's very interesting … here are some more raffle tickets for you to sell.'
>
> To make matters far worse, I wrote a piece for the *Guardian* about the school which was supposed to be a funny, innocuous account of the teachers and classes, but which caused extraordinary fuss. A parent-governor created an enormous scene at a public event, shouting and screaming at me for having betrayed the school. For about two terms, there was a deathly atmosphere at the school gates, a definite chilliness in relationships. I found I was no longer spoken to.
>
> But all this changed in Year 5, when the arrival of a new deputy head entirely changed the atmosphere of the school. He had been making use of parents in his previous schools and had found that the enthusiastic ones could be helpful. I was asked to run a drama club and my partner helped with listening to pupils read. My partner and I ran and directed the school pantomime for two years. I had enormous fun and the school appreciated it in the end. They loved it. A former pupil who was dyslexic and

had one-to-one help from my partner still stops her in the street and congratulates her for helping him read.

In the end, it was all colossally exciting so, you see, the story has a happy conclusion.

The PTA saves the day

I found Gareth scowling outside the Dylan Thomas Community School, John Street, Cockett, Swansea. He appeared to be agitated and aggressive, chain-smoking with pin-prick eyeballs. An ex-pupil at the school, he claimed he had stolen a senior member of staff's laptop computer, assaulted him and then tried to escape in that teacher's car, having pinched his car keys. The police pursued him and this had resulted in a car crash. 'I've got attention deficiency disorder, you see, and the school didn't know how to deal with me. I would disrupt the lessons, smash things up, chuck things around the room, bully people. I was a menace,' he admitted.

No one at the school would confirm whether his story was true or not, but a survey of the school's 2004 Estyn (the Chief Inspector of Education and Training in Wales) report says that the school has 'many and significant challenges'.[3] Sixty-two per cent of the pupils receive free school meals and half of the pupils have special needs of one sort or another. It is also clear that the behaviour of the pupils used to be a real problem at the school, particularly at the time when Gareth claims he was a pupil there. Another former pupil, Lisa, I spoke to confirmed that there had been a lot of bad behaviour at the school. Her father said:

> Being a parent of a girl at such a school made me feel quite protective, and when I heard stories of misbehaviour I felt Lisa should be going to another school. I remember her telling me about the teacher marking the register while the boys were walking over the desks. I think she would have got a better education if she had gone to a better school.

However, Lisa's father did not have the faith in the school that the members of the PTA had. When Mrs Spencer's 13-year-old son, Stephen, raced through the door of his home in May 2005, and told her with tears in his eyes that the school was going to close, she and other members of the PTA went on the offensive to save their children's school. 'Up until then, we just raised money to pay for teas and coffees at parents' meetings and to pay for our NCPTA membership. Suddenly all that changed,' said Mrs Spencer, 42, who looks after her disabled husband John full-time.

The PTA raised parents' awareness of the school's plight, taking their campaign to the local media, councillors and the Welsh assembly. More than 350 parents turned up for the first public consultation meeting. 'We badgered everybody and we just kept going, and we saw a community spirit we had not seen before,' said Mrs Spencer, who with PTA chairman Sheila Lewis went to Buckingham Palace on Tuesday to receive the school's £1,000 reward. In November 2005, they were told the school would not close. 'This is a deprived area, but we are not deprived. Just because we live here doesn't mean we are in the gutter. We felt we were being picked on, that we were an easy target and we didn't like that.'[4]

This sort of parental involvement appears to have significantly improved the behaviour and results of the school, and shows the power of an active PTA. In England as a whole, PTAs raise about £⅓ million a year. On average a PTA raises about £5,600 per year for its school. They do make a real difference.

THE NEW SCHOOL RULES
for parent associations

1. **Get stuck in** Remember, even contributing a tiny bit helps. Don't be frightened when you see a member of the PTA approaching you in the playground. Be prepared for trouble ahead if you want to do something a bit different

▶

though; schools are generally very conservative places. Nevertheless, fight for what you think is right; an active PTA is much more powerful than you think.

2. **Investigate** For more information on what PTAs can do, get in touch with the National Confederation of Parent Teacher Associations (NCPTA), (see www.ncpta.org.uk/).

Being a school governor

I was sitting in a very small chair around a table crowded with anxious men in suits and women in floral dresses, surrounded by scribbled drawings and a sandpit. It was my first meeting as a governor, and the atmosphere was fractious to say the least. The chairman of governors and the head teacher were looking at the local council's proposals to close the school. There was a falling roll, and significant problems with the results and teaching. Everyone was grumbling about the council and Ofsted, about how unfair it was that the school had been judged as failing, that parents loved the school and didn't want it to close, that the teachers were doing a great job.

I had been approached by the chairman of governors at a party to be a member of the governing body and help take the school out of 'special measures' and stop it closing down. Even though I had a lot on and I wasn't a parent of a pupil at the school, I decided to see what I could do. I was flattered to be asked.

At the first meeting, I was voted on to the governing body, and allocated the role of monitoring the senior management team and sitting on the curriculum committee. In the pub outside the school, the chairman confessed to me that the real problem was the head teacher, who was on an 'action plan' because she wasn't doing her job properly. He sighed as he sipped his Guinness, 'I think we're going to have to get rid of her if we are going to save the school.'

He was a local businessman and resident who had charitable intentions and professed a desire to give 'those poor benighted children' a better start in life. The school was an inner-city primary school which had a phenomenally mixed intake – Turkish, Caribbean, African, East European, Bengali, white working class to name a few – and lots of children on free school meals.

As I examined the paperwork with him, I saw the inspectors felt that the school's poor teaching was at the heart of its problems: there were no proper lesson plans or schemes of work which the teachers or pupils were working from, and, as a result, the school days were characterised by aimless, disorganised drifting from topic to topic.

If the first meeting was bad tempered, the next one I attended was volcanic. The chairman, who had been sucking on a particularly explosive bullet finally bit into it, and decided to take 'competency proceedings' against the head teacher: in other words, he was going to try to sack her. This is no mean feat in the state sector: there are mounds of paperwork to go through and lots of committees to oversee the process. This was his first step: to meet the staff and head teacher with the governing body and explain that she wasn't meeting the targets set for her by the governing body.

The staff were apoplectic with rage. Many of them clearly liked their head, who had probably given them a pretty easy time of it. A few of them stood up and shouted at the chairman, jabbing their fingers in his face while accusing him of betrayal of the worst kind.

'You are supposed to be our friend, not someone who is trying to destroy us,' an elderly teacher with a hoarse voice yelled.

The meeting really put me off the whole process. Everyone appeared to be at war: the governing body and the teachers, the council and the school, the inspectorate and the school. A few weeks later, I took some time off work and observed a few lessons, speaking to some teachers. The lessons I saw were not inspiring: children counting numbers on number lines, an assembly where the children were simply told to be quiet, a literacy lesson which the pupils clearly didn't understand. There were no detailed schemes of work, only a few words covering weeks of work. Then I learnt that some senior teachers had been absent from the school for months. Staff sickness was endemic. Because of a falling roll and the poor reputation of the school, some of the classes were only half full. My heart sank. Maybe the school deserved to close?

The head teacher left before she was properly pushed, and the school then had to find a new head while the two deputies ran the school. I collected mounds of DfES paperwork so that I would be able to carry out the deputies' performance management. The trouble was, though, I had enough of this sort of paperwork as a teacher too, and it made me fall asleep just looking at these turgid documents. One of the deputies was asking for more money, but she had had real problems with absence. I didn't see why she should be given a rise, given that she had hardly been in school for the previous year. However, the chairman disagreed with me, and at an acrimonious meeting we argued over the pay rise. No one else supported me in my query. The deputy was duly given her pay rise.

After that, I lost interest completely: I failed to attend a couple of performance management meetings with the deputies and the governors, and a full governors meeting. I was very busy with other things, and ill for one of the meetings. I read in the minutes of one of the meetings that my apologies for absence were not accepted and then I received a letter from a chairman asking me to resign, which I did immediately, grateful to be shot of the whole process.

I was a poor school governor because I was simply not willing to put in the time and effort required. I think this is something that many people who become governors are not aware of: it requires a great deal of time and effort, and people in full-time jobs with families may find it very difficult to do. If you become a governor of a failing school, or a school which has serious problems, the atmosphere may well be very tense and emotional.

A governor's tasks

Parent-governors have to be elected by the other parents at the school and then join the governing body in order to set the strategic direction of the school. The governing body work with the head teacher to improve the quality of education in a school by:

- Deciding how to spend the school's budget.

- Setting targets for the senior management.

- Monitoring and enhancing the curriculum.

- Assisting with issues to do with school discipline by listening to cases of pupil exclusion and expulsion.

- Responding to inspection reports.

- Dealing with admissions to the school.

- Hearing and judging complaints and appeals from pupils and staff.

It is not a thankless task, but to do it properly you need either quite a bit of time on your hands, or a really determined interest in improving or helping the school. It is not a role for dilettantes, as my case so sadly shows.

Linda Humphrey has also been a parent-governor for ten years, and is certainly no dilettante. She told me:

My husband was a governor at the primary school, and thought I would be good at it. I wasn't working at the time, I had plenty of time to spare, and I put myself up for election and got on the committee as a parent-governor. The first meeting was very much listening and finding out what was going on and the new governors were sent on courses that explained all the different facets of being a governor. You need to insist on getting some really in-depth training if you want to be a governor because it is a big job.

It is a stressful job, particularly when you start. At first, I was very confused about the curriculum and didn't have much of a clue about what was going on. But you pick it up as you go along, especially if you have been on some good training courses.

I would say if you have a doubt, you have to question what is going on. As a new governor, it takes real guts to do that. You ask yourself: am I actually going to question what the head teacher has suggested or any member of staff? But you must remember that the governing body is there in order to have a proper system of checks and balances.

I get really cross with the parents for not getting involved both on the governing and PTA side. After all, why should a tiny number of parents sweat their guts out to raise money and sort out the running of the school? Many parents take everything for granted, and don't want to help at all. They are totally apathetic.

THE NEW SCHOOL RULES
for governors

1. **Investigate** Make sure you have the time and commitment to be a governor. Find out where the power lies. If there is a strong head teacher and a weak governing body, or vice versa, there will be problems. The ideal is where there is a genuine balance.

2. **Learn the lingo** Make sure you're given some decent training. Be prepared to digest a great deal of jargon and educational double-speak, but don't be defeated by it. Most of it is obfuscation and cant. Use your position as a non-professional to demand that concepts and plans are explained in clear English.

3. **Be cautious** Do your preparation before causing a fuss. Remember that parent-governors are a different breed from foundation, staff and LEA governors. Parent-governors often feel vulnerable, particularly if the head is strong

▶

with a weak governing body and chairman. They feel their child may be picked on and no long selected for the school team, choir and so on in a small primary school if they cause a fuss. They do need to be careful. They should meet longer-term parent-governors, and find out where to get support before they raise a problem at a meeting.

▶ CHECK OUT

www.governornet.co.uk/

schools.london.anglican.org/Governors/governors-index.htm, website of The London Diocesan Board for Schools (LDBS) which runs excellent unbiased courses for governors.

Joan Dean, *The Effective School Governor*, Routledge, 2001.

CHAPTER 6

Your experience and your child's experience

How different schools used to be

James looks up at the flashcard which has the letters 'oa' printed on it. His teacher points to the letters with a smile and asks him to sound them out. The little boy's fingers quiver over the letters. He's forgotten what sound 'oa' makes. His teacher reminds him patiently that it makes an 'o' sound as in 'boat'. She shows him another flashcard. This time he is totally defeated. He has no idea what 'igh' sounds like. All around him in the classroom, children are examining their flashcards and sounding out their 'phonemes' – their letter sounds. Many pupils are racing through them, and then picking up books which they read out aloud in groups to each other. A small number really are struggling like James.

This is the children's first experience of the literacy hour, which is conducted in all state primary schools in the country and many private schools too. From reception to Year 6, the pupils will read their phoneme charts, read books in groups, listen to the teacher explain salient points of grammar, analyse writing aimed at different audiences, and learn to develop their writing skills. Many of my pupils now at secondary school have commented to me that they found the literacy hour rather sterile. 'Why couldn't they have called it something fun like story hour?' one bright pupil said to me, adding, 'I found it quite boring to be honest because we did so many grammar exercises that I got turned off reading and writing. And I still don't know my parts of speech.'

But this is the reality of English schools today. Every school does it. And I felt it was vital that James did his best.

I never thought I would be this nervous. But I am trembling. There is a person sitting in front of me who is going to be making judgements about my child.

The dreaded words emerge from her lips. 'I'm afraid that James is not where we want him to be.' I tremble. In my mind, I am thinking: James has already failed to make the first hurdle. I think about him. I think about his little face. His innocent eyes. I think about the way he looks with puzzlement and exasperation at the phonemes that he is supposed to be studying. I think about the funny way he shakes his head, and fiddles with his fingers when he doesn't know the answer. I think too at my own shameful anxiety. The way I sometimes lose my temper, and say, 'Come on, James, you are not concentrating.'

His tears drop to the ground, and he puts his fingers to his eyes and shakes his head. I hold him tightly and feel his warm face in the crook of my chest, and let the tears flow. Then we return to the phonemes chart. He's fine with 'o', and 'i', but the bigger phonemes like 'igh' and 'ight' defeat him.

He is four years old.

Is he supposed to be reading?

I gaze at his two teachers, and try to hunker down lower in my tiny infant pupil chair. It jabs into my bottom as I hear the teachers explain that in Year 1, when James is five, he should be reading whole books.

I nod. The teachers are kind people but I sense that they are under intense pressure: parents, the school, and their own consciences. It is a small prestigious private school with a reputation to maintain. James is very lucky to get into the place: most applicants are rejected.

Fortunately, Erica is calm. She nods and says without emotion, 'Yes, we know this, but James is only four. The thing is we only want him to be happy. He seems very happy at the school, but we don't want him to feel like reading is a chore. Both of us are writers. We love reading. We want James to like reading.'

I interject. 'Yes, and I couldn't read properly until I was seven. I think it might be in the genes. You've got me to blame for this one. I don't think he's going to be a fast learner. But when he does get it, he will really get it I think.'

I notice that both the teachers breathe a sigh of relief here. They've said what they have to say and we've said our bit. We've said, 'we don't want him pushed'.

It is agreed that James will have some extra reading lessons in the morning for the rest of the year, but that we won't push him. That reading should always be fun.

He duly turned up for his reading lessons in the morning, before the rest of school has started, and participated in what one parent of another struggling child dubbed 'illiteracy hour'. His reading improved. By the beginning of Year 1, he was reading simple books. And most importantly, he seemed to be enjoying it.

However, this is just the beginning. On the bus, I meet a parent of another child at the school who is playing hangman with her five-year-old. This girl, Daphne, is a terrific reader. She has graduated onto the Mecca of Year 1: 'Chapter Books'! James and I aren't interested in playing hangman at this early hour. James has never played it. Daphne proudly brandishes the half-completed word that she has written: 'Even James could get this word,' she says without malice. Her mother is embarrassed. 'Daphne, don't be so rude!' Fortunately, James is unphased. He shrugs and carries on chatting amiably with Daphne.

I smile. The girl's comment doesn't shock me in the least now. I have been conducting my own clandestine research and have found out that the children could almost place themselves in league tables of reading.

They are now five.

As the rain lashes down on the bus, and James continues to play with Daphne, my mind wanders.

It is 1917, and I am imagining that I am watching my grandfather and my great-uncle play in the sunlit fields outside

Carrickfergus in Northern Ireland. My grandfather was the son of a navy commander who was in charge of the coastguards there. When Cecil, my grandfather, was only two years old his mother died, and he was brought up largely by his father's house-keeper Mrs Lemon. Neither Cecil nor Stephen was educated 'properly' at a school until they were eleven years old. Until then, they more or less roamed wild across the countryside in Northern Ireland. Both Cecil and Stephen would tell me about this time. It was perhaps the happiest time of their lives: Cecil would go birdwatching, and spend endless days lying in the long grass looking up at the sky, listening to the tweeting of birds, and marking them down in a notepad. Sometimes, he would play with his next-door neighbour's son, Louis MacNeice, in the rectory garden. My uncle would sketch pictures of the scenes around him. None of them had any formal schooling.

From the ages of five to eleven, my great-uncle and grand-father went bicycle riding all around Ulster, up to the bogs and the cliffs at Larne, where there was a winding path that led down to the sea. They were taught by a local woman for a few hours a week when they were eight, and only learnt to read and write then. Later on, in the evenings, Jane Mitchell, the aunt of their father's housekeeper, would teach them English and Maths for a few hours.

When they were 11, they moved to London where they had some coaching to pass the exam to get into University College London School. They both passed the exams. My grandfather went onto to be a lecturer in mathematics, and my great-uncle an artist who exhibited painting and sculpture in the Tate. Perhaps most pertinently, they never retired from their work. When he died, my grandfather, at 92, was still working on an incredibly complex astronomy paper which was attempting to reinterpret Einstein's General Theory of Relativity. My great-uncle died when he was 97 and was still practising as an artist until a week before he died. Their playmate, Louis MacNeice, who had a similarly chaotic schooling until he went to boarding school, went on to become one of the foremost poets of the twentieth century.

As I got off the bus with James and made my way to the school, clutching his hand tightly as we crossed the busy road, I thought about my grandfather. When he was five, he was mucking around in the countryside. There was no pressure to read or write, or do his sums. He was expected to occupy himself, and as long as he was out of sight and out of mind, he could do what he wanted.

As I passed through the security doors of the school, and saw the faces of the anxious parents hastily kissing their children goodbye and rushing off to work, I thought: what a different bloody world.

Most middle-class parents nowadays would be horrified if their children spent all day unsupervised, 'learning nothing', in the fields.

And yet, I knew that there was some very sound educational philosophy that argued the case that my grandfather's 'education' was far superior to most modern schooling. Jean-Jacques Rousseau, considered by many to be the philosopher who set up the foundations of thought on which the entire Western education system is based, felt that children should roam free amidst nature until they were 11 or 12, and not be forced to learn anything until they were ready to engage with rational, intellectual thought. His philosophy is perhaps no better illustrated than in Mary Shelley's wonderful novel *Frankenstein*. Contrary to almost all the films, the monster in Shelley's novel is the most intellectual of all the people in it. He's the cleverest precisely because he grows up surrounded by nature, learning initially by his senses, learning to survive by eating berries and drinking from the streams. After this initial stage of survival, he becomes curious about the world, and copies the speech he hears in a lonely cottage in a wood. A family are housed there, and unknown to them, the Creature – as he is named in the novel – listens to them speaking and reading to each other. He also acquires some books that they read to each other: *Paradise Lost*, and *The Sorrows of Young Werther* by Goethe. By this time, he is at the right stage for literature: he has sufficiently matured to fully absorb the importance of reading. It is a source of absolute wonder to him as a consequence. This preposterous storyline was not intended to be realistic but symbolic: the Creature's advanced intellect is due to his education 'within nature'.

When my grandfather got to school he found mathematics fascinating for precisely the same reason, he met the intricate complexities of algebra at the right age. He was living in an age when teachers had the discretion and power to provide their pupils with what they felt was appropriate; not what was dictated to them by a centralised curriculum.

My father, growing up as he did in the fifties, attended the Royal Grammar School in Newcastle, where teachers had the power to let their bright pupils skip O levels, and go straight onto A levels. As a consequence, he only has a few O levels, but five A levels in all the Sciences, and an A level in English Literature. He went onto Cambridge University where he attained a first in Natural Sciences, and then a PhD in molecular biology. Again, most importantly for me, he is still interested in his subject. At sixty, he still carries out theoretical research into the workings of the brain.

I myself was criticised quite considerably at school for my failure to read 'properly'. I remember the look of exasperation on my elderly teacher's face in my final year at primary school as she listened to me stumble slowly over the words in the book I was reading to her. Books meant little to me then, beyond being a source of pain and humiliation: a reminder of what I couldn't do. A metaphor for my general failure to succeed as a person.

The only time when words came alive for me was when singing. I loved the melodies of the hymns we would sing in assembly, and I read the words there effortlessly without ever really understanding their meaning. But when I went to secondary school, the hymns became oppressive, and once again the words failed to come alive. I was happier with the dead language of Latin at the public school I attended: it had none of the negative connotations of English. Added to which, there appeared to be a steady, reliable logic to it. You learned the rules, and it all fitted together. It had none of the twisted unreliability of English with its arbitrary rules.

Having attained a respectable but unexceptional B grade at O level English, it was only when I was seventeen and I read *The Catcher in the Rye* that words began to sing again for me. Holden Caulfield's demotic speech, the easy, natural fluency of the cadences, his sneering dismisal of authority blew me away. I can still remember reading the book in one night.

It was a school night. Although I resented it at the time, I am now grateful that I was not welcome by the adults downstairs in the house after dinner. My mother and my stepfather would sit and watch TV there, and expect my brother and I to be out of the way. The only option was to stay in our rooms and make as little noise as possible. My school doled out hefty amounts of homework and this usually kept me occupied from the ages of 11 to 16, but after my O levels, there was a lot more spare time. Fortunately, I had an inspired English teacher who gave me a reading list, which had Salinger's book at the top.

My life was never the same after reading *The Catcher in the Rye*. As I am writing this, the hairs are already prickling on the back of my neck as I recall the way I read the last pages with tears in my eyes and a charging, surging exhilaration and sadness in my mind. The book spoke directly to me, as it has done to so many teenagers over the decades. Holden Caulfield's lies and doubts, his foibles and evasions, his feelings and anger, his loathing of school, of his family, of the society he was living in were all mine, but I had never come across anyone who had articulated them so well before.

The words sang.

I had, at last, a reason to read.

I read all the other books on the list given to me by Mr Holden: *The Prodigy* and *Demian* by Herman Hesse, *Look Homeward Angel* by Thomas Wolfe, *Sons and Lovers* by D.H. Lawrence, *The Trial* by Kafka, *The Magus* by John Fowles, *The Outsider* by Camus, and *The Outsider* by Colin Wilson. These were far more difficult books to read than *The Catcher in the Rye* but I read them quickly because I was now enthused.

Mr Holden was not my actual English teacher. He had simply seen me wandering in a disconsolate fashion down the corridor, and had said that I looked like Holden Caulfield, and had lent me the book several days later.

The consequences of that chance meeting in a corridor for me are incalculable. I have no doubt that sooner or later I would have come across Salinger's book, but it may have been too late. It is a book that has to be read at exactly the right moment. I look at it now, and it is only the memory of reading it that excites me, not the actual words themselves, which seem far too full of self-pity for my liking now.

But reading it then made all the difference. The book gave me confidence in so many ways: it made me feel entitled to feel sorry for myself, and angry at adult authority. It also made me search for that anger in other books, and that quest took me through most of the classics, all of which explore alienation in various different forms.

That inner drive, that burning desire to search out the truth from literature, made me sail through my A levels, two degrees, and a PGCE in English. It fired me up enough to teach English and English literature in various comprehensives throughout the country for over fifteen years.

And it was to Salinger's example that I returned when I wrote my books, *I'm a Teacher Get Me Out of Here*, and *Teacher on the Run*. I wanted to bring the cut-the-crap honesty to the teaching world that Salinger brought to adolescence. I'm afraid to admit that I also sprinkled in a little of his self-pity.

It was Salinger who partially alleviated my anxieties about my son's reading. Sooner or later, Theo would find his *Catcher in the Rye* which would propel him into exploring the world of literature for himself.

Or would he?

Maybe he would never enjoy reading and writing. Maybe he would always associate it with classroom contests about who was reading 'Chapter Books' and who was not, who could win at hangman and who could not, who could get 10 out 10 in their spelling tests and who didn't, who got house-points for their work and who didn't.

Listening to other parents' stories about their school days

My worst interactions with James over his reading gave me pause for thought. I was losing my temper when I shouldn't have done. I wasn't going to make him love reading if he associated it with temper tantrums. He would land up hating it, fearing it.

In the end I had learned to love reading but it had taken a long time because I had been surrounded people who thought that the way to make me learn was to frighten me. My mother had shouted at me when I hadn't performed well at school, and had made it clear that it could be catastrophic for me if I didn't get a good education. I still have very vivid memories of her sitting me down at the kitchen table and ordering me to learn my spellings and do my reading when I was at primary school. To a certain degree, this had worked. I had performed well for a week or so after getting a rocket from her, but then sank back into doing badly when I wasn't shouted at.

I had also had teachers who had done the same thing, who had become angry with my poor scores, and shouted and threatened terrible things if I didn't improve. I had then tried harder and improved my marks a little. But the customary poor marks returned when the adrenaline wasn't pumping around my veins.

I realised, looking back at my education, that I had absorbed the unconscious lesson that shouting and instilling fear into a pupil produced better results and this was what was at the back of my mind when I shouted at James. The rational, intellectual part of me knew that this was a terrible prescription for teaching. While it might produce short-term results, in the long run it meant that people associated whatever they were learning with anger and fear.

I needed to learn this lesson from my own education that the way I had been educated wasn't perfect. In fact, quite a bit of it was pretty poor.

Talking to other parents, I found that some of the most enlightened were aware of the shortcomings of their own education. Doug in Chippenham, whose daughter Sophie went to a local state primary, told me:

> In the thirty years since I was at school, the contrast between education now and then is absolutely massive. All this stuff in the media and the negatives you hear is bollocks because the standard of the teaching, the standard of the facilities, the way the kids are respected and treated is miles better. Schools are obviously much better resourced: the computers, the interactive whiteboards, the teaching assistants, the brand new classrooms, and the displays are fantastic. The quality is so much better than it used to be because teachers are better trained and know how to motivate, and they have the resources to do it as well.

His wife, Sally, spoke in similarly enthusiastic terms about the primary schools in Chippenham, and felt they were much better than the one she had been taught in: 'I moved to Yorkshire in the 1970s and went to a tiny school with three members of staff. It was near Hebden Bridge. It was in the wilds. We really lived right out in the hills. There were three classes who all sat in the same classroom. I spent the last three years with the same teacher and he was terrible. And he was the head teacher as well! Everyone thinks it sounds so sweet, but it wasn't at all. I was trapped being taught by an idiot for so many years. I can remember laughing out loud at a book. The head heard me and was furious. I tried to explain about the humour in the book and he was very angry. I was eight and I knew that I had to adapt, keep my head down, never laugh out loud and never comment on anything. It was a terrible school; a head teacher like that wouldn't survive nowadays. Things have definitely got much better.'

Both Doug and Sally had reflected upon their own schooling because they realised that it would affect how they perceived their daughter's education. They hadn't fallen into the trap of romanticising their own school days, and believing that things had been better then. Sally was determined not to employ the humourless, angry approach of her head teacher upon her daughter.

Parents can be overly nostalgic about their education and believe that the system decades ago was far better than now. While many people romanticise the old grammar schools, David Parry offered me this scathing insight into his own education:

I went a boys' grammar school in Wrexham. It was an awful school. It was very basic in terms of the curriculum. It was a case of: 'Do this! Do that! Move along boy! Chin up! Behave!' It was a Dickensian place with some grotesque caricatures patrolling the classrooms. All the masters had the cane, and used it frequently. I was caned for failing to do some music homework. I still remember that very vividly: the entire lesson consisted of all the pupils, none of whom had completed the homework, aged 11, going into the stock cupboard and being caned.

A few years later, I was caned for going out at lunchtime without permission. My third time for the cane was for pulling a face behind a teacher's back. He turned around and saw me. The fourth time was when I was caught climbing out of a window, trying to escape the nightmare of that hellish school.

Bullying was rife. The teachers had minimal control, and I never did any homework. I made sixty stool legs in Year 9: the entire year consisted of making a stool. The teacher never came into the lesson so we just mucked around.

I went on to a sixth-form college. This was the first sixth-form college in Wales, and it was a very strange place because it had the trendy, liberal ethos of do-what-you-want, but it was staffed by the old fusty grammar teachers. It was an uninspiring place. There was a big paradox: you had the highly qualified teachers from Oxbridge who were very arid, and taught from notes.

However, it would be a mistake to make blanket judgements about schools being far worse in previous decades. Clearly, many of them were amazing schools. In the days before the National Curriculum, before Ofsted, schools had much more autonomy to set their own agendas. Unregulated and unaccountable to anybody except for the LEA and the odd visit from Her Majesty's

Inspectorate, many schools were laws unto themselves, some got away with blue murder. However, some thrived. I heard a number of stories from parents who felt that they had been very well educated at grammar schools, far better than they felt their children had been at comprehensives. Angela Sharpley told me:

I had a wonderful schooling at a mixed grammar school in Somerset. It was very academic. The norm was that everyone sat 12 O levels. I had a brother who was eleven months older who did the same. I sat 12 O levels and did well at them. Everyone did. You weren't allowed to stay onto the sixth form unless you did well. I did a lot of sport. The school was a rural idyll. The teachers were strict and formal with full gowns and canes. Very firm discipline but fair. The fear of being punished stopped us from misbehaving. Society was different. You didn't kick against discipline but toed the line. It was a marvellous education.

However, while Angela said that she had had an amazing academic education, she felt the system failed her ultimately because of the very poor careers' guidance offered to girls. She said:

There was no careers guidance in those days. I just studied my best A level subject at university. Looking back now, I would have loved to have read Medicine, which my daughter is currently doing. But I simply didn't think about what career I might do, despite being very good at all my subjects. It wasn't the sort of thing a girl did in those days. I am very pleased it is different for my daughter in that regard. While I don't think she has been pushed like I was, I think the career guidance and expectations for girls are so much better.

One of the most interesting parents I spoke to in this regard was Oxana, the parent of a child attending English state schools, but who had been educated in Soviet Russia. She told me:

I was born in the former USSR, in a small republic called Bashkrya, near the Urals. We had very bitter winters, and warm summers. I went to kindergarten there but when I was six we moved to another town, which in the central part of Russia, not far from Moscow, in a town called Koscroma.

From when I was seven till 17, I was educated there in a Soviet state school. The schools didn't have names, they all had numbers, and my first school was number 32, then I moved to school 18 which I didn't like, so I moved back to 32. The system was very uniform: the same curriculum was taught in every school. I felt the schools educated me very well. I learnt Maths, Russian literature and language, Geography, History, Geometry, Physics, Chemistry, English, Art and Technical Drawing, Information Technology, which my school specialised in. We had the first generation of computers. Every term, all of your marks were added up and you were given an average mark, and if you failed to get past a certain grade you had to resit the year again. Pupils were anxious that they might fail and worked hard as a consequence.

My daughter has been educated entirely in the English state system, and, in my view, it is not nearly as good. When she was in Year 1, she was really struggling with her English and Maths, and so I asked someone to bring me Russian textbooks for Year 1. It was so good to have them in my hands. Straight away, it struck me, why don't they use proper textbooks in the English system? In Russia, we have textbooks that the whole country uses. They are good and colourful and they go from topic to topic, and they cover everything. However, because Alice wasn't used to textbooks, and because I had to go through them after school when she was tired, they didn't go down too well. I just wish that they would use something like them in English schools.

What is fascinating about hearing Oxana's story is that her education was so clearly and simply structured. This is something the English system with all its long history and labyrinthine rules and regulations never has been and probably never will be. But perhaps we could all learn from Soviet Russia; perhaps every child could be issued with a textbook which contained all the relevant information. Then parents would know where they were.

THE NEW SCHOOL RULES
for nostalgic parents

Remember the past accurately. Use the past to put the present into perspective. Remember how you learned to read and write: those memories may well help you with your own child's education. Recall your own struggles when you see your child struggling. Don't romanticise the past too much.

CHAPTER **7**

When schooling causes conflict

Niall buried his head in his hands, and rubbed his eyes. I asked him if anything was the matter. He was on the red wine tonight, and took a large mouthful before speaking. It was a year on from our first 'school' conversation, and we'd had many since. Tim and I had started to tease Niall about his conversion to Christianity, asking him how the Baby Jesus was. He had become more and more defensive. Once he burst out that I was a smug, self-satisfied git who would no doubt send his child to a private school. After that, we had all avoided the school topic during our monthly outings to the pub and stuck to safe conversations like politics. Schools were far too emotional.

This Sunday night, things were different. Niall wanted to talk about 'it' for the first time in months. He looked dreadful: washed-out and unshaven with dark rings under his eyes.

He said, 'I can't stand it. His sermons are so dull and empty, so anti-life. And he grins at us in such a smug way. Looking down at his packed-out church so cheerfully, he just talks. He won't stop. The sermons go on for over half an hour. And they are about nothing. Often some obscure aspect of scripture which could have interested no one, even a believer. The Christians can't stand him either. But we have to grin and nod and bow and scrape.'

'Maybe it's all for the best in the long run,' I suggested gently.

Niall sighed. 'Vicky and I are getting into these terrible rows about it. I've started saying maybe we should send Martin to a non-religious school so that we don't have to go through all this crap. She hits the roof. She's paranoid that Martin will turn into a moron if he goes to the other school. She's complains I'm unsupportive when it counts. Apparently, I yawn too much in church, and I shouldn't cross my legs. Can you imagine? It's a crime to cross my legs. But I know she has a point. When it comes to our character reference, the vicar might doubt our motives.'

Niall's experiences are not so rare. Peta Pryor, a married mother of two school-age children, told me:

> Getting your child into the right school is one of the most nerve-wracking experiences I have ever gone through. I would even go so far as to say that it is more stressful than getting a nasty disease. Sometimes it has felt like that anyway. I have seen and continue to see the process reduce parents to fits of weeping, cause friends to fall out with each other for ever, and, at its most extreme, divorces to happen.

Why do people let it get to them so much? Unfortunately, the potential for conflict over choosing schools is endless. This chapter explores the different types of conflict that parents get into over schools, looking at the most common themes.

Religious warfare

Megan is a mother of a nine-year-old daughter, Mary, and they live in Dorset.

6 Sometimes it feels like our household has become like Northern Ireland in the 1970s: you never know when you're going to get ambushed by some nasty bomb. You see, I really want Mary to go to the local comprehensive, which is not religious at all, but my husband is adamant that she's going to the all-girl Roman Catholic secondary

school which is outside the borough. Mary should get in there because we do go to church most weeks and we're friendly with the priest. But in Dorset the comps are really good. They're not like the kind of sink schools you find in the big cities. And they're healthy, sensible places where girls can mix freely with boys and make up their own minds about things. I went to a Catholic girls' school and I hated it. I still believe in a loose kind of way, but I don't like the rigidity of the Catholic Church and certainly don't agree with the way they teach things like sex education. 9

Megan's more liberal Catholicism contrasted with her husband's more traditionalist approach. The subtle nuances in their beliefs had never been a problem until the matter of Mary's secondary school education came up. But Megan's husband was determined that his daughter should be kept separate from boys and that she should learn about Catholicism day in, day out. Megan told me:

6 We can't stop arguing about it. If there's the slightest bad report about the local comp in the press, he'll leap on it. Like the other day, two boys from the comp had been caught shoplifting. My husband brought home the paper and slapped it down on the table and said that this was proof that there was no way Mary could go there. "Catholic girls don't steal," he said proudly. I then told him that that wasn't my experience when I went to my Catholic girls' school. This blew up into a fully fledged row. We were shouting at each other by the end of it. 9

What is interesting here is that both Megan and her husband are Catholic, and yet they were still arguing over schools. This illustrates just how easy it is to get into rows over religious schools: you can actually more or less believe the same stuff and still be arguing. Sometimes, it can be easier if both parents have different beliefs because then it is likely that they have already considered compromise. I spoke to a couple who were Protestant and Catholic, but had agreed to send their child to a non-religious school because they felt this was the best compromise. However, like Megan they lived in the shires where the local comprehensives were good.

Some of the most fevered conflicts I came across were in London where many parents feel that the best schools are religious and are desperate to get their children into them, no matter what they believe. I spoke to several couples who had been worn down by the sheer grind of having to turn up dutifully to church and listen to countless boring sermons. Steve told me:

> We always have rows on Sunday. We have a row in the morning about whose turn it is to go to church, a row about what we are doing with our lives sitting in this draughty hall for hours on end, baking cakes and sitting behind stalls, and then a row after church when one of us makes fun of the other one about suddenly being so religious. The whole thing is such a sour, unchristian business.

But Steve and his partner do it anyway, despite not being at all religious, because they feel it is best for their child.

'Selective school' warfare

It was the ultimate act of hypocrisy. Diane Abbot, the firebrand left-wing MP for Hackney North and Stoke Newington, who believes that private schools 'prop up the class system in society', decided in 2003 to send her son to a £10,000-a-year private school instead of a comprehensive.

She said, 'It is inconsistent, to put it mildly, for someone who believes in a fairer and more egalitarian society to send their child to a fee-paying school.'[1] But she did it, risking open warfare with her constituency, the Labour Party, and an outraged British public who were aghast at her breathtaking, self-confessed hypocrisy.

Diane Abbot is perhaps the most egregious example of a left-winger preaching one message to the masses – that we should all send our children to state-funded schools – and yet doing precisely the opposite herself. She is not the only one. She herself attacked two other prime hypocrites: the Labour MP Harriet Harman, and the Prime Minister himself, Tony Blair. When Prime Minister Tony Blair sent his eldest son, Euan, to the London Oratory, a selective school, she criticised him, saying people voted Labour because they believed in equality. And when Solicitor General Harriet Harman sent her son to a selective grammar school in Orpington, Kent, Ms Abbott said, 'She made the Labour Party look as if we do one thing and say another.'[2]

If Diane Abbot, who had spent so many years publicly attacking the private school system, could eat her own words so spectacularly then what hope is there for the rest of us? Not much.

Selective school warfare is common in the households in the country where parents have the money to send their child to a private school but have moral scruples about doing so. Conflict occurs when one parent wishes to have their child privately educated, and the other doesn't. Private schools offer a social cachet, allowing the child to make the right kind of connections.

Sometimes, one spouse sees this as despicable elitism and social mimicry.

I know of a woman who has been preparing her husband, a hardened socialist, for sending their child to a private secondary school. She is carrying out a ten-year plan: each year she subtly leaves articles about the problems with state schooling in their area around the house. With each year, she intends to intensify the number of articles she shows him, and then, when the child is seven, start to bring it up in conversation. 'I'm frightened he'll divorce me if he finds out what I really think,' she confessed to me. 'But I am determined to get my way.'

Up and down the country, warfare of this kind is going on covertly and overtly in the homes of teachers, lawyers, doctors, social workers, and politicians.

School choice warfare

In any system where there is a degree of choice, conflict can occur. Sally and Doug in Chippenham, Wiltshire, had a number of arguments about the secondary school they should sent their daughter to. Sally told me:

❛ I looked around all four secondary schools during their open days when Sophie was in her last year of primary school. Sophie then spent a day each at all four schools and I let her choose which one she wanted. But the trouble was I wasn't happy with her choice. She'd chosen the school with the best results but not the one I'd envisioned for her, which was the local comp. My husband though was delighted, and agreed with her choice.

I knew all Sophie's friends were going to other schools and that made me question our decision. I thought how can all the other parents choose another school? What were we missing that they were getting?

It was all signed, sealed and delivered by Christmas. Sophie virtually had to do the whole of Year 6 knowing she was going to a different school. I felt that I was no longer part of that group of parents. All through the primary school, I was constantly ringing up friends asking them to help me with child care or whatever, and now I realised I wouldn't be able to in the future. I saw my social network crumbling before my very eyes. I felt lonely in not being able to talk to any of my friends about the new school.

I knew that I had to build up a whole new social network. Unfortunately, secondary school doesn't work like that. There are no mums at the gate with prams.

But my husband, Doug, thought this was irrelevant. He got really frustrated with all my fussing and worrying about it. But he just didn't understand what a big thing it was for me.

Perhaps, it is because of this that we are always having arguments about whether parental choice is a good thing or not. I definitely don't think it is, whereas he always argues the case that the competition between schools in the area has improved the standard of education for everyone. I don't think it has. I think it is leading to segregation. It is a real shame that all of Sophie's friends have gone to different schools. It's just increased the potential for conflict and worry and deprived us of our old friendships. ❜

Other types of common warfare

Moving house warfare

One parent believes it is time to move house and live in the catchment area of a good school. The other parent loves the house they spent all those years nesting in: a lovely, comfortable home, where they are surrounded by friends. The potential for conflict here is enormous: bickering about the quality of relevant catchment areas is potentially inexhaustible.

School-run warfare

Is the school nearby better because it's more convenient for dropping off and picking up offspring? Or is it better to go to the one further away because it gets better results? One parent favours convenience over academic excellence. This is often the parent who has to do the daily school run.

Equally, arguments can occur over who is going to drop off and pick up the kids at school particularly if both partners work similar hours.

Class warfare

One partner has fixed views about the kind of social group their child should be mixing with. This 'snobby' parent wants their child to go to an institution where the children talk with 'well-spoken' accents, and where it is clear that the child can 'socially better' him or herself. The 'inverted snob' wants the opposite. He or she wants his child to 'know the poor' and to feel at ease with children from socially deprived backgrounds, believing that going to a school which has a socially deprived intake will assist with this.

Who-should-be-helping warfare

'You're just not helping him with his reading at all, are you?' I overheard one parent snap at his partner as they were leaving a parents' evening.

His wife retorted with the stock answer, 'Why does it always have to be me? Why is it always my fault if he can't read properly? You could listen to him read as well.'

The husband sighed. 'You're pathetic, do you know that? You just don't get it, do you? I am working, you are not!'

The wife glanced behind her and saw that I had heard what was going on, and hurried away from the confrontation, storming boldly along the school corridor in such a way as to suggest that she was going to give as good she got in the privacy of their car. The husband's shoulders drooped. He knew he had made a mistake. He tried to catch up with her, saying that he was sorry, but it was too late.

Warfare over bullies

Parents are naturally defensive of their children and never more so than when they hear from their child that they've been bullied. One long-serving head of year at a comprehensive in Yorkshire told me that he's had to split up a number of fights between parents at the school gates over bullying. He said:

Usually, a child goes home crying that they've been beaten up by so-and-so, and the parent decides to take the law into his own hands by confronting the parent of the bully. That can end up in fisticuffs. I've had to call the police on a couple of occasions. What these parents don't realise is that they are making it more likely that their child will be bullied by making such an exhibition. These acts of aggression just inflame enmities and do nothing to stop them. My recommendation would be always to go through the school and to let them speak to the relevant parent if necessary. Some parents of hardened bullies are real nutters – they've brought up a bully after all – and they love a good fight.

Warring with your neighbours/friends

No one I spoke to wanted to go on record about these particular phenomena, but it is much more common than you might think. This usually happens when there is fierce competition to get children into the one good school in an area. Most of the cases I came across had happened in London where there are such perceived disparities between schools. The parents who manage to get their children into the so-called great school often fall out with the parents who don't. They nearly always fall out if the parents who have lost out think there has been skulduggery. One couple I spoke to fell out permanently with their best friends because their friends got their child into the good school by using the address of a relative to claim that they were in the immediate catchment area. The parents who lost out felt that this lie meant that their child was deprived of a place which was rightfully theirs. There were no more neighbourly Saturday night barbecues or Christmas parties after that.

But this sort of thing isn't confined to the capital. Another parent in Leeds told me:

> There have been terrible ructions over the last few years in our neighbourhood regarding the myth of 'parental choice'. Certain parents still believe there is a parental choice in Leeds and yet make sure that they move into the catchment area of the school, or use relatives' homes to lie about their addresses.
>
> I've also known parents to fall out with all their friends because they've taken a child out of a state school mid-stream and moved them into a private one. This has caused huge resentment because suddenly the state school isn't good enough for their little darling anymore.

THE NEW SCHOOL RULES
for avoiding warfare about schools

1. **Talk it through calmly** Don't let arguments about school ruin your life. Talk to your friends about schools in a reasoned, calm way. Don't let your anxieties run away with

▶

you. Realise you are dealing with a very imperfect system. Your child is in competition with all the applicants to your chosen school and not just his classmates. So if you know that there are parents 'cheating' at your child's school, you should be aware there will be parents cheating at other schools. There are cheats everywhere. Try not to hold too many grudges.

2. **Don't be paranoid** about what your friends and relatives are up to. You can't control them. If they are cheating, they may well get found out.

3. **Be honest** Don't lie to your friends who are parents of pupils in the same class as your child. Be honest with them, but remember you don't have to discuss your choices with them if you don't want to. Remember, your child will make new friends at his or her new school. Some children want a complete break from their primary school.

CHAPTER 8

What makes a good school?

It all depends on what you're looking for. If you want a safe, kind, caring environment for your child to grow up in, to make friends in, and to learn to be a responsible, considerate adult then you might not want to send him to a top private schools like St Paul's, where cut-throat competition – in all spheres – is the name of the game. However, if want your child to achieve amazing grades at A level and get into the best Oxford college, then St Paul's may be your place – if you can afford it.

Most parents I interviewed didn't see it this way, however, their primary consideration was the happiness of their child. Sure, they wanted their offspring to do well but not at the expense of their overall well-being. This is the perspective I have taken in this chapter. I have decided to judge schools on a range of issues: their academic attainment and their ability to produce happy, fulfilled children. Sometimes, these two things are a little at odds, as we will see.

Bad private schools

There are as many views about what makes a good school as there are parents, and consequently it is impossible to pinpoint what makes a good school, although obviously many politicians, philosophers, teachers and inspectors have tried. However, there are some fairly common views about what makes a bad school. Some of the worst schools I heard about appeared to be in the private sector. Being unregulated and unobserved, I have heard horror stories from children and parents about private schools where the pupils were forced to copy out from the board for days on end, where no discussions were permitted, where pupils from the ages of four and five were expected to sit in silence for long periods of time, where there were no proper facilities for play.

Even private schools with good 'liberal' reputations can have significant problems. One mother told me about a prep school in the south of England where one of the teachers was well known for having a drug problem. She told me:

The school my son attended for three years was owned and run by a tyrannical woman and her daughter, let's call her Ms Leslie. Ms Leslie taught my son from three to six years and the ambulance regularly arrived to take her away. She was a hysterical, drug-addicted loser. She had just done a tour of South America before coming to teach at the school but nobody had any suspicions when she took the post. My son would come home and say, 'Mummy, my teacher collapsed today and had a terrible nose bleed. It was really scary!'

Now the thing to understand about the school is that it had a very trendy reputation in the area. The children were allowed to choose whether they wanted to stay in the classroom. So if the teacher was boring them, they were free to leave the classroom and go into another zone. It sounded all very enlightened but I think it was an excuse for poor discipline. It meant that for much of the year the children learnt nothing and were frequently bored, with nothing much to occupy them. Then the headmistress would get into a panic and insist that the children did mock tests all day long.

The irony is that she preached this philosophy about free thinking, but she was the most controlling person I came across. One year, the headmistress threw out 60 per cent of the pupils because she had no space. Because she was an incompetent planner, she took in far too many children for the actual space she had.

The headmistress was brilliant at wooing parents who were running away from the state sector but wanted a liberal school to send their children to. Quite a few media and artsy types sent their children to the school. At the open evening, she would say, 'Don't put your child into the machine. They'll spit them out at 11 or 13 and they will be droids.'

When I learnt the truth about what was going on there, I took my son out immediately. But it is so difficult to know when you are a parent. It took me three years to figure out what was really going on.

Phil Beadle believes that the teaching in most private schools is far inferior to that of state schools. He told me:

I am of the passionate belief that the teaching in state schools, particularly the teaching in inner-city schools, is infinitely better than that in private schools. Private school teachers are faced with a raft of compliant, charming children with a high boredom threshold. These children are already well educated when they get to school. They don't need good teachers. So consequently they don't get them.

The teaching in an inner-city school has to investigate every possible way of inducing learning. They have to be experts on behaviour management, near geniuses in creativity, and rigorous and encouraging markers. If your choice of sending your children to a private school is not openly motivated by racism, or classism, then you are committing a mistake. If you decide to send your child to a private school on the basis that you are racist or frightened of the working class, then that's fine. At least, you are honest about it. Just don't dare try to perpetuate the fundamental lie which continues to heft the great divide in our society, that is, you will get better teaching at a private school. You won't.

Poor state primary schools

Not everyone, though, has Phil Beadle's faith in state schools, especially parents who feel that their child has been let down by them. Peta Pryor told me her disturbing story.

❧ We were very happy to get her into the oversubscribed primary school near us, but things didn't work out as we had wished. Phoebe had a really excellent reception teacher and Phoebe blossomed. She did very well. But this made me complacent about monitoring her progress.

In the succeeding years, because she was above the expected level she was allowed to cruise. What we did do was to develop our outside activities. Phoebe already did ballet and tap at the Italia Conti Theatre Academy, and swam regularly for charities. She later joined a competitive swimming club, our church choir and the Islington Music Centre.

But Phoebe did not meet anything like her academic potential, achieving top grades when she was seven years old in her Key Stage 1 tests but very average results when she was 11 in her Key Stage 2 results. For a child of her ability, this was poor. Particularly since she had supportive parents and did every single piece of homework she was set. We weren't given any mock Key Stage test results in any of the intervening years. This was the school policy. So I had no real idea about her attainment. Phoebe did regularly say that she was bored witless. Because of where we live, the head teacher said that there was quite a bit of movement out of the school in Years 3, 4 and 5. What I didn't appreciate was that the children that were brought in to fill up the vacant places tended to have special needs. These children had the benefit to the school of bringing funding from other boroughs.

The net result of this was that a mentally disturbed child came into the school, and since there was only a one-class intake, one child can make a big difference. Much of the teachers' attention was taken up with dealing with this child, and, as a result, my child and the class did not get the education they needed.

When we asked the head teacher for information he would explain that we had a map of what they were going to study during the term. But we were not allowed to see the children's books, except by special appointment. We felt apprehensive about doing this more than once because it seemed we were taking up too much of the teachers' time. The school did not offer an open day to view all books, although selected best work was always on display around the school. 9

State schools at their best

It appears though, that at their best, nothing quite compares to really good state primary schools. Sarah's contrasting descriptions of her son, Angus, being taught at a really good state school and her older son, Tom, being taught a private school, illustrate the gulf between a really good state primary and a perfectly good private school.

6 My youngest son, Angus, goes to St Mary's, which is an amazing Roman Catholic state primary. The teachers are very accepting of every child. They seem to have the right mental attitude towards children. Above all, they are very inclusive. They see where the child is, and where his ability is, and then they adapt what they are doing in the class so that he can participate fully in the work.

Angus is six years old and is on the autistic spectrum. Because of this he has been taken out of the class with a group of six other children and has had extra word and sound games to play in order to learn to read. In his reception year, he would just not go into the classroom. He was terrified of the noise, the children, the teacher, the strange surroundings. He has a real problem with transitions, entering new places. Even re-entering a familiar place is difficult for him. The school was fantastically understanding about it all. They tried loads of things. A teacher assistant helped him by putting a computer out in the corridor so that he could play on the computer to calm himself down before he went into the room. His teachers were so positive about everything he did. They did a lot of things in the classroom about why we like people in the class, and what they have got to offer.

Despite the fact that Angus is on the autistic spectrum, he has progressed marvellously.

The one mistake of my life is that I did not move Tom to this school. I moved him to a private school. He went to a prep school which has been good but it does not compare with St Mary's. There is a different attitude in the school. Many prep schools are obsessed with appearances rather than being concerned about what is really going on with the child. St Mary's has such a huge heart whereas the prep school is accountable to the parents but does not have the same inclusive spirit. The prep school is very good at picking up where the children are in terms of their work. The teachers are really on the ball about his academic attainment but they don't have much of a sense of him as a person.

Academically, they have been good. There are 16 in his class. He can finish work and it is all part of a natural progression. It is quite formal and orderly. Serried ranks, and quiet working are expected.

They do have a laugh but it is not the jolly spirit of St Mary's. There is a lot more practising of exams. The main purpose is to get the children into the top private schools in the area. They offer a package and either you buy into it, or you don't. For example, we got one letter the other day saying that they had changed our half-term holiday. We protested but they said they can do that. They are not answerable to a local authority or central government in the way state schools are.

I have decided to put Thomas in the local comprehensive because I have had such a good experience with St Mary's. State schools can get it right. The place has a good reputation. Lots of our friends with kids who have gone there say it is good. I do look at the league tables and it has great scores. I want Tom to feel of the community by going there.

With Angus, I am amazed at the power I have to lead and shape the education I want for him. ❥

THE NEW SCHOOL RULES
about good primary schools

1. **They include everyone** They adapt work so that everyone can understand and enjoy it. They have an inclusive spirit. They celebrate everybody. They have high expectations for all their pupils. They are fair to all pupils with no favouritism: they are not racist but nor are they so politically correct that it is the ethnic pupils who receive all the help and funding. Merits are given out for consistent good work and not to a problem child who has caused grief all week and then gets an award 'for walking down the stairs nicely'. Good, quiet kids are rewarded for their efforts and not overlooked. Such schools have clear merit and sanctions processes so all children know where they stand and what to expect.

2. **They are fun** While private schools tend to be more formal in their atmosphere and approach than state primaries, they should be enthusing their pupils about learning.

The importance of social class

So head teachers are important, but the wider community – in the form of the general neighbourhood, the parents, the governing body, the LEA, Ofsted, the DfES – are very important in defining a school's character. The most vivid illustration I came across was in Ebbw Vale, in the Welsh valleys. I had researched this area in some depth for my book *Yob Nation* because it has suffered from huge problems in terms of social deprivation and anti-social behaviour. Once a world leader in its production of steel and with a strong mining industry, most of the pits and factories have now closed down leaving mass unemployment and despair.

Sitting in the heart of this community is Glyncoed Comprehensive school, surrounded as it is by the magnificent mountains and valleys, and row upon row of terraced houses. Perhaps surprisingly, this is one of the top achieving comprehensives in the country, attaining results well above the Welsh and LEA average. As I walked around the school, I could immediately see that it was a lovely school: both staff and pupils were friendly and relaxed, holding doors open for me and my five-year-old son, and asking us questions about our backgrounds.

Colin James, the head teacher since 2003, but a teacher at the school for seven years, explained to me what he felt was the secret of its success:

My own impression of this area is that it reminds me of the area where I lived as a boy. It is an ex-coal-mining, steel-working community, very like the one I was born and bred in. I am from the upper Afan valley, which was a coal-mining area which served the Port Talbot steel works. The parents remind me of my own community. It is a very working-class area but there are middle-class values because they really believe in school. It is an area of high social deprivation. The pupils taking free school meals is 22 per cent, with an LEA average of 20 per cent, and the Welsh average is 16. The Efstyn report said, 'The area is one of the most socially deprived in Wales.'

Having worked in an area with a selective school system, and coming here, I realise, actually, that the comprehensive school idea works here because the local community is really encouraged to play a proper role in the school. I married a girl from the area, and my in-laws still live here. My father-in-law came to the school. There is a real sense of community here, and the school is at the heart of maintaining the community's identity. The vast of majority of parents are proud of the school: we have very high attendance figures. The school is 'highly regarded in the locality'. A parents' questionnaire indicated that they were very happy with the school in terms of the information it gave them, the support for the pupils, the happiness of their children and the education provided. Nine out of ten parents are very happy with the school.

We try not to forget anyone here. In assembly and at staff meetings, we will praise the local people who are the cleaners and caretakers of the school. During the recent inspection, the local people were coming in to clean the building at five in the morning. My head cleaner has a grandson in the school and her children came here as well. She wasn't going to let the school down!

Above all, there is an open door for parents to come in and talk to us when they like. As a result, parents are confident that the school will respond to their concerns. We send letters home quite a bit, and we do a community letter once a term and that goes everywhere, into the fish and chip shops, the local businesses, onto youth clubs' noticeboards and so on. 9

Colin James persuasively argues that it is the parents' support of the school that makes it such a success. In many ways, the area should be one where all the schools are failing if you believe that social deprivation and poor results go hand in hand. Drugs, vandalism and gang violence are all prevalent in the area. However, the school is now changing expectations. Many of the parents I interviewed in Ebbw Vale had not done well at school and the majority had not gone to college or university, but they clearly had different expectations for their children. Lisa, the mother of two children at local schools, one of whom was at Glyncoed, told me that the ICT resources of the school had really motivated her son.

She said, 'My oldest son loves working on computers at the school and at home. He loves spreadsheets, databases. He has chosen ICT as a main subject. I am very pleased about this because there was very little of this when I was at school.'

In common with many of the best schools I came across, Glyncoed offers a lot of extracurricular activities: sports, music and drama clubs, as well as things that are a bit off the wall. Glyncoed even holds after-school classes in making stained-glass windows.

One parent in Northumberland told me:

A good school allows the children to do other things than straight exams. We wanted a school which had a lot of other things happening, where there is a lot of music and drama going on. Our son, Callum, is in a pop band while our daughter has done no end of drama and music while she's been at the school. There are 13 rock bands in the school, there is an orchestra, and even cameras and editing facilities so that pupils can make their own films.

However, it isn't just a pro-active head, good results and extra-curricular activities that make a good school. Glyncoed undoubtedly benefited hugely from the attitude of the parents, the majority of whom are from stable, hard-working backgrounds. In many ways, the school illustrates the fundamental point that it is the social class of the parents which is the decisive factor in making a good school: while the school has many pupils from deprived backgrounds, they are balanced out by children from more affluent ones. On the whole, social class does play a decisive role in a school's results. Nick Davies told me:

> In general, it's clear that the most important single factor which determines whether a school produces good or bad results is the intake of children; and, within that, the factor which has most impact on the motivation and ability of children is social class. In Lewes, where I am, the middle class overwhelmingly still buy into the state system. It's a self-fulfilling judgement – if the middle class reckon the schools are good, they send their kids there, and so the schools get good results, so the middle class carry on sending their kids there. There is an irony there, because schools with good results find it very difficult to recruit energetic and imaginative head teachers. The heads in a town like Lewes tend to be below par but the intake of kids disguises their weakness.

Dynamic head teachers like Colin James are not particularly drawn to teach in stable, middle-class schools like those found in Lewes. As Davies convincingly argues, this doesn't seem to particularly affect the results of the schools, but it does mean that these schools in middle-class catchment areas can be a little moribund.

Are the best schools religious?

It was definitely one of the best schools I had ever taught in. The school took Catholic girls from a wide catchment area – girls from both tough and more 'polite' backgrounds – and it demanded that they worked and behaved. Every lesson the girls would stand up and greet me by saying in unison, 'Good morning (or afternoon), Mr Gilbert' and would sit down, ready to work, being prepared if necessary to listen in silence for long periods if I wanted to lecture them. Strict tabs were kept on them: if they were falling behind with their work, the form tutor would write a note in the homework diary – which was always checked by teachers and parents – and a dialogue with the parents would begin. During my four years teaching at the school, I never came across any truly bad behaviour.

At the heart of the school was the religious ethos. Although there weren't prayers every day, there were always prayers and sermons in assemblies – which were frequently led by the pupils – and regular masses where the local priest would come into and lead a whole school celebration of Christ's life. The religious ethos gave the school a drive and focus which I hadn't come across in any of the more secular schools in which I had taught.

Perhaps, most strikingly, I felt that this was a school that genuinely cared about the pupils' moral and spiritual well-being. This overused concept was not just a word that was regurgitated in policy documents, you could feel it in just about every classroom, and you could particularly feel it in every tutor group. In many schools, the tutor is mainly a glorified administrator, who registers their allotted pupils every day, hands out letters, and checks the reports and progress of the pupils intermittently; but in this school, tutors were expected to work hard for their money. Tutors were expected to know the pupils very well, and were turned to by other teachers if any of their charges misbehaved or fell behind with their work. The tutor was genuinely *in loco parentis* and seen as an important 'spiritual' figure, a guardian of a pupil's moral well-being.

None of this was explicitly stated, it was implicit because of the religious ethos of the school. Although I am an atheist, teaching there I could see how religious schools could be extremely effective.

Religion, motivation and educational success

My thoughts were echoed by Hassan, my pupil who felt so let down by his secondary school in Tower Hamlets. Although that school was nominally Church of England, there was no religious emphasis in any of the lessons, assemblies or form tutor period lessons. In terms of the teaching, except in religious education lessons, it was a God-free zone.

Quite frankly, when Hassan contacted me I was astonished at how well he had done. Most of the pupils at that school I knew of were essentially unemployed or working on the black market in the restaurant industry in and around Brick Lane. Hassan explained to me how he came to be such a successful, articulate financial journalist. For him, religion played a major part in it. He told me:

> Islam ensured that I took responsibility for myself. In a ghettoised area, it is very easy to get stuck in a rut and accept the stereotypes you are labelled with. Therefore, after I left that terrible secondary school, I started to apply myself at college and university. I also immediately started working part-time when I left school and I believe that added to my learning curve. I think intelligence is not just based on academic achievements: immersing oneself in different social settings and dealing with people at varying levels allows you to pick up skills and traits no book can provide.
>
> I knew I had to break away from the clique I was in and went

to a college completely different from everyone else. I associated with new friends and generally had a different mentality to learning. Discipline was less of an issue at college. Naturally at that age, no one wanted to come across as a kid. So more often than not, we got our head down to learn. Islam was beginning to play a part in my life. I was always religiously minded as a child but went through a period of not giving a damn. But Islam started to come back into my life. Eventually I became a practising Muslim in my last year at university.

It put a perspective to my life and I knew that I could not wallow in self-pity. I could have easily slumped into the defeatist, victimised mindset, complaining about my failings caused by a 'racist' society and my bad education. But Islam is a religion of common sense. Whenever I felt like that, common sense would kick in, and I would feel that compared to other people in the world, I was quite fortunate.

Procrastinating, being lazy and generally unproductive is scorned upon by Islam, while being part of the community and society is encouraged and good deeds are seen as acts of worship. So it was beneficial to be good.

Hassan went on to explain to me why he feels there should be more religious schools. He said:

I do not think there is anything wrong with state-funded religious schools, since their discipline and approach seem to be better. Why is the discipline better? It's easier to rebel in a secular state school because it does not have the same culture of reverence as a religious school. For example, you're probably less likely to swear in a church than you would in a shopping mall. When discipline is less of an issue, teaching and learning is easier. Islamic state schools only number a few. Most Islamic schools are private, run by a community driven to distraction and action by failing local schools.

I posed the question though that perhaps such schools would lead to more sectarian divisions? Hassan answered:

I don't think religious schools will make sectarian tensions any worse. Religious schools allow kids to be proud of their culture but also, certainly in Muslim schools, they teach about other religions and cultures. Religions can teach 'tolerance', i.e., you may not agree with someone else's view but you acknowledge the fact that they have a view.

Sectarian and racial divisions already exist regardless of religion, that's a convenient excuse used by agnostics and atheists to attack religion. Was my secondary a Muslim school? It was nominally C of E. And yet how many non-Muslims were there? My primary school was 50–50 whites and non-whites; by the time I left it was 80–20 in favour of Asians. White people moved away towards Essex, Ilford, Barking, Dagenham. I know two primary schools in Shadwell probably 100 yards from each other; one all white, the other all Asian. For whatever reason, the white parents didn't want their kids in all-Asian schools. Segregation already exists! Religious schools will make no difference.

Unless you have experienced the chaos of a poorly run inner-city comprehensive, you may find it difficult to appreciate Hassan's point of view. But I have, and I feel sympathetic towards his plea for more state-funded Muslim schools. They do tend to be better disciplined and more focused than their secular counterparts.

However, many parents are resentful about their exclusivity. One parent, Tony, who lives in Wolverhampton told me:

My bugbear is church schools. I would like to send my daughter to the school around the corner, but I am not able to send her there because it is a church school. You need a detailed reference from the vicar to go there and you are interviewed as well. I find it extraordinary that you have to do this in this day and age.

I went to a religious school myself but no one asked us about whether we were religious.

Tony's views speak for many parents here who are not particularly religious. Why should they have to pay taxes to fund schools which they are barred from? In this sense, there is an

inherent flaw in the English education system which has provided state-funded religious education for over a century.

Some commentators are very troubled by the rise of religious
schools for this very reason. They feel that the public purse is
being hijacked by religious fanatics of all persuasions in order to
perpetuate their rigid dogmas. The investigative journalist Nick
Davies told me:

> There are some signs of an attempt by Christian fundamentalists
> to infiltrate state schools in Sussex. One became head at a school
> on the south-east coast, and, according to a friend who was
> teaching there, banned Roald Dahl's book *The Witches* from the
> library for promoting paganism and being irreligious. Another
> became head at a rural primary school in Sussex and caused huge
> ructions by talking about redemption and salvation in assembly
> and generally imposing a very conservative regime – she ended
> up splitting the parent body into two factions, with the oppos-
> ing parents eventually abandoning the school en masse to get
> away from her.
>
> The LEA promoted her – that may have been because it was
> the only way to get her out of the school, or because the head of
> the LEA at the time was also a Christian fundamentalist and he
> wanted her at HQ. Once she had gone, the school settled down
> again. The Christians have the law on their side. In order to get
> his 1988 Education Reform Bill through the Lords, the then Edu-
> cation Secretary Kenneth Baker evaded a mass of objections by
> peers by making an unholy deal with bishops and right-wingers
> who agreed to shelve their objections if he introduced a new
> clause requiring all schools to hold an act of collective worship
> every day, that act to be 'broadly or mainly of a Christian char-
> acter'. It is a testament to the independence of secondary head
> teachers that, since then, they have run the longest and possibly
> the most successful campaign of industrial action in contempo-
> rary Britain, simply defying the law day after day and running
> their schools without compulsory Christianity every morning.
> Which may be why some of the Christians want to get in there
> and become head teachers.

It is a very tricky issue. England has never made the separation between church and state, and, as a consequence, many religious schools have been and continue to be funded by the taxpayer. Since this is the state of affairs, it would be hypocritical to deny Muslim schools state aid if there is a legitimate demand for them. Unfortunately, because many secular schools are so poor, there appears to be a need for them. It is clearly preferable to have Islamic schools drawn into the state sector where they are subject to governmental legislation and regulation. Fundamentalism of all kinds is an increasing concern, but as we will see, all state sectors are obliged to teach the National Curriculum which insists upon the teaching of such subjects as evolution. In this sense, let's hope Nick Davies's concerns are exaggerated. If the school inspectorate is doing its job properly fundamentalists shouldn't have a decisive influence in shaping the curriculum.

However, in private Muslim schools, fundamentalism flourishes. A Bengali father, Mohammed, told me about the private Islamic school he sends his child to:

> They have an excellent curriculum. The children are taught science in an Islamic way: there is none of this rubbish about evolution. The children learn that the Koran tells the truth about the origins of the universe. Every day, the children learn the Koran and learn that Allah's word is law. It is an excellent school.

Mohammed was very pleased with the discipline in the school; the children worked in silence and never misbehaved. He was, though, concerned that his son was not learning very much English. Although he was largely pleased with the school, it was clear to me that this school was not educating its pupils very well: the curriculum was almost all rote-learning and copying.

Such schools and any school that preaches a rigid doctrine, need to be brought into the state sector if society is going to stop generations of children being indoctrinated by fundamentalist dogma.

Academically selective schools

Just how good are grammar schools? If you measure them by results, then they number among the best schools in the country. All grammar schools are focused upon achieving the top results in the country, and they do this by rigorously testing their pupils at frequent intervals, and often weeding out those who are going to achieve sub-standard results before they take public exams.

Educational journalist and author Francis Beckett had this to say about the school where his son went:

I went to grammar school when I was 11. It was lovely and I have nothing but happy memories. In those days, it was so close to the 1944 Education Act that the very idea that you had working-class children being given an education was radical, and so, in their own way, grammar schools were thought of as egalitarian and enlightened.

In my view though, grammar schools nowadays are decayed, rotting institutions which are desperately status conscious and trying to pretend to be public schools. This was certainly true of the grammar school which my son went to.

That school ruthlessly pruned the kids who were not going to do well academically both at the eleven-plus stage and as the pupils passed through each year, with a final very heavy prune after GSCE and before A level so that no boy was allowed to take any subject at A level unless his teacher had given a firm prediction that he would get an A. As a result, my son's school always appears top of the league tables for state schools. It looks as though this is due to the masterly teaching at the school when in actual fact those fantastic results can almost exclusively be explained by the fact that the school creams off the top pupils at the eleven-plus, and then forces any under-achieving pupils out.

I saw this happen with my own son. One of the A levels he wanted to take was French. He got an A at GCSE but the staff insisted that he took a different A level to enter the sixth form because his teacher said she was not sure that he was willing to work hard enough to get an A at A level. He left and went to a sixth-form college and got an A at French there.

What this grammar school tends to do, and other grammars do to a lesser degree, is pick on parents with 'under-achieving children' but who are not confident and not that well educated. They drag the parents in to speak to the head. The head with his deputy sit looking grim with gowns on and frown as they explain that so and so will be much better off at another school. They'll find some minor misdemeanour that the child has done and threaten to expel the child. Then they'll add that it will be better for the child's future if he doesn't have such exclusion permanently on his record.

This is a classic way that unscrupulous schools get rid of undesirable pupils.

While Beckett obviously has an axe to grind, his comments should be taken into account because the reality is that grammar schools today are cut-throat places that tend not to tolerate under-achieving pupils because they affect their place in the league tables. On the whole, they feel under threat because the Labour government has an agenda to stop selective schooling. As a result, they are extremely keen to prove their credentials by attaining marvellous results – which they do year after year.

City Academies

Their shiny plate-glass walls glitter and shimmer amidst litter-strewn streets, emerging from the dirty ground like a hi-tech beast rising out of a swamp. The aim is that these leviathans should swallow the pupils in these deprived areas and spit them out as successful, high-achieving pupils. Until these academies arrived it appeared that improving the results of children in the local area was very difficult indeed: all academies are being built where once there was a failing school.

They are undoubtedly one of Tony Blair's big ideas. He has been desperate to make them succeed, so desperate it appears there are suspicions that he and his party may have considered political favours in return for financial support. However, none of the suspicions has been proved.

City Academies have proved very popular with parents because they are so wonderfully resourced but it remains to be seen whether they will make good schools. Since 1997, 19 City Academies have been built, usually on the grounds where failing schools used to be. Nearly £5 billion is being spent on building these schools without much evidence that they are better than their predecessors. A Commons education committee, which had conducted a two-year inquiry into the academies, said that they were increasingly choosing pupils and that it was 'difficult to detect a coherent overarching strategy in the government's proposals'.[1]

The main message here is: be wary about government propaganda regarding City Academies. The government claims that they are improving faster than other schools were recently thrown into question by an analysis by the *Times Educational Supplement*. In October 2005, Tony Blair said, 'We have seen academies – still relatively new independent state schools – improving this year at more than three times the national average.'

In fact, this was complete nonsense. The increase in the proportion of academy pupils achieving five or more GCSEs, including English and maths, was 1.3 points. The national average rise was 1.7 points. So from this analysis, pupils at academies are definitely not doing as well as they could be at other schools.[2]

Parents and teachers have fewer rights at City Academies than they do at other state schools because of the academies' semi-independent status, which means they are not answerable to the LEA and are not bound by much of the legislation that affects other state schools. Potentially, this could mean less influence for parents on governing bodies, fewer rights for SEN pupils and fewer rights over exclusions. At a number of the academies there are significant worries that special interest groups, particularly religious fundamentalists, are dictating the way the schools are run and the content of some lessons.[3]

Having said all this, my own investigations into the schools have not confirmed many of the liberal left's worst fears about such schools. Having looked at a number of different academies, it appears that many of them seem to be bending over backwards to accommodate a real mix of pupils, with many of them favouring SEN pupils in their admissions criteria.

It is still very early days. We need to see how they progress over the next ten years before any really genuine judgements can be made. In the meantime, I am inclined to give them the benefit of the doubt. I would certainly much prefer to send my child to an academy than the failing school that languished on the same land in previous years.

Good points about City Academies	Things to look out for
They are well resourced, and certainly look like good learning environments.	Don't be blinded by the architecture: check to see the academy offers a good, balanced curriculum.
They promise to have a firm grip on discipline.	Be careful that this is not just PR. Talk to parents with pupils at the school about the discipline.
Their results appear to be an improvement upon the schools they replaced.	Don't trust the figures completely. Make sure to use the guide earlier in the book to check that the academy is teaching the pupils well.
They are very popular with parents.	Parents aren't always right.

Are single-sex schools the best schools?

They are definitely a dying breed. In the last 40 years, over 2,000 single-sex schools have vanished from England because, in recent decades, society has taken a dim view of the separation of boys and girls at school, feeling that it is detrimental to the psychological development of children to be segregated from the opposite sex.

However, myths about single-sex schools persist: many parents assume that girls in particular do better academically in single-sex schools where they are not distracted by horrid boys. However, recent research by Alan Smithers, Professor at Buckingham University and director of the Centre for Education and Employment Research, has claimed that there are not 'any dramatic or consistent advantages for single-sex education' for boys or girls. 'The reason people think single-sex schools are better is because they do well in league tables,' said Smithers. 'But they are generally independent, grammar or former grammar schools and they do well because of the ability and social background of the pupils.' Smithers said head teachers made 'exaggerated claims' about the benefits of girl-only schools because they were under threat.[4]

Boys' problems

But there is no doubt that the education system as a whole is failing many boys. The gulf between the sexes has remained stubbornly high in the past few years, with 10 per cent more girls than boys gaining five or more A*– C GCSE grades in 2003. More than six per cent of boys leave school with no GCSEs and boys are five times more likely to be excluded from school.[5]

Some educationalists believe that boys fall behind in exams and the jobs market because teachers do not nurture male traits such as competitiveness and leadership. Instead, they argue, schools celebrate qualities closely associated with girls, such as methodical working and attentiveness in class.

It is important to remember that single-sex schools are doing just as badly as mixed-sex schools at dealing with the problem. They are better placed to give boys more competitive and outdoor activities to take part in. Many do exactly that, but still can't manage to raise the boys' game.

The problem for me is not so much that the curriculum is not 'boy-centred' enough, but that it fails to give boys the proper literacy skills at an early enough age. Many of the boys I have taught simply do not know how to read and write decently by the time they reach secondary school and are always struggling to catch up as a result. It doesn't matter whether they do all the outdoor activities in the world, whether they are taught by a woman or a man, whether they are in a competitive atmosphere or a cooperative one, if they can't read!

The problem really lies with the way boys are taught to read at a very early age. Many have not learned to read by the synthetic phonics method and, consequently, they simply don't have the tools to tackle the reading of difficult words.

The Literacy Trust (www.literacytrust.org.uk) and other educationalists are currently trying to promote 'boy-friendly' reading lists which might enthuse boys to read more. Unfortunately, this can lead to some pretty crude gender stereotyping whereby boys are supplied with texts that adults think they will find 'cool': violent, action-packed texts which are the antithesis of 'girly' books like Jacqueline Wilson's. In my experience, boys are turned off areas in the school library which are obviously there to attract them; they need to be encouraged subtly.

Ultimately, boys need to be challenged and enthused to read what the teachers and parents think are worthwhile texts, not what they think boys will find cool. One of my greatest successes in my teaching career was with a recalcitrant, difficult boy called James Allchurch who refused to read anything during the first year of his GCSE course. Instead of choosing a 'boy-friendly' text to read with the class such as *Of Mice and Men* I demanded that my mixed-sex class, which contained some naughty boys, read one of the most 'girly' books in the world, *Wuthering Heights*. James moaned and groaned about this, but I persisted, insisting that the novel was one of the greatest stories of obsession and family dysfunction ever written. In his mock exam, James achieved an unclassified grade, but then was eventually stirred to read the book properly. He attained an A grade in his final exam because he read the book carefully. It was the highest GCSE grade he achieved.

If I had been teaching James in an all-boys school I probably would not have taught *Wuthering Heights*, but the mixed-sex school environment meant that I considered both genders and chose Bronte's classic instead of the more masculine and much easier to read Steinbeck. It paid off because I refused to be swayed by stereotypes of what a boy should and should not read.

Advantages of a single-sex school	Disadvantages
It allows teachers to cater for gender-specific interests.	It leads to stereotyping of the sexes.
Hormones don't distract in lessons.	Boys and girls fail to learn about each other from an early age and this causes all manner of confusion later on.
Results are better in selective single-sex schools.	A careful analysis of the results of single-sex schools shows that while some selective single-sex schools achieve great results, overall, single-sex schools are no better or worse than their mixed-sex counterparts.

Are private schools the best?

I attended state primary schools and spent half a term at a comprehensive before my parents decided that enough was enough and that I had to go to the local private school. I sat a simple entrance exam, where my maths and English were tested, passed it, and then had to catch up on the work I had missed. It was only then that I realised the gulf between the private and state sector: I had to learn pages of Latin and French vocabulary, read about the Tudors, complete English comprehension exercises and work through a great deal of maths. It was a real shock. The sheer volume of work was huge compared with what had been asked from me in my state schools.

When I joined the school I was bullied for having long, red hair and for generally being a shy, unconfident boy who had joined the school late. I found the all-boys school, which was dominated by the sons of wealthy East End businessmen, a yobbish place: weak teachers were mercilessly mocked by pupils and often forced to leave due to stress. In the playground, the games were much more violent than anything I had encountered at the comprehensive or primary school.

Nevertheless, I thrived there because most of the teachers were knowledgeable and confident. They demanded high standards from the pupils, they set proper homework, they marked the pupils work regularly and effectively, and reported every half-term on pupils' progress in all subjects and provided a written report every term. All pupils sat formal, internally assessed exams twice a year and rankings of pupils were posted on the school noticeboard. Playing sport was a big part of the timetable with games on Wednesday and Saturday afternoons: although I wasn't that great I played in house teams at football, hockey and cricket.

On the whole, I enjoyed the curriculum; I loved studying Latin, learning the vocabulary and grammar and reading its literature. I liked writing essays for history and English, I felt fulfilled completing lots of repetitive exercises in maths and was perfectly content making notes and doing the odd experiment in science. I was grateful for the homework too, because it meant that I could escape from the silences and tensions that existed at home. Often I would spend three hours a night on my homework. At that point, I wasn't a 'naturally bright' student – I struggled with my reading and writing until I reached my teens – but my ability to learn the content of the curriculum and to regurgitate it in an exam meant that I actually did rather well.

Among the top pupils in my class, which was one of the bottom 'bands' in the year, there was a really competitive work ethic. We were called 'swots' by the other boys but we wore this badge with pride. We liked being top of the league tables of boys at the end of every term, we counted the number of 'Vs' (Very Goods – the top effort grade) that we got in our reports and we basked in the glory of having our essays read out to the class.

The competition motivated us but it broke some of the other boys who were down at the bottom of the class. My brother, who was in the top stream of the school a year below me, didn't appear to appreciate this sort of competition. Even though he was very high achieving for his age he did not do well in class; he frequently got into fights with other class members and actually was made physically ill by this Darwinian academic system. I remember following him down a corridor and watching him being sick outside the school kitchens; he wasn't happy at all.

He was removed from the school and sent to an inner-city comprehensive which my mother thought would be better for him than the slack comprehensive I initially attended. He hated it there too, and was frequently involved in fights. He still speaks of the school in bitter tones: knife fights frequently occurred at the school and he often felt frightened for his physical safety. Nevertheless, he got ten GCSEs there and went back to the private school for the sixth form, from where he managed to get into Cambridge to read Law.

I continued at the private school and did well, getting ten O levels and four A levels. However, the older I got the more I fell foul of the school, finding its rules and regulations restrictive and unenlightened. But I remain grateful to the school because it taught me what hard work really is. The work ethic it instilled in me has never left me.

In many ways, my experiences of the school are instructive. While state schools have changed immeasurably since the 1980s with the introduction of the National Curriculum and numerous other initiatives, my school has remained more or less the same: many of the staff are still there, the reporting and examination system is very similar, games are still a big thing and the rules and regulations haven't changed much. League tables of pupils have been abolished, and pupils are called by their first name, but apart from that, a boy's experience there will be quite similar to mine. I flourished there because I was a particular type of student: hard-working, competitive, and conformist. My brother didn't get on well there because he resented the competitive atmosphere, didn't want to conform to the strict rules and had the sort of natural intelligence that baulked at the sheer volume of work he was presented with.

This remains true of private schools today. They are institutions which welcome hard-working pupils who look like they will do well, but will expel any troublesome pupils without much delay. They are not bound by the legislation which prevents state schools from expelling pupils.

Myths about private schools

There are a number of myths about private schools that parents should be aware of before they consider sending their child to one:

- **Myth 1** Private schools can take any child from any background and turn him into a winner. This is a pernicious myth perpetuated recently by the media, where pupils who have failed in state schools go to a top private school and appear to succeed. Many private schools are uniquely poor at adapting to pupils who do not conform to their rules and regulations and nearly always expel them before they reflect badly on their results.

- **Myth 2** You have to go to a private school to get into Oxford and Cambridge. It is true that a disproportionate number of pupils from private schools study at Oxbridge, but recent pressure from the government suggests that you might even benefit by sending your child to state school in the sixth form if you want them to go to Oxford or Cambridge: these universities have been asked to discriminate positively in favour of state school children.

- **Myth 3** The best teachers teach in private schools. Much teaching in private schools is 'lecture based': pupils listen to a subject specialist and take notes. Lessons can be quite dull and repetitive. Certainly my observations of the teaching in private schools confirms this; it is much more interested in spoon-feeding pupils than the teaching you will find in the state sector.

- **Myth 4** There is no bullying in private school. Many public schools are choc-a-bloc with bullying. For example, I have heard reports of serious bullying at boarding schools where older pupils supervise younger pupils.

However, there are some myths which are true. It appears that the top jobs in the country are still dominated by people educated at private schools. Research by the Sutton Trust education charity shows that the percentage of top positions in the British media going to former private school pupils has risen by more than 10 per cent since 1986. The percentage attending private schools: judges 76 per cent, barristers 68 per cent, solicitors 55 per cent, members of parliament 32 per cent, frontbenchers 42 per cent, life peers 56 per cent, top media journalists 56 per cent, top TV journalists 56 per cent.

I think the overwhelming reason for this is because private schools are excellent at instilling a very strong work ethic in their pupils, which means these people leave school feeling confident that with persistence they can overcome most obstacles.

Advantages of private schools	Disadvantages
They instil a genuine work ethic.	Too much passive learning.
Have highly competitive atmospheres.	The competition can demotivate certain pupils.
Don't have the social problems of many comprehensives.	Lack social diversity.
The best schools are good for extracurricular activities such as games, music and drama.	Pupils don't have any time for themselves during term time.

Private tutors

The one area where parents do have some degree of genuine choice is in the private tutor they might select to help their child with his or her work. The majority of parents may not have the money to pay for a private school but they usually have some spare cash to pay for the odd lesson with a private tutor. It appears that a huge number of parents hire private tutors; one research study suggests that a quarter of parents have hired a private tutor to help their children with school work.[6] The most famous person is Tony Blair. According to the *Spectator* magazine, the Blairs' sons Euan, 18, and Nicky, 16 at the time, had been receiving private tuition from teachers at Westminster School to supplement their lessons at the state secondary they attended in west London.[7]

Before you hire a private tutor you will need to ask some important questions, including: does your child actually need one? It may be that the extra pressure might actually demotivate him or her and make their grades worse. You will need to talk carefully about this.

However, once both of you have agreed that you need one, you need to do your research. Most crucially you must make sure that your tutor is properly qualified and is able to teach the same syllabus that your child is doing. I have come across a number of children whose parents have hired private tutors that have been worse than useless because they have taught the wrong syllabus! Ideally, you should talk to the teacher at your child's school and find out all the relevant details before you hire the tutor. Some primary schools actively encourage them, others do not. You will need to make your own judgements about these attitudes, but you should be very wary of schools that are virtually blackmailing you to get a tutor in order to disguise their own faults.

THE NEW SCHOOL RULES
for private schools

1. Talk it through Always discuss the decision to hire a tutor with your child. You must get his or her agreement.

▶

If you can, talk to your child's teachers and see what they think. Ask for the relevant syllabus they are studying and copies of previous exam papers: you are entitled to do this. It may be that you can help your child yourself and save yourself the money. If you can, discuss whether to get a private tutor with your child's school. Don't be blackmailed into getting a tutor though; if your child has a learning difficulty they should receive extra funding and help from the school (see Chapter 4 Does Your Child Have Special Needs?). Equally, if the teaching in your child's school is substandard you need to address this matter urgently with the head teacher and, if necessary, the governing body.

2. **Be cautious** of teachers at your child's school who are touting for extra money. Many teachers run revision lessons free of charge, recognising the need for these lessons.

3. **Investigate** Always ask to see the tutor's qualifications yourself, including their passport, their degree certificate(s), two reputable references and a Criminal Records Bureau (CRB) check. All qualified teachers in England have to have such a document which proves they have no criminal convictions, and all private tutors should produce one. Don't trust the agency you have signed up with to do this unless they explicitly say they do it. Ask the tutors how familiar they are with the syllabus your child is studying and what resources they have to offer which are relevant. The Internet has a whole host of different private tutoring sites. Many of them offer free access to tutors. You will need to check their documentation very carefully. Remember, do not reveal your phone number and address to them until you are satisfied about them.

Crammers

The most famous attendee of a crammer was Martin Amis, the notable novelist, who had performed very badly at all his other schools. He was rescued by a small tutorial college which did nothing but teach him how to pass the relevant exams to get him into Oxford University, something which he managed to do. It appeared that the crammer suited Amis's obsessional mind: its sole focus was upon cramming as many facts as possible into him and enabling him to regurgitate them in a form which would please the examiners. In many ways, this is typical of the modern day 'crammer' or 'tutorial college' as they like to be known.

These utilitarian places are best when they have very, very small class sizes. Usually, sessions are one-to-one or one-to-two and the main thrust of the lessons is that pupils complete test papers and then go through them with their tutor. Pupils have more often than not failed to get the right grades to get into university or a decent sixth form and are attending the college for a year or a few months in order to improve their grades. The quality of the tutors is paramount here: all good ones will have the syllabus to hand and will spend some considerable time working out a pupil's strengths and weaknesses in a subject and acting upon them.

THE NEW SCHOOL RULE

about crammers

Investigate As with private tutors, check out the quality of the tutor in your chosen subject: is he or she a trained specialist? Has he or she been an examiner in the subject? You will be paying hefty fees so it is worth knowing what you are buying. Make sure your child is organising his or her time properly and not drifting around doing nothing

▶

during the periods when there are no lessons, or no test papers to complete. Don't assume that your child will make great friends at the college. Most of the 'extras' of school will be entirely absent. Much of the time will be spent outside the classroom completing test papers. When being taught, pupils will not come into contact with many other pupils. It can be a lonely business. If your child requires more of a social life, check to see if the crammer makes provision for this with social functions and so on.

CHAPTER 9

Getting the most out of the National Curriculum

The National Curriculum is like the Amazon rainforest; it has its own ecosystem, which was grown from scratch in the late 1980s and was officially protected by the law in 1989. The first National Curriculum was so complicated and contained so many tangled thickets of information that much of it was chopped down by a review in the 1990s. It has been revised a bit since then, and was due for another revision in 2006, but essentially the content remains the same as it was after the revision in the previous decade.

I will admit it. I have loathed the National Curriculum for many years. As a teacher, I've seen the worst of it: the constant changes, the seemingly arbitrary content, the foolish systems of assessment. I've complained about them all – as have many teachers.

And yet, to a certain extent, I am going to have to eat my words. Suddenly, looking at it from the perspective of a parent, and not a teacher, I can see that it's been a good thing.

If a parent is reasonably knowledgeable about the National Curriculum, they could not only learn some pretty interesting stuff but also help their child substantially, while keeping tabs on whether their child's school is doing its job or not.

It is a jungle of information, and it is impossible to know all of it, but it is perfectly possible to learn the basic lie of the land in an hour's concentrated reading. This is well worth doing because you will understand the shape, scope and content of what your child is being taught in school, and be able to make a significant contribution to their education as a result. Even if your child is being taught in a private school, which is exempt from doing the National Curriculum, most schools follow its structure now.

Common themes

There are some common themes that are reinforced in subject after subject, in Key Stage after Key Stage. These are:

- Literacy skills: the use of key terminology, the structuring of texts, the way texts are shaped by their different audiences.

- Numeracy skills: the practical use of numbers and maths in everyday situations.

- Analysing texts and data.

- The difference between facts and opinions.

- Investigative methods.

For all its entwined forests of content, the National Curriculum is not actually about content at all. It is about giving children the tools to analyse any given situation when they have left school, to make them at the very least competent readers and writers, and reasonable mathematicians and scientists. These are fairly straightforward aims, but, too often, teachers, parents, bureaucrats and politicians forget them as they become mired in the detail of the project.

The central problem with the National Curriculum, then, is not its aims, which are laudable, but its implementation. It is very confusing for teachers, pupils, and anyone else who cares to examine it. Depending upon your point of view it is either not prescriptive enough or too prescriptive! I see-saw between both points of view depending upon my mood. If I was a hardened prescriptivist I would want a curriculum which laid out exactly what was to be taught day by day, week by week, and enjoy knowing that up and down the country, the same content was being taught everywhere. However, you definitely can't be sure of that with the National Curriculum; there is no government-issued textbook for all the subjects which schools in the country have to work through. Schools and teachers have been left to interpret it themselves. This has led to huge variations in execution.

And yet, the National Curriculum is prescriptive enough to stifle quite a bit of innovation. There is a lot of content to get through: the government wants everyone to be busy. It has not laid down a clear path so teachers frequently find themselves wading laboriously through swamps of information as fast as they can just so that they cover everything. This has led to uninspired teaching.

THE NEW SCHOOL RULES
about the National Curriculum

1. **Talk it through** Throughout your child's education emphasise the unity and relevance of knowledge by talking to him or her about the ordinary world. While they may be learning English, maths, science, design and technology, art and design, geography and history as separate subjects in schools, all these facets come together in so many ways in the ordinary, normal everyday world. Take, for example, a simple shop front – which might contain elements of art, design, poetic techniques, a knowledge of other cultures and history, mathematics in the way it was measured, science in the way it is lit up, and so on.

▶

2. **Have fun** You have one massive advantage over all your child's teachers: within reason, you can go places. It takes an awful lot of paperwork for a teacher to go on a trip, and mostly they don't. But a trip to a museum can be worth a thousand lessons. Playing an instrument helps your child's intelligence in all areas. There is a big correlation between academic achievement and playing a musical instrument and it is worth the effort to encourage it, even if it is just playing the recorder. It appears that playing an instrument stimulates the brain in a way which really assists with academic subjects.

2. **Be curious** Ask key questions which assist analysis and thought, again and again. What did you like best about that? What didn't you like? Why? What's your favourite? What do you like least? These sort of evaluative questions are at the heart of the curriculum, which is trying to cultivate the spirit of investigation and enquiry.

3. **Focus on the big three subjects** English, maths and science, and the rest will fall into place. If your child has a grasp of these subjects, then they won't fail.

The Key Stages

There are five Key Stages in the National Curriculum. At the end of each stage, pupils are tested and are expected to reach a minimum level.

Key Stage	Age range and School Years	Minimum level expected in Key Stage tests
Key Stage 1	5–7-year-olds (Years 1–3)	Level 2

Key Stage	Age range and School Years	Minimum level expected in Key Stage tests
Key Stage 2	8–11-year-olds (Years 4–6)	Level 4
Key Stage 3	12–14-year-olds (Years 7–9)	Levels 5 and 6
Key Stage 4	15–16-year-olds (Years 10–11)	Grade C or above in GCSE, pass at GNVQ
Key Stage 5	17–18-year-olds (Years 12–13)	E grade or above at A level

Key Stage 1

What subjects are taught at Key Stage 1? All state schools have to teach all the National Curriculum subjects:

- English
- mathematics
- science
- design and technology
- information and communication technology
- history
- geography
- art and design
- music
- physical education

They also have to teach:

- religious education
- personal, social and health education and citizenship is optional but most schools teach these subjects

Not every subject will be taught in separate lessons.

Key Stage 2

At Key Stage 2, all state schools have to teach all these National Curriculum subjects:

- English
- mathematics
- science
- design and technology
- information and communication technology
- history
- geography
- art and design
- music
- physical education
- personal, social and health education and citizenship is optional but most schools teach these subjects.

Not every subject will be taught in separate lessons.

Key Stage 3

At Key Stage 3, all state schools have to teach these National Curriculum subjects:

- English
- mathematics
- science
- design and technology
- information and communication technology
- history

- geography
- modern foreign languages
- art and design
- music
- physical education
- citizenship
- religious education
- personal, social and health education is optional but most schools teach this subject.

Not every subject will be taught in separate lessons, although most are at secondary school.

Key Stage 4

The compulsory National Curriculum subjects at Key Stage 4 are:

- English
- mathematics
- science
- design and technology
- information and communication technology
- physical education (at least two hours a week)
- citizenship
- religious education, careers education, sex education (these are compulsory but not National Curriculum subjects)
- a modern foreign language is no longer compulsory
- other subjects the school chooses to make compulsory: these might include, for example, personal, social and health education, or an arts course

Options:
Other courses that your child can choose might include: modern languages, history, geography, art, music, business studies, health and social care, leisure and tourism.

At Key Stage 4, pupils can take vocational qualifications or more academic ones such as GCSEs. This area is becoming increasingly complex and is changing from year to year.

Key Stage 5

Pupils can take either A levels, which are academic qualifications, or vocational qualifications.

Education is voluntary after 16, and there are no compulsory subjects that must be taken. However, some schools can make certain subjects compulsory if they wish to do so.

Key Stage tests

All the tests your child will be given in their school career from Years 1–9 will be inextricably tied up with the National Curriculum. Get clued up on your National Curriculum content and you're much more certain of success.

Key Stage 1 tests

At the age of six or seven, during Year 2, your child will have English and maths tests. Pupils are asked to complete a series of preparatory tasks between January and June, and then take the tests during May.

Don't be scared of the tests. Many parents I have spoken to have got in a real panic about them, only to find that their children actually enjoyed them. The English Key Stage 1 tests assesses your child's reading, writing, handwriting and spelling skills, while the maths tests contain questions on addition, subtraction, multiplication, division, graphs, money, shapes and problem solving.

The tests provide what is called 'baseline' data upon which all your child's other performances are measured. Your child should be scoring approximately a Level 2. Within this level they may be assigned a Level 2a: the highest score, a 2b: a mid-ranking score, or 2c: the lowest score within the level. If they score a level 3, they are above the national average.

THE NEW SCHOOL RULES
for Key Stage 1 tests

1. **Don't panic** Your attitude is more important than your child's at this stage. If you get in a real panic about the tests then your child will, afterwards, forever associate panic with tests. Try not to be anxious. Read to your child, talk about reading, encourage the writing of thank-you notes, play games like draughts, battleships and Monopoly to develop their maths and social skills.

2. **Be suspicious** of schools that are drilling the children for the tests or are doing very little to prepare for them.

3. **Investigate** Examine your child's results carefully. Ask for a breakdown of the scores. If he or she is below average in any of the scores, that is achieving a Level 1, you should investigate and see if they have a learning difficulty (see Chapter 4 Does Your Child Have Special Needs?). Above average, then ask about gifted and talented programmes for your child: is he or she being stretched enough?

Key Stage 2 tests

These are the tests that primary schools in England are ranked on, and are notoriously unreliable. Unfortunately, far too many schools drill their children for these tests and this leads to real pupil disenchantment.

Your child will be tested once again on English and maths in Year 6. The tests follow a strict format and there are many revision guides on the market that will assist considerably with all the different varieties of question. Pupils should attain a Level 4 in both tests: Level 3 is below the national average, and Level 5 is above the national average.

THE NEW SCHOOL RULES
for Key Stage 2 tests

1. **Keep calm** Be the voice of reason. Don't let your child panic about the tests, and protest if your child is being bored to death with completing numerous practice tests during Year 6. All the research evidence shows the best schools that attain the highest results do not drill their children for the tests, but teach a balanced curriculum which includes some practice tests, leavened with far more interesting material as well.

2. **Investigate** Examine your child's results carefully. Most crucially, has he or she progressed from Key Stage 1? There should be a rise of at least two levels: so a Level 2 at Key Stage 1 in maths, should now be a Level 4 for maths and the same for English. For English look at the breakdown of scores for reading and writing. Are scores higher on one than the other? Many pupils' reading scores are comparatively low compared with their writing scores because, unfortunately, too many pupils are being switched off reading by the time they come to the end of primary school. Compare Teacher Assessment (TA) scores with test scores: do they match? Do the teachers think he or she is brighter than the results actually show? Is your child panicking in tests? If so,

▶

why? Or is it the opposite? Also, ask to see any other data the school has on your child. Most schools test pupils' IQs at some point. Does the IQ score for verbal reasoning match the Key Stage test scores? For example, if he or she is above average in Key Stage 2 English tests, is there a corresponding above average IQ for verbal reasoning? If there's no match, why is this? Ask the teachers.

3. **Never forget** Don't forget your child's results when she goes to secondary school: compare the levels assigned in Years 7–9 with primary levels: do they match? If they don't, why not? What is going on? Many, many pupils suffer what is known as the 'Year 8' dip where they actually do worse in Year 8 in English and maths than they did in Year 6. Beware of this.

Key Stage 3 tests

In Year 9, all pupils at state schools take tests in English, maths and science. The average level pupils should be scoring in these tests is a Level 5 or low Level 6 (i.e., 6c). However, pupils should be moving up at least one or preferably two levels. Real alarm bells should be ringing if your child stays on a level or has only moved up one level.

These are the most pressurised tests your child will have taken. Believe me, I know all about them because I have taught the Key Stage 3 English tests since they started in the early 1990s. Once again, the danger for teachers is that they teach far too much for the test and bore their pupils to death. I have been guilty of this on occasions because I have been paranoid about getting poor test scores. I am less anxious now, knowing that if I teach some good books and engage the children with the basics, then they'll do well. However, I am aware that much important work is done in Years 7 and 8, where preparatory tests should be given, and mock marks issued to pupils and parents.

THE NEW SCHOOL RULES

for Key Stage 3 tests

1. **Watch out** Keep an eye on your child's National Curriculum assessment scores during Year 7 and 8; don't leave your concern until Year 9 and have a great big panic then. If your child is slipping or achieving below average scores in Year 7 and 8, you must demand that they receive extra help. Again, it may be that a learning difficulty is at issue (see Chapter 4 Does Your Child Have Special Needs?).

2. **Be enthusiastic** With English, getting your child enthused about Shakespeare is important because he will be tested on a Shakespeare play in Key Stage 3 tests. Again, going to plays and watching films from Year 7 and 8 will help with this. It doesn't matter if they are not the 'set' play; simply making your child familiar with the language and theatricality of the plays helps a great deal.

3. **Investigate** There are millions of revision guides on the market. Ask your school about the most suitable one or refer to Appendix B in this book.

4. **Get extra help** If your child achieves a low Level 5 or below in their tests, you really should seek extra help if you want A–C grades in English, maths and science GCSEs. Ask the school about this, or hire private tutors if necessary.

GCSEs

I have frequently been asked what the secret to good revision is. My answer is simple: do the work in the lessons. Far too many pupils think they can muck around in lessons, buy the revision ~ide and then get a great grade.

If your child has good literacy and numeracy skills then he or she will almost certainly do well in their GCSEs. Get the 3 Rs right and success follows. Most GCSEs nowadays are not content driven. In other words, your child does not have to remember vast quantities of material in order to do well. They are much more skills based, which means pupils are often provided with the content they need in the exam and then are asked to interpret, analyse or rewrite it. These sorts of interpretative skills are not acquired by a few nights' revision: you need to have listened carefully over a period of a few years to attain the highest marks. It is true that good literacy and numeracy skills and a high degree of common sense will probably get you a C grade, but really the top pupils are expected to attain A or A* grades. To do this, you have to have listened pretty carefully and been well taught.

THE NEW SCHOOL RULES
for GCSEs

1. **Focus upon the important stuff** English, maths and science are the really important GCSEs. Your child should be aiming for a C or above in all of them.

2. **Investigate** Choose the other GCSEs carefully. Some are taken more seriously than others. A good grade in a modern language GCSE is a prestigious award. Some of the vocational GCSEs have yet to prove their worth.

3. **Talk it through** As with everything, talk through all the different choices with your child explaining the pros and cons of each one.

The importance of the Assessment Objectives and revision

I have had excellent pupils coming to me in tears because they have scored poorly in their GCSEs and haven't had a clue why. They've known the subject inside out, and without fail write coherent, knowledgeable essays. When we've asked for a copy of their exam answer, we've found out the reason they've done badly and been more than a little outraged. It wasn't that they had written bad answers, they hadn't. Under the old system of marking GCSEs they would have attained top marks. Not so now. You see, the answers, despite being well written and valid, didn't meet the Assessment Objectives laid down in the subject.

With all GCSEs and A levels now, each exam or piece of coursework is marked on the basis of what are known as Assessment Objectives (or AOs in the jargon). It is important that pupils know these Assessment Objectives while studying their courses and revise their subjects according to them.

THE NEW SCHOOL RULES

for revision

1. **Support those teachers** Stress this blindingly obvious but much ignored point to your child: there is no better revision than working in lessons. Use the teacher first before relying on revision guides.

2. **Help your child be organised** Draw up a revision timetable: a little bit each day. Revise using the relevant Assessment Objectives for the subject. If you don't know what these are, ask your teacher or consult the websites of the exam boards (www.aqa.org.uk, www.edexcel.org. uk, www.ocr.org.uk). This may take some research as they

▶

can be buried in the syllabi (see pages 334–68 for the Assessment Objectives of the major National Curriculum subjects).

3. **Have fun** Make the revision interesting. Use spider diagrams, colours, posters, poems, music, tape-recording and videoing relevant material. However, don't get so bogged down in learning about revision techniques that you don't do any revision. Sometimes the best revision is simply copying out key phrases from the relevant texts! I passed all my O and A levels this way.

4. **Talk it through** Ask your child to explain to you the key concepts in each subject.

5. **Get them to use their friends** Ask your child to buddy up with a trusted pupil and get them to explain key concepts to each other. One of the best ways of remembering or understanding something is to speak about it out loud.

6. **Be cautious** Don't trust the web for revision, except for the really reliable sites such as the BBC or sites recommended by the school. I have had pupils who have spent hours reading rubbish on the web when they could have spent that time actually reading the books they were being tested upon.

Choosing A levels – don't believe the hysteria

The press have become hysterical about the 'gold standard' of the A level being dumbed down recently, and have pointed an accusing finger at so-called 'Mickey Mouse' subjects like media studies being responsible for a massive upsurge in pupils getting A grades. This kind of hype is exceptionally misleading. Some parents and pupils might think that media studies is the thing to do because it's easy to get an A grade in, whereas maths and chemistry is much harder. The reverse is actually true. In the summer of 2006, on average one in four pupils received an A grade at A level, but in some subjects this average was either higher or lower. Most interestingly, in maths, 41 per cent of pupils received an A grade, whereas in further maths a staggering 56 per cent received an A grade. In chemistry, 30 per cent attained A grades. However, in media studies only 11 per cent attained A grades.

There is an important message here: don't think that opting for what is thought of as the soft option subjects will mean a pupil has a better chance of getting a higher grade.

THE NEW SCHOOL RULES
about the sixth form

1. **Investigate** Choose a mix of A levels, try to include maths, a science subject or a foreign language if you can – these are all highly regarded by the universities.

2. **Talk it through** Think carefully about applying to university before choosing A levels. For example, taking English language A level will significantly hinder a pupil from studying English literature at university if he or she hasn't taken English literature A level as well.

3. **Don't believe in media myths** Don't assume the soft option subjects are the ones where it is easier to get an A grade.

The truth about reading

The real test, for me, comes when my pupils start to read Thomas Hardy's *Far From the Madding Crowd* for their GCSE course. Most of my pupils have done well at school and in tests but that doesn't necessarily mean that they are hugely literate. Many of them scratch their heads at Hardy's complex prose, unable to even pronounce some of the longer words. I ask them, 'Weren't you taught in primary school all the different letter sounds?' Half of the class shake their heads.

One boy told me, 'I was one of the best readers in my school but I didn't learn much about letter sounds, only the simplest ones.' Millions of pupils, both high- and low-achieving ones, have found school life very difficult for one simple reason: they haven't been taught to read and write properly.

Since the mid-1990s, most primary schools have spent an hour a day teaching literacy because tests revealed that children leaving the schools were not properly literate and, as a result, were unable to cope with the demands of the secondary curriculum.

The Bullock Report

There is no doubt that the English education system has struggled to teach reading and writing very well for the past 50 years. Successive governments have chopped and changed over the issue, unable to decide what it is best for our children. In the 1975 Bullock Report investigating the issue it was stated, 'There is no one method, medium, device, approach or philosophy that holds the key to the process of learning to read.'

The Bullock Report led to a free-for-all which allowed some crazy – and sane – ideas to flourish in schools. Frank Smith, a highly influential reading guru of previous decades, argued that children should learn to read by doing it, the way they learn to speak. However, neurological research has discredited the idea; speaking is a natural function, reading is not. Smith's method of shoving books in front of children led to all sorts of problems:

children looked like they could read, when in actual fact they could not. Having being taught by the 'whole-book method', these pupils hadn't learned the sophisticated code that lies behind the written English language.

Finally, the bureaucrats in Whitehall have seen sense and are now insisting that schools teach 'synthetic phonics'. This is where children first learn the 44 individual phonemes, or sound units of the English language such as 'a', 'b', 'ie' and so on, rather than decoding whole words first by breaking them down phonetically, or by trying to work them out from the context of the book.

This is the method that James, my son, learnt to read by. Now I can see that he is actually, in essence, a better reader than I am. I was taught the whole-book method and I still struggle to break down an unfamiliar word into its constitute parts. Because he knows all of his phonemes he is able to read unfamiliar words very easily. Some serious studies into the issue have revealed that children who learn by the synthetic phonics method are much better readers and writers than those who don't.

A 2006 government review[1] into reading concludes that synthetic phonics offers 'the vast majority of beginners the best route to becoming skilled readers'. It says children should be taught:

- The links between sounds and letters in a clearly defined, incremental sequence for example, S, M, C, T, G P, A, O.

- The skill of blending sounds all the word in order to read it, for example S-T-R-E-E-T.

- To split words into sounds in order to spell them.

But rather than advocate one or more of the phonics programmes on the market, the report sets out common features of all good synthetic phonics programmes.

Speaking and listening are stressed as being very important. Play, stories, songs, rhymes and drama are vital, as well as pre-reading activities such as sharing stories with adults.

At about the age of five, children should have short 20-minute sessions to help them with their reading. Multi-sensory methods such as copying letter shapes with arms should be used and letter names taught as well as sounds. But children should not be denied access to favourite books at any stage.

Teachers should explicitly teach irregular words such as 'the' and 'was'. But crucially, children should not be taught to infer words from context or pictures, contrary to the previous government pronouncements on the matter.[2]

Many of the best schools have sought to make 'synthetic phonics' a little more interesting than just the repetitive learning of letter sounds. At Kingshott prep school in Hitchin, Hertfordshire, the denizens of Church Farm all talk in vowel sounds. The cows say 'moo', the scarecrows yell 'oi' and the farmer says 'arr'. Church Farm is the setting for Church Farm Sounds, a phonics scheme invented by the school which aims to make children associate specific sounds with particular characters. For example, the scarecrow shouts 'oi' at troublesome crows in early books. While children may have trouble sounding out 'boil' or 'soil' in more advanced books, they will associate the 'oi' sound with the scarecrow. In a collection of 40 stories, each character on the fictional Church Farm introduces a different sound. Sheila Wearmouth, head of pre-prep at Kingshott, said,

> We're building up the links between pictures and sounds. Phonics can be taught the wrong way round: sounds first, and then association with words. It can be hard to remember a sound. But if children have a picture in their mind, that picture reminds them of a sound. You only need to draw a little sketch, and they have a clue what the sound is.[3]

Dyslexia or bad teaching?

Test scores from recent years indicate that one in four 11-year-olds is unable to read properly. Former head teacher and reading expert Ruth Miskin told *The Sunday Times*, 'I've seen plenty of kids from affluent families, pupils at private schools, the 4 x 4 parked in the drive. These children are often labelled dyslexic or SEN. Not a bit of it: what they are is, to borrow an American acronym, ABT – Ain't Being Taught.'[4]

If you have a child who is struggling with reading, apathetic about it, reluctant to bring books home or has clearly memorised books but not progressed any further, it is worth checking to see that they have been taught the letter sounds of the alphabet properly. Many teachers might describe such children as dyslexic or SEN, but it may be that they are ABT.

While a good school should give your child the tools to read and write with by teaching them synthetic phonics, the most exhaustive studies have shown parents play a huge role in a child's linguistic development. In her illuminating book, *Why Children Can't Read and What We Can Do About It*, Diane Mc-Guinness highlights the American study which Betty Hart and Todd Risley carried out several years ago. They studied 42 families from three social groups and recorded how mothers spoke to their young children during the first two and a half years of life, recording everything which was said to each child for one hour per month. McGuinness writes:

> The average number of words addressed to the children ranged from 1,500 to 2,500 words per hour in homes classified as 'professional', 1,000 to 1,500 in middle-class homes, and 500 to 800 to children on welfare. By the age of three it was estimated that children in professional families had heard nearly 35 million words, middle-class children 20 million words, and welfare children 10 million words. These differences were found even though welfare mothers spent more time with their children. Mothers in the professional group used a more complex sentence structure, a richer vocabulary, and highly affirmative feedback style: 'That's right', 'That's good' along with a more positive tone of voice. Welfare mothers often used a negative tone, and lots of explicit disapproval 'stop that', 'don't spill it' and 'don't do it that way'. However, welfare mothers did not differ in other ways, affection, concern for their children, the cleanliness of home, appropriate reactions to children in need. Nor was race a factor.[5]

McGuinness's vital point is that reading is so much easier if the word already exists in the memory. This American study has been endorsed more recently by some exhaustive research carried about by the DfES which showed conclusively that children who achieved most highly were the ones who had supportive parents.[6] Perhaps most importantly, this research shows that children growing up in these sort of caring homes do the best – irrespective of the social and ethnic background of their parents. The message here is more hopeful than the Hart and Risley research, and to some degree, appears to contradict it: pupils do best when parents communicate regularly with their children.

Clearly though, schools have an important role to play even with children who come from supportive homes. They need to be teaching children how to read and write. If you look carefully at the figures, they are quite shocking. In 1998, seven out of ten pupils achieved the expected Level 4 in reading in English, while only five out of ten achieved the expected Level 4 in writing. If you track this cohort of pupils to 2003, when they all took their GCSEs, you'll discover that only six out of ten achieved a C grade in English GCSE, which is fairly dismal considering 40 per cent of the exam is coursework, and I know that many of those results are vastly inflated. That's four out of ten school leavers exiting the system without a decent grade in English. It begs the question: what have they been doing all that time in the system?

The trouble is that too many schools benefit from having pupils who can't read because they then get put on the SEN register for dyslexia and the school receives extra funding. The system is so ridiculous that it is actually covertly encouraging poor literacy skills.

So where does that leave the poor parent and pupil? Well, you need to be wised up. You need to check to see if your child knows his or her phonics and whether they are reading fluently. Get them to read to you regularly. Talk to them about how they are getting on. Support them.

If the school is not teaching the basic phonic code, you need to be pro-active and complain. Show your head teacher the current research if he or she is not aware of it.

Tick-box culture

Don't underestimate the scale of the problem with children's literacy. Recently, the Royal Society of Literature carried out a detailed survey of undergraduates' writing skills. The Royal Society of Literature's spokesperson, eminent biographer Hilary Spurling, wrote:

> Until they reach university, most young people have never felt any need to write. They belong to a tick-box culture based on speeded-up electronic responses in education as in other fields. Children brought up on video games, PlayStations and the Internet are masters of the search engine and text message. They read little, if at all, and so have no models or more subtle searching or expressive writing to set beside their own.
>
> Meagre vocabulary, slack phrasing, tortured syntax, incompetent punctuation mean that teachers in higher education spend an increasing amount of their time correcting grammar, spelling and punctuation, and trying to explain how an essay is meant to be structured.[7]

THE NEW SCHOOL RULES
about reading and writing

1. **Talk it through** Think aloud with your child. Chatter about anything and everything. Tell stories about your day at work in a way they will understand. Articulate your feelings.

2. **Go over the basics** Teach your child at an early age the very basic letter sounds: 'b', 'c', 'g', 'o'.

3. **Set a good example** Read in front of your child and talk about what you are reading with them.

4. **Investigate** Find a good educational psychologist or

▶

reading specialist (your LEA will help you here) if your child has been diagnosed as having learning difficulties or being dyslexic.

5. **Don't be too pushy** Don't force your child to read. Avoid saying that some reading material is better than others. Encourage reading in any shape or form. Comics and magazines are all good to read from, if they are balanced out with reading from other sources such as novels, plays, poetry.

6. **Use reading schemes** For the very early years, many parents and teachers favour particular reading schemes. The Oxford Reading Tree remains the favourite. My sixth-form pupils still talk in glowing terms about Biff and Chip, the heroes of this particular reading scheme aimed at 4–8-year-olds. If your child is struggling with their reading at this age and they haven't seen the Oxford Reading Tree, you should definitely insist the school tries it. If it won't, go online and get the books yourself: they can be bought quite cheaply second-hand.

7. **Be poetic** Poetry is often the best reading material for children: it is short and thoughtfully written.

Brain checks

What follows in this section, and in all the 'Brain check' sections, are some selected questions which will help you see whether your child is learning the appropriate content in the National Curriculum; all the questions are based on criteria culled from the National Curriculum. I haven't provided the answers, but, for the most part, you can find them easily from any encyclopaedia or by logging on to: www.parentscentre.gov.uk/education andlearning/whatchildrenlearn/. This website contains the information which enabled me to formulate my questions.

An English brain check

English – Key Stage 1

Speaking and listening skills Can your child recount a short anecdote to you clearly? (Ask them to tell you about the most enjoyable trip they have taken recently.)

Reading Can your child read a short book to you? (See if they can read *The Twits* by Roald Dahl.)

Writing Can your child write you a story with a clear beginning, middle and ending using legible handwriting and largely correct spelling? (Give them the title 'The Day My School Burnt Down' and see how they get on.)

English – Key Stage 2

Speaking and listening skills Can your child use some formal English appropriately? (Ask them to pretend that you are the King/Queen and that they have to ask you for permission to use their palace as a holiday home.)

Reading Can your child read the first Harry Potter book, *Harry Potter and the Philosopher's Stone* by J. K. Rowling?

Writing Can your child write a formal letter, which is punctuated and spelt correctly, to their teacher asking for an extra week's holiday?

English – Key Stage 3

Speaking and listening skills Are you are able to carry out a mock job interview with your child, where formal language is used extensively, explaining he wants to become a lawyer/astronaut/politician, etc.?

Reading Does your child know in detail about the story, characters and themes of the Shakespeare play being studied for the Key Stage 3 English test?

Writing Can your child write an analytical essay, using correct spelling and punctuation, explaining why the central character in a chosen Shakespeare play behaves in the way he or she does?

English – Key Stage 4

Crucially, does your child know the Assessment Objectives (AOs)? Can she explain what the following AOs mean in plain English and when they will have to use them? Remember the different questions in the exam test separate AOs. They are not tested in every question. (Your child should consult her teacher if she doesn't know the answers. The different AOs are used differently by different exam boards, but candidates should know when and where they are being tested on them. All exam boards use the same AOs.)

AO1 – Speaking and Listening

Candidates for GCSE English must demonstrate their ability to:

- **AO1 i)** Communicate clearly and imaginatively, structuring and sustaining their talk and adapting it to different situations, using standard English appropriately.

- **AO1 ii)** Participate in discussion by both speaking and listening, judging the nature and purposes of contributions and the roles of participants.

- **AO1 iii)** Adopt roles and communicate with audiences using a range of techniques.

AO2 – Reading

Candidates for GCSE English must demonstrate their ability to:

- **AO2 i)** Read, with insight and engagement, making appropriate references to texts and developing and sustaining interpretations of them.

- **AO2 ii)** Distinguish fact and opinion and evaluate how information is presented.

- **AO2 iii)** Follow an argument, identifying implications and recognising inconsistencies.

- **AO2 iv)** Select material appropriate to their purpose, collate material from different sources, and make cross references.

- **AO2 v)** Understand and evaluate how writers use linguistic, structural and presentational devices to achieve their effects, and comment on the ways language varies and changes.

AO3 – Writing

Candidates for GCSE English must demonstrate their ability to:

- **AO3 i)** Communicate clearly and imaginatively, using and adapting forms for different readers and purposes.

- **AO3 ii)** Organise ideas into sentences, paragraphs and whole texts using a variety of linguistic and structural features.

- **AO3 iii)** Use a range of sentence structures effectively with accurate punctuation and spelling.

English Literature

Please note English Literature is a separate GCSE and has different Assessment Objectives. Candidates must demonstrate their ability to:

- **AO1** Respond to texts critically, sensitively and in detail, selecting appropriate ways to convey their response, using textual evidence as appropriate.

- **AO2** Explore how language, structure and forms contribute to the meanings of texts, considering different approaches to tests and alternative interpretations.

- **AO3** Explore relationships and comparisons between texts, selecting and evaluating relevant material.

- **AO4** Relate texts to their social, cultural and historical contexts and literary traditions.

Mathematics crisis – the truth

Britain desperately needs more mathematicians. Our economy depends upon the subject, more than any other. Every aspect of technology – from mobile phones, to the Internet, to washing machines – requires mathematicians to design and make them. However, it looks increasingly like it won't be British pupils who will be at the technological forefront. The number of A level maths pupils has slumped from 85,000 in 1989 to 66,000 in 2001, to just 52,000 in 2004.[8]

Simon Singh, the science populariser who has just spent a week in school teaching maths for Teachers' TV, is pessimistic about the state of affairs. 'The state of science and maths teaching in this country is catastrophic,' he says. 'And I'm not sure that there is anyone in government who is taking it seriously enough. We need to inject some passion into lessons, but most people are just so lacklustre.'[9]

One reason often cited as to why there are fewer mathematicians is because the subject is too difficult. And yet it is a lot easier than it used to be, when many more pupils were studying it at A level. A long-standing head of maths at a top comprehensive in the north of England, Geoff Noakes, explained to me why maths is a lot easier than it used to be:

In the days of O level, the exam was designed for only about the top twenty per cent of pupils. This was not satisfactory, and so they introduced the GCSE, which was aimed at including everyone. The old O level was simplified considerably. The old exam required quite a sophisticated knowledge of algebra and the GCSE made that considerably simpler. There were other areas like calculus which were simply removed.

There is a further change coming about in GCSE maths which is a further effort to make maths relevant to everyday life. A large proportion of the exam papers will be asking mathematical questions about such things as wallpapering a room, laying a carpet, going shopping, and supervising personal finances. The reason why maths is so unpopular with many kids is because they don't see why they have to do it. I hope this will improve the situation.

So are maths teachers getting worse? Geoff Noakes swallowed hard and then told me the truth:

There is no doubt that people who come into maths teaching now have not had the rigorous training older mathematicians had. It does mean that for A level teaching you have got teachers who have not got the depth of understanding that once they had. That sounds awful but it is true.

I can recall many times over the last 20 years when I have found myself explaining key mathematical concepts to staff. This is because they have gone through the GCSE system and the new revised A level and just don't have the subject knowledge that someone who did the old O level and A level would have had.

The vital thing to remember is that someone going through the new system is not required to prove things mathematically in the way they would have been before. Having to prove things was part of the old O and A level system. The A level now is, in general, more superficial.

Depending on the type of university they've been to, maths graduates have varying experiences. At the top flight universities, it is still rigorously mathematical. But there are no end of possibilities with degrees now: maths with economics, maths with psychology and so on and so forth. Somebody who has done one of these joint degrees won't have the mathematical grounding to teach the hardest parts of A level.

There's always been shortages of maths teachers. When we advertised for six consecutive weeks in the late 1980s for a maths teacher, we didn't attract one applicant. We had to get somebody from an agency. This is the experience up and down the country.

A good maths graduate ends up in accountancy, banking, commerce, the City, or in an actuarial position. It is an excellent degree to have if you want to make money.

I asked Geoff why, in the Far East, the maths teaching seemed to produce much better results from the pupils?

He explained:

In the Far East, young children are doing drill and learning by rote. The kids here rarely do things like that because it is so frowned upon by the educational establishment. You'd fail your Ofsted if you were observed doing mathematical drill. But in China, there is a lot of rote learning and drill. As a result of intensive drilling, the processes of arithmetic and algebra come to be second nature to children as young as six, seven and eight years old. A lot of the teaching done in China would be regarded as archaic and formulaic and stifling of creativity and free thinking. Nevertheless, it does seem to produce a lot of very competent mathematicians. They may not have the flexibility of thought of our pupils, but they certainly have a lot more knowledge.

THE NEW SCHOOL RULES
about maths

1. **Talk it through** Talk to your child's maths teacher. He or she will have a whole host of statistics and ideas that they can talk through with you.

2. **Set targets** Give your child some revision guides to work through. These days, there are no end of aids to help with maths. It is a whole industry that has sprung up on the back of angst and worry.

3. **Investigate** Have a basic knowledge of the National Curriculum requirements (see following page) and give your children little tests on what they know.

4. **Go over the basics** Send your child to a Kumon school. These schools are very good. They are amazing to behold.

▶

It is like stepping back 40 years. The Kumon method consists of page after page of carefully structured questions that slowly become more difficult as they progress. The kids are given a sheet where they have to get 20 out of 20, and then, and only then, can they move on to the next concept. The Kumon method is completely based on traditional rote learning and drill (www.kumon.co.uk/).

A maths brain check

Maths – Key Stage 1

- Can your child double and half any even number between 1 and 100?

- Does your child know the 2 to 10 times table by heart?

- Can your child use a ruler to draw and measure lines to the nearest centimetre?

- Can your child tell the time to the half and quarter hour?

Maths – Key Stage 2

- Can your child reduce a fraction to the simplest form? For example, can they reduce 8/16 to its simplest form (e.g. ½)?

- Does he or she know all the times tables from 2 to 12?

- Can he or she use a protractor to measure angles to the nearest degree?

- Can he or she tell the time on a 12- and 24-hour clock?

Maths – Key Stage 3

- Can your child add, subtract, multiply and divide using written methods?

- Can he or she transform algebraic expressions?

- Can he or she use a ruler, protractor and a compass to construct two- or three-dimensional shapes?

- Can he or she interpret graphs containing mathematical data?

Key Stage 4 – GCSE Maths

Does your child know the Assessment Objectives in maths? These are:

- **AO1** Using and applying mathematics.

- **AO2** Number and algebra.

- **AO3** Shape, space and measures.

- **AO4** Handling data.

The truth about science teaching in schools today

Penny Wilson, head of chemistry at the comprehensive where I teach, explained to me why science teaching is also in a parlous state in the country:

> Science has lost valuable curriculum time on most school timetables. It used to be the case that a pupil could study THREE sciences, physics, chemistry and biology at GCSE, and, before that, at O level. Now most schools do what is called 'Double Science' whereby all THREE subjects are stuffed into the time that used to be given to TWO science subjects. This is because most schools don't have the trained staff to deliver the old subject specialisms anymore.

Science isn't trendy anymore. I find it sad that I talk to bright kids in Year 11, who say to me that they want to be a lawyer and need three As at A level and can't take the risk of doing chemistry because it is much harder than psychology and economics. Take the story of Fred, a lovely student and very clever. He was predicted As in maths, biology, chemistry and physics at A level. In his upper sixth before Christmas he decided that he might want to do economics at university so he took it up then and got an A grade. You could never do that with any of the sciences.

Science teaching is in decline because we are producing too few scientists who are willing to teach. It is a tragedy for the country because we are not producing top scientists or even mediocre scientists. They are disappearing from view and it is all because of the centralised planning of the system which has allowed easy qualifications to have parity with chemistry and physics.

So what is good science teaching? Miss Wilson told me:

What children like is experiments that they can do, test-tube experiments. Things that are theirs. And then if they have done the experiment, you can talk about why it worked. They are interested in that because they did it. Whereas if you are talking about things that are relevant to everyday life, which is the government's thinking at the moment, the science can be very dry and dull because you can't possibly replicate an industrial process in the classroom. What children need to do is to learn how to observe, to get sets of results and come to their own conclusions. To do experiments you need technicians, labs, equipment. We have one of the best resourced schools in the area for science, but even we don't have the lab space to do experiments as often as we would like. Also, if you are a popular school, there is pressure to have big classes and that leads to a health and safety issue.

In a lot of schools, kids don't get the hands-on experience. They watch videos to see the experiments. But science is practical and you should develop dexterity as well as everything else.

It's like the English student who says I haven't read the book but I've seen the video, and possibly looked at the Letts Revision Guide.

There is a problem with training teachers. You need a lot of time to teach new staff how to do experiments, particularly with the more dangerous experiments. There is a lot more worry with poisonous gases and so on. A child burns their finger on a Bunsen burner and you used to say, 'Run it under the tap' and then 'There you go, don't moan, it was your own silly fault.'

Now you have to fill in forms and do a risk assessment, and then possibly get sued, if you are not careful.

Some old-fashioned schools still carry on the tradition of encouraging pupils to experiment wildly – and appear to be indifferent to the health and safety implications. One parent told me about such an institution, where the teachers still wear mortar boards and gowns:

> I was drawn to a laboratory where there was the foulest pong and lots of flashing lights. The sixth-form boys were happily larking around in the dark, putting washing-up liquid on their hands and pumping gas into the soap bubbles and setting fire to the bubbles as they floated to the ceiling. It was wonderful fun!

Alas though, this sort of experimentation is all too rare and much of the fun has gone out of science teaching today. It is nothing short of a national disaster.

A science brain check

Science – Key Stage 1

- Does your child know that every living thing eats, grows and reproduces?

- Can your child describe how some materials change when they are heated, cooled, stretched or twisted?

- Can your child make a bulb light up using a simple circuit with a battery and switch?

- Can you child classify living things using words such as: 'loud' or 'quiet', 'hard' or 'soft', and 'faster' or 'slower'?

Science – Key Stage 2

- Does your child know about solids, liquids and gases?

- Can your child name the main body organs, and know where they are?

- Can your child predict whether changes can or cannot be reversed? Do they know, for example, melted chocolate goes hard again, but cooked egg stays cooked?

- Can they explain what happens to light and sound when they see and hear the earth, sun and moon? Can they explain why their positions change?

Science – Key Stage 3

- Can your child explain all the main functions of the human organs like the heart and lungs?

- Can your child describe some of the properties of metals and use these properties to sort metals from other solid materials? Does your child know, for example, that all metals conduct electricity?

- Does your child know how to increase the current in a circuit by using a larger battery, or reduce the loudness of a sound with insulation?

- Can your child explain why a year or a day has a specific length of time?

Science – Key Stage 4

Does your child know his Assessment Objectives for science? Can he explain in plain English what these AOs mean (giving examples where relevant)? These are:

AO1 Knowledge and understanding of science and how science works. Candidates should be able to:

demonstrate knowledge and understanding of the scientific facts, concepts, techniques and terminology in the syllabus

show understanding of how scientific evidence is collected and its relationship with scientific explanations and theories

show understanding of how scientific knowledge and ideas change over time and how these changes are validated.

AO2 Application of skills, knowledge and understanding. Candidates should be able to:

apply concepts, develop arguments or draw conclusions related to familiar and unfamiliar situations

plan a scientific task, such as a practical procedure, testing an idea, answering a question, or solving a problem

show understanding of how decisions about science and technology are made in different situations, including contemporary situations and those raising ethical issues

evaluate the impact of scientific developments or processes on individuals, communities or the environment.

AO3 Practical, enquiry and data handling skills. Candidates should be able to:

carry out practical tasks safely and skilfully

evaluate the methods they use when collecting first-hand and secondary data

analyse and interpret qualitative and quantitative data from different sources

consider the validity and reliability of data in presenting and justifying conclusions.

Design and Technology

A head of design and technology at a comprehensive in London offered this advice for parents who want their children to become great designers:

- **Get them using their hands** Get the kids off the computer, and get them working with real materials. Encouraging them to play and design with Lego is excellent at an early age: it means that children learn about interacting with physical objects. Later on, children can play Jenga or work with wood. Jenga is a superb game to play and cultivates important D and T skills because the players intuitively learn about the different structures of an edifice as they stack wooden blocks on top of each other.

- **Be enthusiastic** Encourage a spirit of exploration. Don't make your children frightened to try to test out different technologies: let them rig up the new DVD player, the music player, and so on.

- **Talk it through** Get them to analyse the technology around them. Talk to them about what they think of the shape of the TV, the car, the washing machine and computer and discuss whether they think the designs could be improved.

A design and technology brain check

Design and Technology – Key Stage 1

- Can your child come up with good ideas for new designs for bookshelves, cupboards, cars, gadgets?

- Can she talk about these ideas and plan what to do next using pictures, words and models?

- Can she explain how these ideas might be improved?

Design and Technology – Key Stage 2

- Can your child explain design ideas, and work out how to achieve them in a step-by-step plan?

- Can she put together materials with some accuracy? For example, can she make a basic container?

Design and Technology – Key Stage 3

- Is your child able to make models and drawings in order to develop their design ideas?

- Can he draw up a list of aims and features for designs, taking into account the needs of the user, environmental issues and health and safety issues?

Design and Technology – Key Stage 4: GCSE product design

There are a number of different D and T GCSEs, but one of the most popular is product design which includes these Assessment Objectives. Candidates should be able to demonstrate their design and technology capability through acquiring and applying knowledge, skills and understanding:

of materials, components, processes, techniques and industrial practice

when designing and making quality products in quantity

when evaluating processes and products and examining the wider effects of design and technology on society.

Information Communication Technology

Computers

Of all the subjects in the National Curriculum this is the most controversial, and perhaps the most relevant to everyday life. Parents' lives today are blighted by the computer. One typical horror story I listened to was Jack's, a middle-aged business man. He confessed to me that he was being bullied by his teenage son. He told me of the nightmarish role the computer plays in his son's life:

> Billy expects everything to be on a plate instantaneously. Even though he is very bright, I worry that he does not have the concentration, willpower, or strength of character to do something worthwhile.
>
> I blame the culture of the Internet and the computer. It is an incredibly valuable tool, but children have to learn that it is your servant not your master. The trouble with Billy is that he is addicted to going on the Internet in his spare time. He will leave his homework to absolutely the last minute, and he will get up at six in the morning and finish it by eight to hand in that day.
>
> He is a boarder at a top public school. For five days a week, he has the most demanding lifestyle of any pupil possibly in the world. He has a huge amount of work to do. He gets up at eight, has lessons during the day and hours of prep in the evening. He is expected to train as a rower, he is learning to shoot, and participates a lot in the theatre.
>
> When he comes home at weekends he wants to relax, and the main way he does this is playing games on the Internet. So he will come home with a large amount of homework to do, but he doesn't get started with the work. This makes me very uneasy because instead of watching him get on with his work, I see him playing this game called America's Army where he is battling against Osama bin Laden. The game is made by the American army, and can be downloaded free. He wastes endless hours doing this. When I threaten to pull the plug, he can get very menacing. Once he put me in an arm lock because I dared to

threaten to switch the game off. He is now six foot tall, and all the rowing that he has done at his boarding school has made him incredibly strong. I told him to stop this nonsense, and said that he could play on the Internet. He let me go.

This weekend he has played non-stop on the Internet. My wife and I don't know what to do. We would like him to stop playing the games but it appears that there is nothing we can do. I certainly don't want to be put in an arm lock again. He has threatened worse.

We prefer not to tell the school about how he is at home. We don't want to damage his opportunities there.

Jack was being physically assaulted by his son because of his addiction to computer games. He didn't know what to do. Like many parents, he felt at the mercy of his son's addiction. It appeared that Billy's work was not unduly affected because he did much of it during 'prep' time at school. However, many pupils really suffer because of their addiction; they are often tired or grumpy in class, or even fall asleep, because they have been playing games late into the night.

One enterprising and forthright head teacher has tried to deal with this problem by seizing the electronic equipment from pupils' bedrooms. Duncan Harper, head of New Woodlands school in Bromley, south London, visits the homes of such pupils and takes away their computers. Harper has temporarily removed computers, Xboxes and PlayStations from nine children in four years. Annie Blake, whose eight-year-old son, Robert Juniper, is a pupil at New Woodlands, said she noticed 'a complete turnaround' in her son after his Gameboy was taken away for a month. Miss Blake, 37, said:

It is a fantastic idea. He wasn't very happy about it but it sends a very clear message that he can understand: 'misbehave and you lose the game; behave well and you can have it back'. After being a child who didn't sleep, would hit out at other children and would be sent home from his old school 10 minutes after arriving, he is now the happiest he has ever been.

Robert was excluded from his first school three times but after only one term at New Woodlands his mother says he began interacting better with other children and showing an interest in learning. 'It is about building up the self-esteem of the parents too, and putting the power back in their hands,' Harper said.[10]

When used properly, computers are a real boon, but parents have to be in control and must stamp out any addiction to violent, mindless games. The parents I spoke to who were happiest with their children using computers constantly felt in charge. Angela, who lives with her three daughters in rural Cheshire, told me:

> Our house is laptop city in the holidays and most evenings. MSN messenger rules, we have a web cam. The web cam is attached to the laptop and we have broadband wireless all the way through the house so that they can take their laptop anywhere. It is a mixed blessing. It is very tempting for my daughters to spend hours in the evening talking to the friends who've they've only just seen at school. I have to be able to walk up to the laptop and read what's going on. I check really carefully about this. I am in charge and the girls know this. The computer goes off if they should be getting on with their work or they are wasting their time.
>
> But by the time they're on MSN, they have done homework, and they like to spend the evening on the laptop even in preference to the TV, chatting to school friends. They don't talk to strangers on the Internet. I check regularly every evening. But we've had our moments on the laptop – the Internet is a scary place and there are a lot of horrible people waiting to prey on naive youngsters. Parents have to keep a very careful eye on everything.

Having interviewed parents and pupils up and down the country, I found that nearly everyone at school now is on MSN instant messenger. Usually, the whole of a particular year group have their own chatroom, and then within the year group, friends form more private chat areas where they can talk to their closest friends. The pressure to keep talking mindless, pointless chit-chat all night is intense. Lots of children I spoke to said that they didn't like to let people down once they were online, that they liked to respond with a kind word to whoever messaged them. There was a real neediness there. An insatiable desire for approval from one's classmates which appears to feed the spectacular rise in popularity of the medium.

In many ways, Laura, a 17-year-old in Northumberland, is a typical teenager of today, feeling totally at home in this brave new world of technology. She told me:

> I trawl the list of names on MSN, and then double-click on a name that I fancy talking to and they come up. If they are online, they are blue, and if they are not, they are red. You can make your own icons. One of my favourites is a dancing panda which shows excitement about something. Me and my friends have little stars that show various body movements, and that avoids misunderstandings. You see, irony and sarcasm can really be missed if you don't use an icon. For example, you can say something is really good, when you mean it's rubbish, and without a glum face beside the word, the sarcasm could be completely missed. I am not addicted to it, but I have a few friends who are. One time I was on quite late and I was trying to go to bed, and my friend was saying, 'Please talk to me! Please talk to me!' Emotionally, I felt I had to be involved because no one else was on line. She didn't have anything to say – as normal. It was just endless, banal stuff about your day and what have you done. You see, you don't talk about anything important on MSN. You start a thread and you keep going until you don't know what you are talking about.

Most parents I interviewed had no problem with children talking to their friends on MSN, but they did have concerns about larger chatrooms. One parent told me:

> I have no problem with MSN within their friendship groups, but when it is a larger chatroom you never know who is there. We have never had the computer in a bedroom, but it should be

in a shared area so you can a glance over their shoulder and see what is going on. He is not locked away with a computer, chatting away forever and forever.

The head teacher at my school, Dr Lloyd, who is also a parent, was less tolerant. She has to deal with the fallout from the bullying that goes on on these messaging sites. She said:

> Stop your children MSNing if you can or at least, track their MSNing. MSN can lead to serious bullying under the guise of being jokey. Unfortunately, pupils can send messages or set up websites that verge on being illegal. It is an offence to send certain types of material over the Internet: threatening to kill people or certain types of pornography are totally illegal.

Mobile phones

While there were mixed opinions about MSN, many parents I interviewed were utterly and totally fed up with mobile phones. Dr Lloyd told me:

> I hate mobile phones. We have created a generation that can't cope without them. It has led to a huge increase in the amount of attacks on young children because their phones are constantly taken off them. It has increased theft and hasn't made children safer. I know about this from the inside because, as a head teacher, I have to deal with the fallout when children have been assaulted for their phones or have had them stolen.

Linda, the mother of two teenagers, resented the pressure that parents are under to spend huge quantities of money on them. She told me:

> Mobile phones have become a status symbol, and the kids have to have the latest up-to-date phone. Often you will find they have more than one phone because they are on different networks. It is worrying because parents are spending hundreds

of pounds on a gadget which is basically only a phone! It's a complete rip-off and yet parents feel compelled to get this sort of rubbish because their children nag at them so much. And the phones are very disruptive in school.

Teacher of the Year, Phil Beadle, is very suspicious of flashy technology. He told me:

> I see technology being treated as a universal panacea for every educational issue as idiotic. Shakespeare wrote all his plays with a feather quill from a duck's arse. In fact, quite often the use of ICT in school is simply a means for a lazy teacher with a hangover getting through a lesson without effort or planning.
>
> If you want to do one thing for your child's education, take their computer games into the garden and burn them. These destroy their attention spans, teach them the doctrine of violence as being acceptable, and make them try out kung fu moves in the most inappropriate settings. Learn to write with a pen or pencil first before you use a computer.

THE NEW SCHOOL RULES
about ICT

1. **Watch that computer** Keep the computer in a communal area where everyone can see what is going on. Track any MSNing or instant messaging. It may not keep your phone bills down, but it could lead to all sorts of trouble if you're not vigilant. Don't let your child keep the computer in their bedroom.

2. **Talk it through** Ask your child to explain some of the concepts that they have learnt in ICT to you, but avoid teaching them yourself unless you feel very confident. Certain skills like using databases, spreadsheets, making

▶

presentations and using a word processor are best taught by a specialist ICT teacher: someone who is not trained may give a child bad habits which are difficult to break.

3. **Be cautious** Don't let them take a mobile phone or MP3 player to school unless they have a very good reason to do so. Despite all their protestations, most children do not need phones at school – and definitely don't need iPods and suchlike. There is usually easy access to phones in any school if there is an emergency. Even though your child won't tell you this, you will be sparing them a great deal of anxiety. Mobile phone thefts are very common in all schools, and peer pressure about such technology is endemic. If you do let them take any technology into school, make sure that it is cheap! One parent, Andrea, told me that she lets her daughter take her old, scratched mobile into school because she travels a long way by tube and train, and if there is a delay or problem she can call for advice. Andrea said: 'Phoebe texts me just before she gets to school and turns the mobile off. It goes on at 4pm when she gets the train home or texts me to advise of a detention or whether she's got swimming and so on. I am so relieved to get a text each morning. But I expect her to respect the school rules and not have it visible or switched on at school.'

▶ **CHECK OUT**
www.bbc.co.uk/schools/digger/

An ICT brain check

ICT – Key Stage 1

Does your child know how to gather information from the computer, organise it, store it and present it to others? For example, can he look up a topic on the computer, save it to the computer and present it in a word processing format?

ICT – Key Stage 2

- Can your child create programs that monitor temperature change, or switch on a light bulb when light levels drop below a certain point using a computer programme?

- Can your child use simulation software and spreadsheets to test theories and explore patterns in data?

ICT – Key Stage 3

- Is your child able to make up sequences of computerised instructions to carry out different tasks? For example, can she use a computer programme to control the movement of automatic doors or the temperature in greenhouses?

- Is she able to discuss the impact of ICT on herself and society?

ICT – Key Stage 4

Does your child know the ICT Assessment Objectives if he or she is sitting the GCSE? Ask your child to explain them in plain English, giving examples where appropriate. GCSE ICT requires candidates to demonstrate their ability to:

apply their knowledge, skills and understanding of ICT to a range of situations

analyse, design, implement, test, evaluate and document information and communication systems for use by others and develop understanding of the wider applications and effects of ICT

reflect critically on the way they and others use ICT

discuss and review the impact of ICT applications in the wider world

consider the social, economic, political, legal, ethical, and moral issues and security needs for data which surround the increasing use of ICT.

Candidates will be assessed on their ability to organise and present information, ideas, descriptions and arguments clearly and logically, taking into account their use of grammar, punctuation, and spelling.

History

Stephen Lawlor, head of history at my school, explained to me how there has been a quiet revolution in history classrooms over the last ten years:

> It used to be the case that pupils were expected to learn a lot of facts about history, and to explain the story of events in some detail. Now there is much more emphasis placed on why events happen. Pupils are no longer required to memorise endless dates, but to know the overall key chronology of history. Most importantly, they have to discuss what I call the 3 Cs: Causation (why an historical event happened), Conduct (what happened) and Consequences (what the historical event caused to happen next). Pupils have to think for themselves about history, study source materials and arrive at their own conclusions, rather than regurgitate facts.
>
> Parents should also be aware – and many of them are not – that at Key Stage 3 pupils study British history for three years, and so should know all about our nation at the end of it. Media hysteria about pupils learning nothing about Britain's past is totally unfounded.

A history brain check

History – Key Stage 1

- Can your child discuss a historical event and explain why it happened?

- Can your child explain why people's lives were different in the past?

- Is your child able to ask questions about the past after looking at old photographs, pictures, using computer sources and visiting museums?

History – Key Stage 2

- Is your child able to describe some of the most significant people, the main events and changes from the periods that they have studied?

- Can they use dates and historical terms to explain these events?

History – Key Stage 3

Pupils will learn about local, national, European and international history through six areas of study:

- Britain 1066–1500

- Britain 1500–1750

- Britain 1750–1900

- a European study before 1914

- an African, American, Asian or Australasian society before 1900

- a world study after 1900.

After studying these:

- Can your child summarise the main events, people and changes in the periods they have studied from the list above?

- Can he explain why the past is depicted and interpreted in different ways?

- Can she use different sources to explore a particular historical issue?

History – Key Stage 4

GCSE history is not compulsory in most schools, but if your child does take it, he or she must be familiar with the Assessment Objectives. (Ask your child to explain them clearly to you.) Candidates must demonstrate:

AO 6.1 **Deployment of knowledge** Recall, select, organise and deploy knowledge of the syllabus content to communicate it through description, analysis and explanation of:

- the events, people, changes and issues studied

- the key features and characteristics of the periods, societies or situations studied.

AO 6.2 **Use of sources** Use historical sources critically in their context, by comprehending, analysing, evaluating and interpreting them.

AO 6.3 **Interpretations and representations of the past** Comprehend, analyse and evaluate, in relation to the historical context, how and why historical events, people, situations and changes have been interpreted and represented in different ways.

Geography

An experienced geography teacher told me there are a few things that parents can do that will really make their child better at the subject:

- **Be nosy** Get your child to ask questions about the world. Geography is not about learning a great long list of facts, it is about having your eyes open and investigating the environment, whatever that might be.

- **Use maps** Get your child to find out the directions to a place you want to go to. Children love looking at maps, and what better way to show them how they work than by making them figure out how to get somewhere using one?

- **Talk it through** Discuss the environment of a place with your child. Get her to guess how the land around them was formed. Get her to observe the environment in general: pollution, the influence of man upon the natural landscape, the influence of the natural landscape upon man-made objects. Never stop talking about where objects your child encounters come from: food, clothes, the materials that are used to build houses and cars.

A geography brain check

Geography – Key Stage 1

- Can your child explain why some places are similar and some places are different from one another?

- Can your child recognise where things are and why they are there? For example, does your child know why a pedestrian crossing is on one part of a road rather than another?

- Can your child explain how people affect the environment?

- Can your child find out about places by observing them, asking and answering questions?

- Can your child use basic maps?

Geography – Key Stage 2

- Does your child know why seasons change?

- Does your child know about the layout of roads in a town?

- Can your child explain about the natural and human features of places?

- Can your child describe how people can damage and improve environments?

- Can your child explain why it is important to protect the environment?

Geography – Key Stage 3

- Can your child explain the following concepts?

  weather and climate
  ecosystems
  populations
  settlements
  economic activity
  development
  environmental issues
  resource issues
  tectonic processes
  geomorphological processes

- Does your child understand how natural and human processes lead to changes in places? Does your child understand, for example, how a flood may cause a river to change its course; how a new bypass may affect an ecosystem or result in people losing their homes?

- Does your child understand how the views and opinions of different groups of people may make them respond in different ways to the same issue?

Geography – Key Stage 4

Geography is not a compulsory GCSE in most schools, but those studying it should know the Assessment Objectives. (Get your child to explain them.) Candidates are required to demonstrate their ability to:

AO1 Show knowledge of places, environments, and themes at a range of scales from local to global and with a consideration of their wider context and interdependence

AO2 Show understanding of their specified syllabus

AO3 Apply their knowledge and understanding in a variety of physical and human contexts

AO4 Select and use a variety of skills and techniques appropriate to geographical studies and enquiry.

Art and Design

The art department at my school gives the following advice to parents who want their children to excel in this area:

- **Be enthusiastic** Try to get encourage your children to draw and paint from life when they are at home, rather than copying from books. Drawing from life is much better for developing artistic skills because it helps children to draw from perspective, and to learn about perspective. One of the things we find with children is that they frequently do not have a proper idea of proportion so they'll draw a cup, for example, but make the handle far too big. Buy them paints and encourage them to paint; too few primary schools really encourage painting now because there is so little time in the curriculum. Urge them to look at the world in detail, not to just scan the world. Get them to look at the way light reflects off the roof of a car, get them to observe the cracks in the pavement. Art is all about analysing and looking at the world in detail.

- **Have fun** Visit art galleries as much as you can.

An art and design brain check

Art and Design – Key Stage 1

- Is your child able to draw a basic picture from real life using colour, shape, form and space in a convincing way? Ask him to draw a picture of his friends at the park.

- Can she suggest ways of improving her own work?

Art and Design – Key Stage 2

- Is your child able to use a variety of different materials to produce a reasonable picture or drawing?

- Can he discuss the ways in which time and place affect ideas and the methods used?

Art and Design – Key Stage 3

- Is your child able to draw from real life using perspective in a convincing fashion?

- Is your child able to analyse works of art critically?

- Can your child explain why art has changed over time and from place to place?

Art and Design – Key Stage 4

Art is not a compulsory GCSE but those doing it should know the Assessment Objectives. Candidates must demonstrate their ability to:

AO1 Record observations, experiences and ideas in forms that are appropriate to intentions

AO2 Analyse and evaluate images, objects and artefacts showing understanding of context

AO3 Develop and explore ideas using media, processes and resources; reviewing, modifying and refining work as it progresses

AO4 Present a personal response, realising intentions and making informed connections with the work of others.

Music

A head of music at a top comprehensive in the north of England gave the following advice for parents if they want their children to be good musicians:

- **Be enthusiastic** Encourage your child to play an instrument early on: start the recorder at six or seven. Being able to play a musical instrument greatly assists with improving your child's academic attainment. There is a very strong correlation between high achievement in exams and musical proficiency.

- **Get involved** Get your child to play and sing with groups of people and sing along with them. Get your child to see that music is a communal social activity. A school which is really serious about music will give your child the chance to sing in a choir or play in an orchestra.

A music brain check

Music – Key Stage 1

- Is your child able to sing songs from memory?
- Can she keep a steady rhythm when singing and playing music?

- Can he make his own musical patterns?

- Can she describe when notes are high and low? When a rhythm is fast or slow?

Music – Key Stage 2

- Is your child able to sing in tune?

- Is your child able to make up his own pieces of music?

- Can she talk and write about music using musical terms?

Music – Key Stage 3

- Can your child pick out the characteristics of different styles of music?

- Can she recognise how one type of music can influence another?

- Can she re-create, improvise and compose music in different styles, and use suitable musical notation when planning or revising compositions?

Music – Key Stage 4

Music is not a compulsory GCSE in most schools but any candidates studying it will have to know the relevant Assessment Objectives which are:

Performing Singing and/or playing an individual part with technical control, expression and suitable interpretation.
Two solo performances are required:

- A solo, which may be accompanied by one or several players or unaccompanied.

- An ensemble in which the candidate must take a significant part and show a sense of ensemble.

Neither solo nor ensemble parts may be doubled.

Composing Creating and developing musical ideas in relation to a given or chosen brief. The brief must describe the stimulus for the composition, provide a clear indication of the candidate's intentions and make connections with Area of Study, Music for Special Events.

Appraising Analysing and evaluating music using musical terminology.

Physical Education

An experienced PE teacher in Wales gave this advice for parents who want their children to be great at PE:

- **Be enthusiastic** Encourage your child to do a whole variety of activities: dance, football, gymnastics, track events, swimming. Don't get them to specialise in a sport until they are 13 or 14. Research shows that the best athletes and sportspeople have had a rounded education in PE before specialising.

- **Go swimming** Swimming is being cut back in schools and yet it is one of the most important physical activities your child can do. Try to make sure that your school offers a decent set of swimming lessons.

- **Talk it through** Remember, the subject has an academic side as well: talking and discussing the science of movement and sport is very interesting and also very beneficial for PE.

At all Key Stages children should be doing at least two hours of planned physical activity a week.

A physical education check

Physical Education – Key Stage 1

- Is your child able to make up and perform a short gymnastic sequence that joins actions together?

- Can she move in time to a beat?

- Can he express his feelings in a dance?

- Does she enjoy being physically active?

Physical Education – Key Stage 2

- Children should do the following: dance, games, gymnastics, swimming activities and water safety, athletics, outdoor and adventurous activities.

- Can your child swim?

- Does your child understand the rules of at least two games and is your child able to to employ tactics in competitive games?

- Can he explain how exercise affects the body and how it helps keep him healthy and fit?

- Can your child compose and perform dances and gymnastic sequences?

Physical Education – Key Stages 3 and 4

- Does your child know how to play a striking/fielding game such as softball or cricket, an invasion game such as basketball or water polo, a net/wall game such as badminton and tennis?

- Schools also teach three of the activities from this list, at least one of which must be dance or gymnastics:
  dance
  gymnastics
  swimming and water safety
  athletics
  outdoor and adventurous activities

- Is your child able to warm up before activities and cool down after them?

- Can he or she explain how different types of exercise help their fitness and health?

Religious Education

A former head of RE gave me these basic guidelines for parents who want to help their children with the subject:

- **Be tolerant** Above all, children should learn to be tolerant of all religions, to see that all religions contain teachings that people agree and disagree with.

- **Talk it through** Try to educate your child about areas that they may be falsely biased about. For example, explaining clearly the fundamental tenets of Islam should correct a great deal of misinformation about this religion that is on TV and in the media generally. The Dorling Kindersley books on religions are excellent for this. Don't allow your child to be brainwashed by any particular doctrine, but allow them the space to arrive at their own views and opinions.

A religious education brain check

Religious Education – Key Stage 1

- Does your child have a basic knowledge of the story of Jesus?

- Does your child understand why religions have ceremonies and know what these ceremonies involve?

- Does he or she understand about the different buildings and places of worship that different religions have?

Religious Education – Key Stage 2

- Does your child know how Christianity has affected Britain?

- Does your child understand the meanings between the stories and festivals of certain religions?

- Does your child have any of their own ideas about religion?

Religious Education – Key Stage 3

- Has your child begun to consider what the purpose of life might be? Does he or she understand how the various religious might try to answer these questions?

- Has he or she thought about why people might suffer?

Religious Education – Key Stage 4

Religious Education is not a compulsory GCSE in most schools but those who study should have a working knowledge of the Assessment Objectives. Candidates must demonstrate their ability to:

AO1 Recall, select, organise and deploy knowledge of the syllabus

AO2 Describe, analyse and explain the relevance and application of a religion or religions

AO3 Evaluate different responses to religious and moral issues, using relevant evidence and argument.

Personal Social Health Education (PSHE) and Citizenship

These are the most nebulous topics in the National Curriculum. They can be boiled down to one big word: responsibility (basically, the government wants everyone to learn to be responsible). This is a very tall order, but schools do try, some with more success than others. If you are looking for a school that is good teaching PSHE, you should be looking for schools that give pupils responsibility, while minimising the opportunities for them to abuse any positions of responsibility. This is easier said than done. I have my doubts about any school which gives too much responsibility to older pupils to look after younger ones because institutionalised bullying – or fagging to use the old-fashioned public school word – can occur. For example, I have heard about some severe cases of bullying in boarding schools where older pupils are supposedly in charge of looking after the younger ones in the dorms, at choir practice and at various sporting occasions.

A school which is good at giving children responsibility will:

- Have an active school council which is listened to. Sometimes, the school council can be the most powerful agent of change in a school. At many good schools now, prospective teachers are interviewed by members of the school council. While obviously pupils shouldn't have the final say in such matters, their opinions should be valued. In one school, I heard about how the disgusting 40-year-old toilets were finally replaced after a sustained series of complaints from the school council. Parents' complaints to the governors hadn't worked, but the pupils' complaints were acted upon.

- Give a wide range of pupils positions of responsibility: good teachers do appoint monitors who help clear up, show visitors around the school, assist with basic classroom tasks, and help out at extracurricular functions such as sports evenings, concerts and shows, parents' evenings. Again, it is a matter of balance. Obviously, pupils must not have too much power, but they should be doing their bit.

- Encourage responsible 'consumption'. The most obvious area here is the way schools are now obliged by law to offer a selection of healthy food in their vending machines and in their canteens.

- Have firm and clear rules. A decent school uniform means that pupils are not forever obsessing about what clothes to wear and not competing about who is wearing the trendiest gear. Likewise, a blanket ban on mobile phones and other gadgets means that the school is challenging the prevailing materialist climate in our society.

- Teach PSHE issues in the relevant subject areas. Primary schools do not have to teach PSHE and citizenship, but they should. It might not be taught as a subject in its own right, but through other subjects. For example, the National Curriculum for science at all the Key Stages says that a child should learn that all animals, including humans, reproduce. While the information is fairly basic at Key Stage 1, by the time your child reaches Key Stage 3, she should know about reproduction in detail. Likewise, children learn about drugs in science.

- Have decent sex education and drugs education policies and lessons. In law, a parent may withdraw their child from sex education lessons, but not from the science lessons where they learn about reproduction. Unfortunately, many schools have a lamentable track record in sex education. Teacher of the Year, Phil Beadle told me: 'The British education system is pitifully bad at sex education. Teachers form the erroneous opinion that if they teach this vital life skill they will somehow be branded paedophiles. This is a national scandal every bit as ludicrous as the scandal of children being given spaghetti hoops as part of their daily vegetable ration. We have the highest teenage pregnancy rate in Europe, and sex education is not taught in schools.'

A recent survey concluded that parents worry more about bullying, drink and drugs than academic achievement when their 11-year-olds start secondary school. More than half (53 per cent) fear that their child will be bullied, whereas one in five worry about the influence of alcohol, drugs and tobacco (for more on these topics see Chapter 3 How to Tackle the Big Problems). Only 11 per cent are concerned about their child's academic achievement.[11] This is fascinating because it indicates that much more attention should be given to this area than is currently the case. Many aspects of PSHE are not mandatory and a school can quite easily get away with covering the topics in the most cursory way without censor.

Interestingly, and contrary to what you might think, it is actually the schools with the worst social problems (and often worst results) that are often the best at teaching these subjects.

One parent, Karen, whose daughters are at a very rough comprehensive in Leeds, told me:

> No moans about Personal Social Health Education (PSHE). One daughter, who for years did not like cheese and wouldn't drink milk, started consuming both after doing work at school on a healthy diet! At both primary school and high school PSHE and comparative religion have been tremendously helpful in introducing them to different ways of thinking about life's big issues – as has being in a high school where there are many religions and 37 languages spoken! They are very laid-back, articulate and open-minded young people who can see others' points of view. We have our big worries about certain aspects of their secondary education, but this isn't one of them. The school has a compulsory half a GCSE in RE, which we don't agree with in principle. But, now that she has done it (our eldest is just doing the exams), she has gained hugely from the philosophy/ethics side of the course. It's led to lots of meaningful discussion at home. If your kids do well in a comprehensive school, they come out wise and with a broader range of knowledge than we did.

A PSHE check

Personal Social Health Education – Key Stage 1

- Is your child independent and confident?
- Do he or she keep themselves safe and healthy?
- Do they think about what's unfair and fair?

Personal Social Health Education – Key Stage 2

- Has your child thought about the different racial, ethnic and social groups that exist within British society and considered how to get along with all of them?
- Has your child thought about how and why rules are made?

Personal Social Health Education – Key Stage 3

- Does your child know about the importance of a loving and stable relationship?

- Does he know about the arguments for delaying sexual activity?

- Does she know about contraception and safe sex?

- Does he know about the different types of drugs and the effects they have on people?

- Does she know about resisting unwanted peer pressure?

- Does he have good personal and social skills which enable him to mix with a variety of different groups and people?

Modern languages

They are not compulsory at Key Stage 1 and 2, although, increasingly, primary schools are studying languages. A modern languages teacher and head of department in the Midlands gave this advice:

- **Be enthusiastic** Get your child motivated about a language and a culture, and everything else will follow. Encourage your child to listen to the music of a foreign language culture, to watch its films, to look at its paintings. Travel with them to foreign countries if you can. Enthusiasm is everything! Once your child is enthusiastic about a place and a language, there are many, many ways of getting them to learn the language: they can do a language course on the Internet, watch training videos, read books and newspapers.

- **Talk it through** Good foreign language teaching teaches the skills necessary to learn any language. This is why it is so necessary that your child learns a language – it doesn't matter which one. Once they have the skills to acquire one language, they will be able to learn another easily. At some point, your child will almost certainly have to know a foreign language, and so learning one at school is crucial. I would thoroughly recommend them studying a foreign language at GCSE and A level. It is a vital life skill.

A modern languages brain check

Modern Languages – Key Stage 3

- Does your child know the way to greet a person and say goodbye in the language?

- Can she ask for directions, make enquiries in a shop and order food successfully in a restaurant in the language?

- Can he hold a basic conversation in the language?

- Can she watch a film and understand most of it without reading the subtitles?

- Can he read a simple book in the language?

- Can she talk about events in the past, present and future?

- Can she read a passage of complex writing and pick out the main points?

CHAPTER 10

Some New School Rules for the government

I am a changed teacher and parent now. Having interviewed so many parents throughout the country, having researched about so many different facets of our education system, having thought so hard about what it must be like to be a parent in all the situations discussed in this book, I feel that, at last, I am beginning to cut through the school jungle. The system, as we have seen, is hideously complex and is becoming more so with the increase in specialist schools, the building of academies, the changes to the National Curriculum, the new vocational qualifications, the changes to the A levels, the changes to the university admissions system and so forth.

A motto for the government

If I were to offer motto one that the government and the DfES should adopt, it would be: less complexity, more simplicity.

School admissions

I feel this motto should particularly apply to school admissions. At the moment, it is a complete free-for-all where many schools are able to set their own admissions criteria – and basically select by the back door. This seems an absurd halfway house: it is not selection based on the merits of the child, it is selection based on the merits of the parent. The government is aiming to clamp down on this in the coming years but as yet it is unclear whether it will eradicate it completely. One plan is to allocate school places by lottery: how this will work in practice remains to be seen. Either the government should say loud and clear that the sole admission criterion will be proximity to the school, or it should allow schools to select pupils based on their merits. Neither solution is that satisfactory: one is selection by postcode and the other is selection by academic ability.

I can still see the advantages of a 'voucher'-type system whereby parents are given a voucher worth the cost of educating a child for a year in the state system, reckoned to be nearly £5,000 at the last count, and can spend it on any school of their choice. For this system to work, you would have to either allow schools to select their pupils or operate a 'first come, first served' principle. You would probably need to put a premium on pupils with special needs or English As An Additional Language so that schools felt enticed to take them on. You would also need to relax planning restrictions on building new schools and the expansion of current ones so that entrepreneurs felt that they could have a crack at setting up a school. There would be failures – as there are in the free market – but there would be winners too. The poor schools would close down, and the good schools would expand. Parents would have real choice – not the phoney kind of choice that is offered at the moment – and could easily vote with their feet if they didn't like a school.

Reading and writing

At the moment, the state has an astonishing monopoly on education, and appears to be doing a pretty rotten job of educating our children: half of all school leavers are not properly numerate or literate. There are thousands and thousands of pages of regulations and guidelines, but they haven't helped with the basics: the majority of our school leavers can't read or write. This is truly terrifying, but the complacent educational bureaucrats are too busy mired in the depths of the jungle to see just what is happening.

If the DfES wanted to do one thing that would transform our educational landscape overnight, it could do this: learn a lesson from Soviet Russia. As we saw earlier in the book, in Soviet Russia, all schools were issued with a basic textbook that covered all the relevant subjects for different ages. As a result, educational standards in the Soviet bloc were surprisingly high. Surely, it wouldn't be beyond the bureaucrats' power to devise some basic textbook for every child in the country which taught them to read, write and be numerate? The government could issue a textbook for each Key Stage. At the moment, parents don't have a clue what is going on in schools: they don't understand the National Curriculum – many teachers don't either – and they don't know what their child should be reading and writing. A basic textbook which provided sample reading material, grammatical exercises, writing tasks and maths calculations, with relevant answers in the back, would assist parents immensely. Then they would know what everyone else in the country was doing, and they could work through the book with their children. It would enable them to monitor what was going on in school as well, and ask questions if work wasn't being covered.

I know that many teachers will be howling with rage at this suggestion, and I probably would have done too before I wrote this book, but my research has been a real eye-opener for me: the school jungle is a terrifying place for children and parents and something needs to be done to make it a friendlier and more benign environment.

Parent helpline

Moreover, if schools are to become easier places for parents to find their way around, I think most schools should have a parent helpline – a phone number and email address – where parents can always call if they have something to discuss, or a problem to sort out. It should be manned by administrative staff who make a note of the issue on a centralised database and then pass the issue to the relevant person. The administrative staff then follow up later on to see if the problem was sorted out. At the moment, many of the parents I interviewed simply didn't know who to contact when they had a problem and were passed from pillar to post, with the problem frequently left unsolved. A helpline would simplify matters and it would also give the school a centralised database of all the problems that do occur. At the moment, most schools do not know what the most pressing problems are because this information is diffused throughout the school.

Naturally following on from this is the fact that most staff in schools haven't had a moment's training on how to deal with parents. I was given five minutes during my training on this, but in my 15 years' of teaching, I haven't had any other training on dealing with parents. Teachers badly need this training, I believe, so that they are less defensive and more open with parents. At the moment, there is very much a 'them and us' barrier in schools which needs to be broken down.

Work ethic

Above all, state schools need to encourage their pupils to have more of a work ethic. Even in some of the best state schools pupils are picked upon for being 'boffs or 'swots' if they work. One of the side effects of having schools focus so obsessively upon achieving good results is that children are constantly feeling like they are being 'kicked in the arse' to work. Day in, day out, teachers are telling pupils that they will get rubbish results if they don't work. This sort of 'kick in the arse' motivation is counterproductive, as we have seen earlier on in the book. Instilling a genuine work ethic in our children means getting them to see the intrinsic value of working; that working is a process that is worthwhile in itself, and that ultimately, it is not about achieving the result but the sense of fulfilment from having worked which is important. This kind of work ethic just is not present in English schools today – but it needs to be if we are going to educate our children properly.

THE NEW SCHOOL RULES
the government should adopt

1. **Simplify as much as possible** Simplify the admissions systems for all state schools. They should also focus on the basics by radically simplifying the literacy and numeracy strategies.

2. **Publish textbooks** As part of this process of radical simplification, the government should publish textbooks for the National Curriculum, issuing engaging textbooks to all pupils so that every parent knows what a child should be learning.

3. **Give all parents easy access to good advice** All schools or LEAs should have a parent helpline, a first point of contact for any problems they might have.

4. **Train teachers** Staff should be given much more training on how to deal with parents.

5. **Put the ethos of the school at the heart of the system** Rather than obsessively focusing upon league tables, schools should be encouraged to generate a genuine work ethic within the hearts and minds of their pupils.

CHAPTER 11

The five essential New School Rules

1. **Meet the criteria** In today's climate, this is definitely the most important school rule. It applies to everything from meeting the admissions criteria of your favoured school to your child meeting the criteria of the examination syllabi he or she is studying. Everything is about criteria nowadays! Every school writes out a list of requirements they need their pupils to meet if they are going to join the school. Match the criteria and you're much more likely to get your child into the school. Likewise, exam boards write a detailed list of what they want their candidates to know and if you meet that criteria, hey presto, a good grade is there for the taking.

2. **Talk it through** Your child is going to need your enthusiasm and attention, and if he or she gets it they should do well wherever they go to school. The most exhaustive research shows that it is the children who have parents who talk to them regularly that do the best in school. Chatter away to them constantly about this and that, play games with them, read to them, watch TV with them, go for walks and discuss everything with them. Be

enthusiastic about the world, love, life and literature and they will do well. Remember that specific praise is the best motivation there is: praise them regularly.

3. **Get into the groove** Establish a clear daily routine with your child so that the use of the computer and watching TV is rationed. Get them into good habits and they won't give you much grief.

4. **Investigate** Listen to his or her conversations in the back of the car, look at their exercise books, discuss them with their teachers – but don't oppress them with your fervent interest. With any serious issue, try to discuss it with someone else before talking to your child. When you give your child a 'Brain check' (see pages 333–373) do it subtly without them knowing that you are necessarily testing them at all.

5. **Don't be bitter, set targets instead** The system is very imperfect and it is very easy to feel short-changed by it. However, instead of constantly moaning about this and that, you should focus on the things that your child can do to improve on his or her current achievements. Focus on the future, don't become twisted and bitter about the past.

A DEATH analysis

Photocopy these pages and carry them around with you when looking at prospective schools.

Name of school: _____ Date: _____

D stands for Discussion, Discipline and Display

Questions to ask

Ask pupils: how are you treated if you work hard? What level or grade are you working at in English, maths and science and what do you need to do to improve? Ask the staff: would you send your child to this school? If you would, why would you? If you wouldn't, why not?

Points to consider

Does the school pass the toilet test: are they nice? Look at the graffiti in the school. Artificial displays are a sign that the school is more concerned about appearances than the pupils' real work.

Your notes

_____

_____

_____

_____

_____

E stands for Ethos, Evaluation and Extracurricular Activities

Questions to ask

Do the pupils and staff know the mission statement of the school? Is there an ethos where work is celebrated not ridiculed or envied? Check out the Ofsted report: is it rated outstanding, good, satisfactory or average overall? What is the rating for key points like discipline and the various departments? What extra-curricular activities are on offer?

Points to consider

Be wary of the school saying that there might be extracurricular activities on offer or there were ones. They probably won't be available when your child arrives. Check to see if there is a choice of extracurricular activities, and whether children/parents choose them, or the school chooses them. Research any costs.

Your notes

_____

_____

_____

_____

_____

_____

A stands for Assets and Achievement

Questions to ask

What is the social mix of pupils? How well do the parents support the school? What books and ICT resources are available to the children? What is the school's ranking in the league? In particular, what are the scores for English, maths and science at GCSE?

Points to consider

Remember the best schools have a substantial number of children from supportive homes. Find out whether the funding for the school is good, and whether the funding matches the school's achievements, i.e., if it is well funded, is it doing well? Look at the school's library and textbooks: are they looked after? A school's attitude towards books is very important.

Your notes

_____

_____

_____

_____

_____

_____

T stands for Target Setting and Turning Up

Questions to ask

What are the targets the school has set for itself? What is the turnover of staff and pupils like? Does the school take in a great many SEN/problem children during the year? What are the exclusion rates and what are pupils excluded for?

Points to consider

Ask a member of senior staff to explain the school's Self-Evaluation Programme. Note that with primaries, if pupils are leaving in Year 2 this may mean the teaching isn't very good. Find out who is dropping out, when and why.

Your notes

_____

_____

_____

_____

_____

_____

H stands for Head Teacher

Questions to ask

What values does the head teacher espouse? Are they in keeping with your values? Is the head an ostrich head, burying his head in the sand about some serious problems?

Points to consider

Do remember that heads are not the be-all and end-all. The above points are more important. But visionary heads can turn around previously bad schools.

Your notes

_____

_____

_____

_____

_____

_____

Revision guides and reading lists

Revision guides

They must be among the best-selling books in the country and yet they are never reviewed and rarely discussed. They are bought in vast quantities by desperate parents. Almost every bookshop in the land now contains racks of revision guides for all the Key Stages. And you have to give these books some credit: they are usually clearly laid out, often nicely presented and cover the relevant points. However, if used wrongly, they can be very destructive. Some parents appear to be buying these books by the bucket load and ramming them down their children's throats until they squeak. If you do this, you're just putting your child off the subject forever. The revision guides are very reductive: the mysteries of English, maths and science are reduced to fill-in-the-gaps exercises and lists to learn. Your children will be probably be getting enough of this at school; a parent's job is to give their child a wider perspective, to give a child an insight into the sheer wonder of knowledge. To do this, you need to be careful about how you encourage your child to read and revise.

THE NEW SCHOOL RULES for choosing the right revision guide

1. **Talk it through** Crucially, wherever possible let your child decide. If he or she, their teacher or you decide they need a revision guide, take them into your local bookshop or library

and let them browse through the relevant revision guides and find the right one. Most good bookshops stock at least two or three books that cover the same topic, with the approach being slightly different in each one. For example, CGP revision guides have no frills but are very clearly written. (www.cgpbooks.co.uk) while Letts (www.letts-successzone.com/) and BBC guides (www.bbc.co.uk/schools/ revision) are more colourful and tied in with their large interactive websites. The old-fashioned Bond assessment papers are still probably the best for preparing children for scholarship exams: they are very old-fashioned but effective (www.assessmentpapers.co.uk/). There won't be much difference in terms of content of the books, it's just a question of temperament and choice.

2. **Hold your child accountable** If he has bought the book but isn't working from it, remind him that he chose it and therefore needs to use it.

Real books

By far and away the best books to read are those that are not specifically tailored to cramming for an exam, but books which open up the wonder of learning. There are an increasing number of great books on the market now which do a marvellous job at this.

Many of the following titles were first discovered on the www.booktrusted.com website, which is a brilliant resource for finding an excellent child's book on a specific subject. There are a number of different ways of browsing for books on the site, and I have found all of the recommendations to be very reliable.

THE NEW SCHOOL RULE for reading

Be enthusiastic Encourage, as much as possible, browsing in bookshops, charity shops, and libraries. Make sure you are a member of your local library. Browsing is one of the most enjoyable activities about book reading: looking at covers, flicking through books, talking about them with people. Encourage your child to read books which are not totally reductive in content, but ones that are obviously designed to inspire. Don't worry if they are short or insubstantial-looking if they do this.

A very select reading list for your child

For the very early years, many parents and teachers favour particular reading schemes. The Oxford Reading Tree, as mentioned earlier, remains the favourite. If your child is struggling with their reading between the ages of four and eight and they haven't tried the Oxford Reading Tree, you should definitely insist the school tries it, and if they won't, go online and get the books yourself.

I have deliberately avoided all the obvious favourites here, but most books for the relevant age by the following are great:

Malorie Blackman (www.malorieblackman.co.uk/),
Enid Blyton, Roald Dahl, Jim Eldridge, Greek Myth cartoon and story books, Carl Hiaasen, Anthony Horowitz (www.anthonyhorowitz. com/), Brian Jacques (the *Redwall Chronicles* www.redwall.org/), E.S. Nesbit, Spike Milligan, Michael Morpurgo (www.michaelmorpurgo.org/), William Nicolson, Michelle Paver, Philip Pullman, Michael Rosen, J.K. Rowling, adapted Shakespeare story books (and the actual plays themselves), Jacqueline Wilson.

English reading books

Age range 0–5

Title, publisher and author: *Fix-it Duck* (Picture Lions), Jez Alborough

Comment: Hilarious cartoon about a spectacularly incompetent duck.

Age range 5–7

Title, publisher and author: *Runny Babbit* (Marion Boyars Publishers Ltd), Shel Silverstein

Comment: An American comic poet whose last book is inspired nonsense where the letters at the beginnings of words are switched around. Very good for developing awareness of spelling and the shapes of words.

Age range 8–11

Title, publisher and author: *Hacker* (Corgi), Malorie Blackman

Comment: A brilliant and gripping thriller about computers and bank robbery.

Age range 11–14

Title, publisher and author: *Powder Monkey* (Bloomsbury), Paul Dowswell

Comment: A gripping adventure story about a boy who is press-ganged into being a sailor during the time of Napoleon.

Age range 14–16

Title, publisher and author: *How I Live Now* (Puffin), Meg Rosoff

Comment: A thrilling book about adolescence. Boys shouldn't be put off by the cover. It is the best cross-over book for teenagers and adults since Mark Haddon's *The Curious Incident of the Dog in the Night-time.*

Maths books

Age range 3–7

Title, publisher and author: *Handa's Hen* (Walker Books), Eileen Brown

Comment: A very entertaining book about numbers which is ideal for bedtime reading or for story time sessions. (www.booktrusted.com)

Age range 5–8

Title, publisher and author: *Number Stew* (Levinson Children's Books), Mike Hirst

Comment: Lots of activities to help children to learn maths, including simple sums, learning about shapes and recognising money. (www.booktrusted.com)

Age range 6–10

Title, publisher and author: *Think of a Number* (Dorling Kindersley), Johnny Ball

Comment: This is a brilliant book about the history of numbers. It is beautifully illustrated and will surprise anyone who reads it.

Age range 11–14

Title, publisher and author: *Murderous Maths* (Scholastic Hippo), Karjtan Poskitt

Comment: Full of bizarre characters and funny insights into numbers. This is the book for putting the fun back into maths for teenagers.

Age range 14–16

Title, publisher and author: *Murderous Maths – Fractions and Averages* (Scholastic Hippo), Karjtan Poskitt

Comment: Another classic by Poskitt.

Fun books about science

Age range 6–11

Title, publisher and author: *The Stunning Science of Nearly Everything* (Scholastic Press), Nick Arnold

Comment: The reader is taken on a glorious tour of the universe, from the very small to the absolutely, unbelievably big.

Age range 11–15

Title, publisher and author: *Blame My Brain* (Walker Books), Nicola Morgan

Comment: A funny and brilliant guide to the biological mysteries of adolescents.

Age range 13–15

Title, publisher and author: *Can You Feel The Force?* (Dorling Kindersley), Richard Hammond

Comment: The best and most compulsive children's book about physics.

Age range 14–16

Title, publisher and author: *A History of Nearly Everything* (Black Swan), Bill Bryson

Comment: Bryson's classic explanation of the origins of the universe and life on earth.

The best book for detailed parental advice on reading is *The Reading Bug* by Paul Jennings, Penguin, 2004.

A–Z of The New School Rules

A is for Admissions

THE NEW SCHOOL RULES for getting your child into a good school

1. **Take note of the talent** Find out what your child likes and is good at first of all and look for a school that meets those needs. Equally, think about what kind of parent you are and what kind of school you want for your child. For secondary schools, talk to your child about what you want and what they want, and come to some sort of agreement about the kind of school you are looking for. Please be realistic and find out their level from a recognised professional in the field, i.e., director of coaching, or the senior county coach, and not from your after-school club. Are they performing at district, county, national or international level? **Dance:** An excellent dancer may get a scholarship to Italia Conti, Anna Scher, or the Royal Academy of Dance if you choose this path. **Music:** A musician may qualify for the Guildhall School of Music, and may also be offered a scholarship or place at a school which specialises in music. **Sport:** A good all-rounder will be welcome at many private secondary schools and will help towards an all-rounder scholarship, particularly if the child also plays an instrument.

2. **Do your research early** Get the most out of your Local Educational Authority (LEA). A few LEAs, too few in my mind, have parent helplines to assist with the whole process. Learn

about these and about the different types of school in your area by logging onto your LEA's website. Log on to www. dfes.gov.uk and type in the name of your LEA, and the website should come up. Learn how to get the most out of Ofsted. Log on to its website www.ofsted.gov.uk and read the reports. Read the admissions criteria early. When your child is in Year 3 of primary school, scan the admissions criteria of your favoured schools carefully and check to see if they specialise in a subject or area which your child is interested in. It can be to your advantage if your child is diagnosed as Special Educational Needs because most schools favour SEN pupils. This point is going to be more and more important in the coming years for all schools because the government wants to make all schools specialist in status. That means that their admissions criteria will probably favour children with the specialism the school espouses. Evidence of your child having expertise in that specialism could give you the edge. Investigate possible scholarships, bursaries and government grants at this time as well. The best place to start investigating this is the Independent Schools' website (www.isc.co.uk/) which will show you the full array of options open to you. If you're going for the state option, find out whether you can hold on to multiple offers. For example, in London where you're not generally allowed to hold on to multiple offers, nevertheless, in 2006 parents were allowed to hold on to an offer of a specialist music place until one week after 1 March to allow the family to decide on their first choice school; so there are sometimes exceptions. Investigate them all! Don't interrogate the secretarial staff at your favoured schools for inside information: they won't give you any. Ask them to send you the admissions criteria for the school and any other relevant literature and read it very early.

3. **Don't trust the gossip** Listen to what other parents have to say about the schools, and take their views on board, but don't trust them entirely. Many parents do have ulterior motives, but the majority of them do not bribe head teachers or lie

about their addresses. Don't become paranoid and don't panic.

4. **Check 'em out** When looking at secondary schools, visit your preferred four choices of school in Year 4 and get the feel of each school's ethos and ensure you like the schools. Then discuss them with your partner. In Year 5, shadow a Year 6 parent going through the process and take your child to visit only your top choices and see what they think. Discuss your thoughts with your whole family. If you have younger children, think about where they may go when you are making the choices for your first child. So for example, if you send your oldest child, your daughter, to a single-sex school then obviously your son will not be able to go there. If you want your younger child to attend the same school, you'll have to opt for a mixed-sex school. Remember that many schools favour siblings. It is important to discuss this when making your choices. Go and see the school while it is in session. Don't be fobbed off with an open evening. See what it is like during a typical school day.

5. **Use DEATH to help you** Learn how to do a DEATH analysis on a school: D stands for Discipline and Display, E stands for Ethos, Evaluation and Extracurricular Activities, A stands for Assets and Achievement, T stands for Target Setting and Turning Up, H stands for Head Teacher.

6. **Be cautious** Do trust your intuitions about a school, but don't solely rely on them. If the evidence from an inspector's report or your own further investigations show that the school is not that good, your intuition may have been wrong.

7. **Don't be complacent** Rules and regulations change every year. Even the most seasoned professionals get caught out. In addition, don't expect that you will be allocated the nearest state school if you have not put it as first choice on your list. Check to see if your preferred school has been criticised by the ombudsman in recent years. If it has, then it is very, very unlikely that the admissions panel will bend the rules for your child.

8. **Meet the criteria** When filling in the forms, make sure you meet the admissions criteria of your choices. Don't forget to mention any 'special considerations' that might be relevant. Many good state schools will favour children who have struggled in one way or another; don't hide any important information with regards to this. Special considerations is a loose term which refers to any difficulties a child may have had, it is different from special needs which is something that has been officially documented by a school. Don't be shy about your child's special needs, which may or may not be a 'special consideration'. Under new legislation, any child with a serious learning difficulty should receive extra time and resources at school, and is entitled to study at the school which best will meet their needs. This means that if you feel a particular school would best meet your child's need and you can prove it, you have a right to send your child there.

9. **Do your paperwork properly** Remember to apply through your LEA and the school if this is required – which it normally is – for voluntary-aided schools. Don't expect you will get your first choice school if you don't meet the admissions criteria. Always put your first choice in first place on the form.

10. **Appeal** to the relevant admissions authority if you have failed to get into the school of your choice. Try to hide any trauma you have about schools admissions from your child. Be aware most appeals fail because parents do not meet the admissions criteria.

11. **Appeal against the appeal** If you are rejected think about going to the ombudsman (www.lgo.org.uk/index.php) who can overturn the appeal panel's decision.

12. **Don't despair** Realise that sometimes there is nothing you can do: you have to accept the school your child is allocated. Remember, children are resilient and most can adapt. Study after study shows that it is parental support that plays a key role in a child's ultimate attainment.

B is for Bullying

THE NEW SCHOOL RULES for doing something about bullying

1. **Tell the school** Your child may beg you not to contact the school after they have confessed that they are being bullied. Ignore their pleas, contact the school immediately. If there is no one obvious to speak to, speak to the head teacher who will normally pass the enquiry down to the relevant person.

2. **Reassure your child** Remember to tell your child that it is not his or her fault.

3. **Investigate** Read the school's anti-bullying policy – all schools should have one. Follow the procedures on this in the first instance. A good school will carry out a thorough investigation into any allegations of bullying, and report to parents about what they have discovered. It will take a parent's concerns seriously and try its best to solve the problem.

4. **Go up the chain** If you are not satisfied with the school's response take your complaint to the governors of the school. If the governors are not able to stop the bullying, go to the police.

THE NEW SCHOOL RULES for avoiding cyber-bullying

1. **Keep an eye on that computer** Always insist that the computer is used in a communal area where you can regularly monitor what is going on.

2. **Talk it through** Tell your child about the dangers of cyber-bullying. Remember again to tell him or her that it is not their fault. Help them to develop a thick skin as some kind of bullying is probably going to happen at some point in anyone's life.

3. **Investigate** If you think that the cyber-bullies are at your child's school, inform the school, saving the relevant messages, emails, and Internet addresses. Make sure you get the ISP address where the abusive message was sent from. Report instances of cyber-bullying to the Internet Service Provider (ISP) which is usually the name of the ISP plus the word 'abuse', e.g., abuse@hotmail.com or abuse@btinternet.com.

> ▶ **CHECK OUT**
> www.dfes.gov.uk/bullying/ for help on bullying.

THE NEW SCHOOL RULES for stopping your child being a bully

1. **Be honest with yourself** Examine your own behaviour very carefully. Do you get angry with your child a lot? Do you attempt to get them to change their behaviour by frightening them? Learn to avoid threats as much as possible. The child who is threatened at home is a child who then threatens others at school.

2. **Talk it through** Learn to talk to your child in a calm way. Talk about your own feelings and try to give them the tools to talk about their own emotions. The first step to changing their behaviour is by getting them talking about their own behaviour. Teach your child to empathise by telling them stories. Psychologists have shown that telling stories about bullies and victims can help children learn to empathise with victims more. Roald Dahl and J.K. Rowling's stories are particularly good for this; they have shown time and again what it's like to be on the wrong end of bullying behaviour.

C is for Complaining

THE NEW SCHOOL RULES to help parents deal with teachers who complain

1. **Work out what's gone wrong** Don't be immediately defensive. Find out what has happened and trust the teacher is telling the truth. Diagnose the past. Find out what has been going wrong and ask whether this has been affecting your child's work and learning. Is your child working at the level expected for his or her age? Is he or she working at the level expected for his ability? What is he not learning that he should be? If your child is not working at the level expected for his age or ability, it may be that they have a learning difficulty. Don't be frightened or defensive if a teacher says this. Your child should be assessed by the special needs department, and could well receive extra funding and teacher time if they are put on an Individual Education Plan (IEP). (See Chapter 4, Does Your Child Have Special Needs?) It may be that your child's learning style is not being catered for. All schools now are supposed to cater for pupils' different learning styles: visual, auditory, kinaesthetic and tactile. There is a belief that if a child is, for example, very 'visual' then the materials given to help them learn should be full of pictures and the exercises set should be focused on drawing pictures and spider diagrams. Each child should be given a 'personalised' learning plan. If your child has not been tested for his or her own particular learning style, ask for this, and ask that the exercises set are focused on their own learning style.

2. **Set some targets** Above all, set specific targets with the teacher and your child. Ask the teacher to draw up an Individual Action Plan (IAP) with the pupil where specific tasks are set with definite deadlines on them. It is crucial that your child understands the action plan, so it should be done with him there and agreed by him and by you. Every child is entitled to an IAP.

It should be realistic, though, and not absurdly optimistic. It should be no more than a page and should have no more than five targets that your child will remember to carry out.

3. **Beware bribes and treats** As a general rule, avoid the carrot and stick approach unless absolutely nothing else is working. The problem with dangling the carrot too often is that it actually demotivates in the long run. Children become more interested and preoccupied with the reward in front of them than actually improving their work and attitude. Punishing children for the failure to do work often fails too because it makes them resentful and angry. By far the best way is to make clear why the work is worth doing. Your child should realise why it is worthwhile without any rewards or punishments. If they don't know why they are doing it, and you don't either, maybe the work is actually pointless.

THE NEW SCHOOL RULES for changing the set or stream your child is in

1. **Work out what's gone wrong** Ask to see all the relevant test data that the school has on your child. In particular, ask to see at the results of any IQ (Intelligence Quotient) tests which your child has taken. Many schools, feeling distrustful of the Key Stage test results, pay for companies to do multiple-choice IQ-style tests (the names vary according to the company carrying out the testing) and see what a pupil's IQ looks like. It may be that your child has scored poorly on these tests and has been put in a lower set or stream as a result of this. In which case, question the result. Most IQ tests are a little discredited now: they usually fail to take into account a child's creativity or their social skills and instead focus upon a narrow range of skills such as their mathematical ability, verbal knowledge, spatial knowledge and reasoning skills. The best schools will always look at a number of test scores and take into account the teacher assessment of a child. The most

accurate assessment is usually the teacher's, if there has been no undue pressure for the teacher to inflate their scores in order to get a pay rise – which in these days of performance- related pay is always a problem. Examine the social, gender and ethnic mix of a particular group or set. Equal opportunities legislation these days means that all classes should reflect the ethnic, social and gender mix of the school as a whole. I have had to teach some disastrous bottom sets where there have been only white work-ing-class and Afro-Caribbean boys, some of whom were pretty clever but who had been placed in the bottom set because of their atrocious behaviour. You are within your rights to ask that your child is moved to a class which properly reflects the social mix of the school.

2. **Don't slag off the class in front of your child** Don't tangle your child in all your enquiries by denigrating the set they are in. It may be that they will have to stay there. If you have done nothing but slag off the group to your child, or allowed your child to indulge in moaning endlessly about it, then you will not have done them any favours when they have to stay.

THE NEW SCHOOL RULES for complaining about bad teaching

1. **Work out what's gone wrong** Contact the teacher you have a problem with first. Don't get aggressive. It may be that you haven't heard the other side of the story: remember children are often not reliable sources of information. They often lie or deceive themselves. Have a quiet chat with the 'problem' teacher. In particular, you should focus upon what your child is learning in the lesson, not the misbehaviour of the other pupils – they aren't your concern.

2. **Set targets** You should ask for an Individual Action Plan (IAP) to be drawn up: a plan of action for your child in the area of difficulty. Specific tasks should be set with specific deadlines, and there should be a definite review period to see if your child

has met those targets. The IAP route is definitely the best for pupils who are working in a badly behaved class because it means that they can get on by themselves.

3. **Go up the chain** If the teaching doesn't get better, contact the teacher's line manager: this is the person directly in charge of that teacher. You don't need to ask the teacher himself who this is: the office staff should know who all the line managers are. Explain the problem, and if necessary go into the school. At this point, if you are seriously concerned your child is not learning anything you are legally entitled to ask for an IAP for your child. This is a series of targets with deadlines that will be reviewed in a few months. The teacher should draw up these targets with the child in order to ensure that he or she learns the right material. If this fails, you should see the head teacher, and explain the situation. If that fails, you are entitled to take your complaint to the governing body. This is a monstrously bureaucratic procedure, but if you are dealing with a very severe problem, you may need to do this.

D is for Disappointment

THE NEW SCHOOL RULES if your child is disappointed with their results

1. **Investigate** Was this result expected? Is it the same as the teacher's predicted grade? If it is not, ask the school's exams secretary or administrator to request a re-mark. You could alternatively ask the school to request a photocopy of the script so that your child's teachers can examine the marking on it; if it is not good marking, they could then request a re-mark if there is time. Remember, the exam boards do not like re-marks. They do everything in their power to make it difficult to get a script remarked: they are often expensive and the deadlines are very tight. See if the exam can be retaken. Most exams nowadays can be retaken. However, do bear in mind

that some exams such as Key Stage tests cannot be retaken except in exceptional circumstances.

2. **Set targets** Make sure your child's teacher draws up a detailed action plan about how, when and where they will learn the relevant skills to help them with the next test. The action plan should be understandable for your child and should have clear deadlines set on it.

3. **Keep calm** While your child should be working for the exam, he or she should also try to put exams in perspective, they are not the be-all and end-all of life: they should learn to see that. This is probably just as important as working for the exam. Your child needs to have the right balance between work and life.

F is for Keeping Fit

THE NEW SCHOOL RULE for stopping your child becoming a slob

Get into the groove Establish a good routine with your children. Establish clear times and places where work is done. Make your children see the intrinsic value of work but also help them see that some work is just boring but has to be done. That's reality! Pay attention to your children by having family meals together and reading stories to them before they go to bed. Ration TV and computer use.

THE NEW SCHOOL RULES for healthy eating

1. **Talk it through** If your child is eating a lot of junk food, don't immediately ban it. Discuss the issue, and find out what she knows about the content of the junk food they are eating. Agree to phase it out slowly, replacing the junk food items a little bit at a time.

2. **Get into the groove** Get your child into the groove of eating healthily. Don't ban junk food entirely. Have it as a treat. Cook fresh food and eat it yourself!

G is for Gifted and Talented

THE NEW SCHOOL RULES about gifted and talented pupils

1. **Don't be ashamed** You must not feel ashamed if your child has a learning difficulty, and therefore a special need. Do not feel it is a stigma. Precisely the opposite is the case; it may well be that your child is actually gifted and talented but has interlinked special needs.

2. **Learn the lingo** If your child is gifted and talented in a particular area this does not mean he or she has a special need, but often the special needs coordinator (SENCO) will deal with gifted and talented pupils as well or will work closely with the gifted and talented coordinator. Therefore it is worth contacting the SENCO if you feel your child is gifted and talented in the first instance. Try to use the correct language for the school. Say, 'My child has learning difficulties because he/she is a particularly talented reader/artist/sports person, etc. As a result of this, he/she wants everything to be related to his/her topics of interest.' Or you could say, 'He/she is becoming easily distracted because he/she is becoming bored with the work; he/she is clearly gifted and talented in such and such an area.' Using this language will help the school tap into the relevant funding.

3. **Set targets** Make sure that a detailed Individual Education Plan (IEP) is drawn up for your child so that he or she receives help which is 'additional to and/or different from' the ordinary work.

H is for Home and School

THE NEW SCHOOL RULES for homework

1. **Make doing homework feel easy and natural** Have a designated time and communal place for completing homework. Do some work while your child is working: set a good example. Encourage the meeting of deadlines even if the school is struggling to do this. Remember, things are different in the real world. Monitor the homework diary very carefully.

3. **Be suspicious** Don't trust the stock remark like 'I don't have any homework' or 'I did it at lunchtime' or 'There was a supply teacher and none was set'. Even if there is nothing in the homework diary, check with the school if this is correct; don't wait until the parents' evening. Some schools have websites now where teachers post the homework on the web so there's no escape.

3. **Don't hover** Don't do the homework for your child, don't hover around them too much. Let them have the freedom to make mistakes.

THE NEW SCHOOL RULE about coursework

Let your child make her own mistakes Insist that your child does her own work. By all means show her how to research a topic, but don't do the research. Do not make your child frightened of failure. Encourage them to have a go. Complain if you think your child's teacher is doing the coursework for him or her. You can easily find this out by picking up some coursework and questioning your child about some difficult passage that they probably haven't written. Remember, in the end, cheating is totally counterproductive. Your child is not learning anything except that being a cheat is the way to get on in life. Sooner or later, cheats in a law-abiding society land up in serious trouble.

THE NEW SCHOOL RULES about home–school agreements

1. **Read them carefully** They are much more than pieces of useless paper. Examine them carefully, looking particularly at the homework and discipline comments: it may well be that you have to talk to the school about both these issues. If the agreement makes promises about the school's responsibilities for homework and behaviour, then the school should be held accountable for these promises. Equally, if you sign up to support the school's ethos and policies, you need to do so, but you should find out what these are before you sign.

2. **Use them to your advantage** If your child is not behaving properly or is not doing his homework, remind him of the home–school agreement. Don't be afraid of re-reading these important bits of paper with your child, they can really help.

3. **You do not have to sign them if you disagree with them.**

THE NEW SCHOOL RULES about letters home

1. **Talk about them** Read the letters. Don't throw them in the bin. Discuss the contents of the letters with your children in a calm way. Do not get into a panic. If you find the contents of a letter objectionable, contact the person who sent the letter in the first place – do not run straight to the head teacher, who may know very little about it.

2. **Reply to them** Remember that schools do pay very close attention to parents' criticisms. They may appear to ignore your complaints in the first instance, but behind closed doors there will be a big discussion of the issue. Your voice will be heard.

M is for Motivation

THE NEW SCHOOL RULES for helping your child learn properly

1. **Talk it through** Engage your child in pleasant non-confrontational conversation every day. The research shows that no matter what you're talking about – whether it's the weather, what your child had for lunch, stories about your life – every little bit counts and helps your child do well at school.

2. **Praise them** Praise specifically and regularly.

3. **Don't threaten** Avoid Kick-In-The-Arse and PULL motivation.

THE NEW SCHOOL RULES for motivating children

1. **Be enthusiastic** Read to your child with enthusiasm. Read in front of your child and show them that you enjoy reading.

2. **Try different approaches** Story tapes can work wonders for slow or poor readers. When the tape finishes they often try to read the next book. Make sure their room has lots of reference and non-fiction books as well as fiction suitable for their age/reading group. Charity shops, church fairs, and libraries are wonderful resources for these.

N is for Needs

THE NEW SCHOOL RULES about SEN

1. **Don't be ashamed** If you think your child has a learning difficulty talk to your child's teacher or the school's SENCO.

2. **Investigate** Find out any relevant test scores such as IQ tests,

Key Stage test results, internal assessments and see whether you child is under-achieving. Ask for a breakdown of the results if necessary: your school will not only have the overall level for your child in English but will have scores for reading, writing and speaking and listening. Survey the general atmosphere of the school: how seriously does the head take SEN? Does the SENCO have an important position on the senior management team or do they have lots of other duties which mean they won't have much time to devote to SEN?

3. **Demand your due** Remember, you are entitled to ask for your child to be assessed by a properly trained educational psychologist if you and the school feel there are significant problems. If your school appears to be hazy about this, contact the SEN department at your LEA. Your LEA is obliged to give you details of reputable educational psychologists who could test your child but, except in certain circumstances, they may not be obliged to pay for the testing. Always use an educational psychologist recommended by your LEA in the first instance. If you have the money you could get your child tested yourself, particularly for dyslexia issues. Look up the relevant contact details on: www.dyslexiaaction.org.uk/. If necessary ask for concessions in public examinations. This has become a bit of scam which is much abused, but if your child has a genuine need then it is worth asking for extra time in public examinations. Potentially, children can receive extra time – up to 25 per cent in some cases – if they have a special need such as dyslexia or they are a slow reader or writer. If motor skills or physical disabilities are the problem, such is the case with dyspraxic children, then they may use a laptop or amanuensis (a person to write for a child).

4. **Be patient** Be prepared to go through a laborious process of assessment and target setting if you want your child to get extra help and resources. The procedure now is: school action, IEP, review of IEP, school action plus IEP, review of IEP and if necessary statement. Remember, acquiring a statement of SEN can take months, even years.

5. **Talk it through** Talk to other parents who have children with similar special needs. Talk to other children with SEN. Listen to their stories.

P is for Parents' Evening

THE NEW SCHOOL RULES for parents' evenings

1. **Be prepared** If there is a big problem, always flag it up before the parents' evening. Come prepared, if you can, with your child's report. Bring a notebook and pen to jot down key comments.

2. **Find out the level your child is working at** Ask for their current National Curriculum level in the subject and find out whether this is in line with the national average: in Year 3, the state expects every pupil to be a good Level 2 which translates as a 2b (a is top, b is middle, c is bottom of the level). Pupils should be moving up 'two parts' every year, so, for example, in Year 4, pupils should be achieving in English and maths a 3c, in Year 5 a 3a, Year 6 a 4b, Year 7 a 5c, Year 8 a 5a, Year 9 a 6b. Ask for any other scores such as IQ tests that have given the school the raw data for their verbal and non-verbal reasoning skills.

3. **Get precise information** Try to pin down teachers when they make generalised comments such as 'he's/she's doing very well' or 'he/she never listens': use the 5 Ws to work out, WHAT exactly is happening? WHEN is it occurring? WHERE is it occurring? WHO is involved? And WHY is it happening? Remember to focus on the 3 Rs above all else: how good is your child's reading and writing and arithmetic?

4. **Be supportive** Always be the teacher's friend – even if you don't like that teacher. Talk about what support you can give and ask them how you can help. That way the teacher will be more willing to go the extra mile to help your child. If it's been

a bad night, don't return and hit the roof. Take time to reflect and review your notes. Follow up by talking to the teacher your child likes best: this may not be their form tutor. Most teachers want to help, the favourite teachers especially. Try to work out why your child is doing well in that teacher's lessons and not others.

5. **Set targets** From each teacher look for a specific piece of positive information and a specific target that your child can work towards.

R is for Revision

THE NEW SCHOOL RULES about revision

1. **Support those teachers** Stress this blindingly obvious but much ignored point to your child: there is no better revision than working in lessons. Use the teacher first before relying on revision guides.

2. **Help your child be organised** Draw up a revision timetable: a little bit each day. Revise using the relevant Assessment Objectives for the subject. If you don't know what these are, ask your teacher or consult the websites of the exam boards (www.aqa.org.uk, www.edexcel.org.uk, www.ocr.org.uk) . This may take some research: they can be buried in the syllabi.

3. **Have fun** Make the revision interesting. Use spider diagrams, colours, posters, poems, music, tape-recording and videoing relevant material. However, don't get so bogged down in learning about revision techniques that you don't do any revision. Sometimes the best revision is simply copying out key phrases from the relevant texts! I passed all my O and A levels this way.

4. **Talk it through** Ask them to explain to you the key concepts in each subject.

5. Make use of their friendships Ask your child to buddy up with a trusted pupil and get them to explain key concepts to each other. One of the best ways of remembering or understanding something is to speak about it out loud.

6. Be cautious Don't trust the web for revision, except for the really reliable sites such as the BBC or sites recommended by the school. I have had pupils who have spent hours reading rubbish on the web when they could have spent that time actually reading the books they were being tested upon.

S is for Settling In

THE NEW SCHOOL RULES about what information to demand from your child's new school

1. **Get the nitty-gritty** Ask for practical information: a map of the school, access to drinking fountains, toilets, wash basins, medical facilities, the phone, procedures for break and lunchtimes. A particular concern for many parents I have spoken to is the toilet: they want to know how often the toilets are cleaned, what type of toilet paper there is, what kind of soap is in the basins. In many ways, the school's response to these questions will be an indicator of its attitude in general: if it is a nice place, it will have nice toilets. Ask for some up-to-date information about the extracurricular activities going on in the school, and the social functions. You should receive a calendar or booklet with dates of parents' evenings, concerts, clubs and so on.

2. **Don't suffer in silence** If your child is being picked on or seems unhappy, ask for a copy of the school's discipline policy – these are the rules for behaviour that the school insists upon – and how it deals with bullying (see Chapter 3 How to Tackle the Big Problems for more on bullying). If your child is finding the work difficult or seems to be making little progress,

ask for a copy of the school's special needs procedures and talk to the SENCO (see Chapter 4 Does Your Child Have Special Needs? for more on this). If your child is bored, you must ask to meet with your child's teachers and tell them about this. If the teacher tells you that there is nothing much they can do, you have a right to ask for your child to be 'given an Individual Action Plan (IAP) which sets out clearly a list of tasks that will stretch and engage them in your child's preferred learning style'. I know this sounds like terrible jargon but it's the way we teachers speak now. An IAP is, effectively, a list of specific targets or goals for your child to work towards that will motivate him or her: it should be drawn up with your child and has his or her consent so that he or she feels part of the programme. A 'learning style' is the way in which your child learns best: it might be that they learn 'visually' (drawings help them remember and understand things) or 'aurally' (they need to hear words read out to them in order to comprehend best) and so forth. To work out your child's learning style log on to: www.bbc.co.uk/keyskills/ extra/module1/1.shtml. So for example, after discussion with your child and teacher, an IAP might be drawn up so that your child has a particular book to read, or a series of drawings to complete by a particular date – and then attitudes and progress will be reviewed. For more on learning styles and IAPs see the glossary at the back.

T is for Tutors

THE NEW SCHOOL RULES for private tutors

1. **Talk it through** Always discuss the decision to hire a tutor with your child. You must get his or her agreement. If you can, talk to your child's teachers and see what they think. Ask for the syllabus they are studying and copies of previous exam papers: you are entitled to do this. It may be that you can help your child yourself and save the money. If you can, discuss whether to get a private tutor with your child's school. Don't

be blackmailed into getting a tutor, though: if your child has a learning difficulty she should receive extra funding and help from the school (see Chapter 4 Does Your Child Have Special Needs?). Equally, if the teaching in your child's school is substandard you need to address this matter urgently with the head teacher and, if necessary, the governing body.

2. **Be cautious of teachers at your child's school who are touting for extra money** Many teachers run revision lessons free of charge, recognising the need for these lessons.

3. **Investigate** Always ask to see the tutor's qualifications yourself, including passport, degree certificate(s), two reputable references and a Criminal Records Bureau (CRB) check. All qualified teachers in England have to have such a document which proves they have no criminal convictions, and all private tutors should produce one. Don't trust the agency you have signed up with to do this unless they explicitly say they will. Ask the tutor how familiar he is with the syllabus your child is studying and what resources he has to offer. The Internet has a whole host of different private tutoring sites. Many of them offer free access to tutors. You will need to check their documentation very carefully. Remember, do not reveal your phone number and address to them until you are satisfied about them.

X is for Sexy

THE NEW SCHOOLS RULES about sex, drugs and rock 'n' roll

1. **Talk it through** When you think the time is right, talk to your child about your fears. It is important to explain that you are frightened for them, and care for them, but try not to ban them from doing things – all the evidence suggests that this approach backfires. Keep your child informed. Tell them the truth.

2. **Investigate** Use the web to keep up to date with the latest news on these subjects. The best place to start is the Parentlineplus website (www.parentlineplus.org.uk/) which provides links to all the best websites dealing with these concerns. An organisation called DARE (Drugs Awareness Resistance Education) has been particularly effective in dealing with this problem. Their website (www.dare.uk.com/) is very good and provides much up-to-date information about various drugs.

Y is for Yobs

THE NEW SCHOOL RULES for battling against yob culture

1. **Investigate** But be subtle with your spying. Don't go stomping into a situation, demanding to know what is going on. Try to figure it out with some gentle questions, by observation and discussion with any other people involved or in the know. Find out what is really going on. Eavesdrop upon your child, talk to them, talk to other parents. Invite other children around to your house.

2. **Talk it through** Educate your child from an early age about society: how it is made up of different social groups, how some people behave differently. Discuss drugs and alcohol, and gang culture. Don't make them frightened, but tell them the truth.

3. **Show them how to avoid trouble** Give them strategies for avoiding trouble. Lead by example: don't get drawn into vitriolic arguments in front of them, show them that you can laugh things off and walk away from sources of conflict you encounter on the street and at home. Help develop a constructive social activity such as a sport or recreation which involves their friends, football, music and so forth.

4. **Be jokey** Help them develop a sense of humour. Making jokes which are not personalised and vicious is an excellent way of avoiding real trouble. Buy them a joke book suitable for their age and go through it with them.

5. **Don't panic** Finally, try not to worry too much. Karen told me: 'It is very, very easy to obsess and feel cheated by the state school system. We really did not want our daughters to go to the school they're in, and appealed twice against our older daughter's school allocation. Yes, I think they might well have had a more pleasant experience in the school up the road which people in our street traditionally went to, but they are bright kids and are taking the best from where they are. Academically they'll do OK because they are able, they tend to go around with other bright kids, and they have positive influences at home. Organisationally, discipline-wise and environmentally, the school is really awful. Socially, they have made friends from many backgrounds, races, creeds which is always a good thing.'

Useful websites

- **www.dfes.gov.uk/bullying** For help with bullying.

- **www.dfes.gov.uk** For government information (and propaganda) about state schools. This site is massive and includes links to many other important sites. It is easy to get lost in. You should look at the parents' centre site (see below) before trawling through this one in detail.

- **www.aqa.org.uk** (AQA), **www.edexcel.org.uk** (Edexcel), **www.ocr.org.uk** (OCR) Examination syllabi and past exam questions, check the wonderful websites of the examination boards. They are chock-full of past examination papers for GCSE and A level and will save you a fortune in revision guides. But before you do make doubly sure you know what syllabus your child is following. Remember a syllabus (an outline of what topics must be covered) for a course is now called a 'specification'. They can all be downloaded very quickly from these sites.

- **www.nagcbritain.org.uk** For information on children who are gifted and talented.

- **www.goodschoolsguide.co.uk** For information on state and independent schools. *The Good Schools' Guide* is published as a book every year with detailed updated information on the top schools in the country.

- **www.isc.co.uk** For information on independent schools. Lots of biased information about the wonders of private schools.

- **www.ofsted.gov.uk** For Ofsted reports.

- **schoolsfinder.direct.gov.uk** For school profiles (schools' annual reports).

- **www.ace-ed.org.uk** For impartial advice on schools, the charity the Advisory Centre for Education is worth a look. It is particularly good if you have a specific problem that requires legal advice, while the FAQ section answers most common queries about choosing schools, bullying, SEN. The BBC website is also pretty good and much more interactive, if a little bland at times: www.bbc.co.uk/schools/parents.

- **www.themindgym.com** For exercises to improve your child's mind it might be worth trying the Mind Gym. It's aimed at business people but it can be used by anyone.

- **www.parentscentre.gov.uk** For government-sponsored parents' advice. This is an excellent website which covers every area of parents and schools. However, do bear in mind that it is a government website so you will not find any advice which is critical of the government or the bureaucrats. The Advisory Centre for Education (see above) is perhaps more reliable when talking about key issues such as admissions.

- **www.parentalk.co.uk** For more parents' information on schools. This is an excellent site which contains a whole host of other contacts and links to their publications, which are clearly and accurately written.

- **www.schooladviceforparents.co.uk** This is my own website specifically aimed at giving parents tailor-made and up-to-date advice about schools.

- **www.teachers.tv** has many of the programmes from Teachers' TV (available on digital) to download which are relevant to any parents who are interested in their child's education. I think it is the one successful initiative the government has launched in recent years.

Glossary

AD(H)D Attention Deficit (Hyperactivity) Disorder If you suspect your child has difficulty concentrating in lessons and is very restless much of the time, he or she may be suffering from this condition. Please refer to the chapter dealing with SEN on how to get your child assessed for this condition. For more information contact the National ADD Information and Support Service (www.addiss.co.uk or www.adders.org). These are both sites which will give you information on the condition and further contact details.

Admissions authority Some types of schools – voluntary-aided, foundation and trust schools – are their own admissions authorities because parents send their application direct to that individual school. They must not forget also to apply through their Local Education Authority (LEA) as well. Some schools – community and voluntary-controlled – have their admissions controlled by the LEA. Parents only apply for them through the LEA.

Admissions criteria It is vital that you read the criteria or list of rules that each school uses to select their pupils. Voluntary-aided, foundation and trust schools can set their own admissions criteria. (See Chapter 1 Getting Your Child into a Good School.)

AS level This stands for Advanced Supplementary level, which is the first part of an A level which pupils take usually in Year 12.

A2 level The second year of A level.

Autism spectrum disorders Autism is a neurological condition which makes it difficult for a child to form relationships or communicate with others. It is wrong to say that a child is 'autistic', they are merely on the 'autism spectrum'. At the mild end of the spectrum there is Asperger's syndrome which might cause a child to be a little eccentric and uncommunicative, and at the other there is extreme autism which means a child will find it almost impossible to communicate properly with people. For more information log on to the website of the National Autism Society: www.nas.org.uk.

Baseline assessment The first assessment made by a teacher during your child's first weeks at primary school. It is an important assessment to get right because your child's performance in tests in future years will be measured against his or her performance in this baseline assessment. Children are assessed for language and literacy, maths, and personal and social skills.

BSP Behavioural Support Plan.

BTECS Business and Technology Education Council.

CAT Cognitive Ability Test (produced by the National Foundation for Educational Research). This is essentially an IQ test which tests a child's reasoning skills with words, quantities and spatial patterns. Many, many schools use the test because it does not require much prior knowledge to do well in. It is a very good predictor of natural intelligence as opposed to learned intelligence. It is well worth knowing what your child's CATS score is (see: www.nfer-nelson.co.uk/education/resources/cat3/faqs.asp?css=1#faq1) for more information.

Catchment area The majority of admissions authorities now give priority to children who live in an area around the school, but there may be other priorities though.

Community school The LEA controls the admissions for these schools.

CVA Context Value-Added. A new way Ofsted is using to measure the performance of schools. The CVA takes into account the social background of the pupils in measuring how well they have done in school. Very dodgy statistics in my view, but they are increasingly being used to make judgements about schools.

County schools The LEA controls admissions for these schools.

CTC City Technology College.

DfES Department for Education and Skills. The government department which supervises the running of schools throughout the country.

Differentiation The QCA (Qualifications and Curriculum Authority) defines this as: 'The organisation of teaching programmes and methods specifically to suit the age, ability and aptitudes of specific children'. All state schools should 'differentiate'. This means that the work set should engage your child and help him or her learn. If the work isn't doing this, the first step will be to ask, 'Is the work differentiated enough to meet the needs of my child?' If it isn't, you should ask that it is by requesting an Individual Action Plan for your child.

Dyslexia This is a learning disability which affects reading ability. Persons with dyslexia may have difficulty remembering, recognising, and or reversing written letters, numbers, and words, might read backwards, and have poor handwriting. For more information log on to www.dyslexiaaction.org.uk. This excellent site gives parents a full and accurate checklist of points for dyslexia. You could also read *The Secret Life of the Dyslexic Child: a practical guide for parents and educators* by Robert Frank, Rodale – Macmillan. Also *Day-to-Day Dyslexia in the Classroom*, second edition by Joy Pollock, Elizabeth Waller and Rody Politt, Routledge Falmer, 2004.

Dyspraxia This condition causes severe difficulty in performing tasks requiring fine motor skills such as drawing or writing. For more information: *Dyspraxia: Developmental Co-ordination Disorder* by Dr Amanda Kirby, Souvenir Press. Also *Making Inclusion Work for Children With Dyspraxia: Practical Strategies for Teachers* by Gill Dixon and Lois M. Addy, Routledge Falmer, 2004.

EAL English As An Additional Language.

EBD Emotional and Behavioural Difficulties.

ESL English as a Second Language.

Every child matters (As if they didn't before this legislation was passed!) This is a new approach to the well-being of children and young people from birth to age 19. The government's aim is for every child, whatever their background or their circumstances, to have the support they need to:

- be healthy
- stay safe
- enjoy and achieve
- make a positive contribution
- achieve economic well-being.

No one in the education field has got their head around what this new legislation means yet, but it appears to give parents many more rights than they had before. For example, it seems that if your child is being badly bullied, you may have recourse to law since he or she isn't 'safe' at school. This is, as yet, untested in the courts (see: www.everychildmatters.gov.uk).

Exclusion The suspension or expulsion of a pupil from school for disciplinary reasons. You can appeal against an exclusion if you think it is unfair by contacting the school governing body disciplinary committee.

Extended schools The government is aiming for all state schools to become schools which open well beyond the normal school hours, with their premises being used for after-school clubs, parenting classes or anything else the wider community requires.

Feeder schools Some admissions authorities automatically accept pupils from specific primary schools. Remember, always check the admissions criteria of your favoured schools a few years in advance.

Foundation schools These schools have the power to set their own admissions, but are nominally run by the LEA.

GCE General Certificate of Education. These are A levels by any other name. It is particularly important to bear this in mind when looking up syllabi on the Internet.

GCSE General Certificate of Secondary Education. These replaced the old O levels.

GNVQ General National Vocational Qualification taken mainly by pupils aged 16 and in full-time education.

Healthy Schools Initiative A multi-faceted initiative aimed at improving the health of pupils and teachers. In particular, it has set strict guidelines for school dinners but has also asked schools to address a multitude of health issues in schools, including encouraging pupils to make their own fresh food.

HMI Her Majesty's Inspectors for schools, otherwise known as Ofsted.

HOD Head of Department.

HOF Head of Faculty.

Home–school agreement Every state school should have asked parents to sign a home–school agreement, after consulting a number of them. The agreement aims to make parents aware of their responsibilities and the school's ethos and guidelines.

HOY Head of Year.

IAP Individual Action Plan, which every child is entitled to. A plan of action that will help him or her learn in the best way possible. You are entitled to have this plan 'personalised' to meet specific learning styles (see: www.bbc.co.uk/keyskills/extra/module1/1.shtml).

IEP Individual Education Plan is a planning, teaching and reviewing tool. It records key short-term targets and strategies for an individual pupil that are different from or additional to those in place for the rest of the group or class. Pupils with learning difficulties should all have an IEP, and gifted and talented pupils may be given one too.

ISIS Independent Schools Information Service (see: www.isc.co.uk/).

KS Key Stage. A child's progress through school is marked out in Key Stages. Each stage covers a number of school years and there is a test at the end of the stage, starting at Key Stage 1 and finishing at Key Stage 4.

Key Stage tests These are sometimes named SATs (Standard Attainment Tests). At the end of each Key Stage pupils must take tests to see how well they have done. No child can 'fail' a test but they are expected to attain certain levels. Within each level there are further 'levels', a: top of the level, b: middle of the level, c: bottom of the level. Children are expected to move up at least two levels every year, so if your child is marked at seven as being a 2c in English, by the time he or she is eight he should be a 2a, by nine a 3b, at ten a 4a and so on. The best website I found to explain this in detail is not a government website but a primary school one. It is not a hugely professional site (some of the links don't work but scroll down the page and you'll find all the answers) but it does the job better than anything else (see: www.woodlands-junior.kent.sch.uk/SATS.html#levels).

Summary:

Key Stage	Age range and School Years	Minimum level expected in Key Stage tests
Key Stage 1	5–7-year-olds (Years 1–3)	Level 2
Key Stage 2	8–11-year-olds (Years 4–6)	Level 4
Key Stage 3	12–14-year-olds (Years 7–9)	Levels 5 and 6
Key Stage 4	15–16-year-olds (Years 10–11)	Grade C or above in GCSE, pass at GNVQ
Key Stage 5	17–18-year-olds (Years 12–13)	E grade or above at A level

LAC Looked-After Children.

LEA Local Education Authority. The term 'Local Education Authority' (LEA) describes a type of council which has responsibility for providing education to pupils of school age in its area. Their overall education remit covers all the ages in their area from early years to adult education. Most crucially, it should be sufficiently organised so that there are enough places at good schools for all the pupils in the area. Whether it does this or not is another matter. Some LEAs have parent helplines: if they do, use the helpline. If they don't, complain!

Learning styles There are four different learning styles: visual (seeing), auditory (hearing), kinaesthetic (moving), and tactile (touching). Children learn in different ways and may benefit from being stimulated to learn by one style above another. So for example, if they are 'kinaesthetic' in their learning style, they may learn better by doing drama and PE. Every child is entitled to have a 'personalised' learning scheme which caters specifically for their learning style. Most schools haven't got their head around this at all.

LSA Learning Support Assistant. LSAs are not fully qualified teachers and usually support children with learning difficulties.

MLD Mild Learning Difficulty.

National Curriculum All state schools must teach the content laid out in the National Curriculum.

National Curriculum Levels All pupils undergo national tests and teacher assessments at ages 7, 11 and 14. The school then must send a report to parents telling them what National Curriculum levels their child has reached in both tests and teacher assessments.

NUT National Union of Teachers. The biggest and most powerful teaching union.

Ofsted Office for Standards in Education: the school inspectorate. Their reports on schools aim to say what a school is good at and what they need to improve upon. Their website is excellent and very easy to use. Their reports should be read before deciding upon any state school (see: www.ofsted.gov.uk).

PANDA Performance and Assessment Reports. Produced by the Office for Standards in Education (OFSTED) and issued every year to schools. These reports compare the results of a particular school with schools in similar areas and see whether the school is doing better or worse than them. They make for very interesting reading but can be unreliable indicators about how good a school is.

Parent Partnership Service Nearly all LEAs have parent partnership services whereby the LEA will provide an adviser for parents to guide them through the SEN process if it is required. Contact your LEA for more information.

PEP Personal Education Plan.

Performance Tables or League Tables. The Department for Education and Skills (DfES) publishes comparative secondary and 16–18 performance tables each year. The tables report achievements in public examinations and vocational qualifications in secondary schools and further education sector colleges. Primary school performance tables are published by LEAs and report the achievements of pupils at the end of Key Stage 2. The key scores to look for are the achievements in English, maths and science.

Personalised Learning Every child is entitled to have a personalised learning plan which caters for their specific learning style (see: Learning Styles above and www.everychildmatters.gov.uk/ete/personalisedlearning/).

PMLD Profound and Multiple Learning Difficulties.

PTA Parent Teacher Association.

QCA The Qualifications and Curriculum Authority. This is the government quango which monitors all the qualifications in the country, issuing the relevant criteria for exams to the exam boards. They are a very powerful body indeed, and have a huge influence over the lives of pupils and teachers in the land. They are unfortunately frequently wrong-headed in their judgements and unaccountable for their actions. Perhaps most disastrously, they have effectively encouraged mass cheating for over a decade now by refusing to abolish coursework. This, they say, is about to change but we will see what happens (see: www.qca.org.uk).

School Action When a class or subject teacher identifies that a pupil has SEN they provide interventions that are additional to or different from those provided as part of the normal curriculum. An IEP will usually be devised.

School Action Plus If School Action fails, a pupil moves onto School Action Plus. The targets should be different from or additional to School Action. A new IEP should be devised.

School Profile A school's annual report. Log on to: schoolsfinder.direct.gov.uk/ and type in the name of the relevant school to find out what your school has to say about itself.

SEN Special Educational Needs. If a pupil has a learning difficulty then he or she will be dubbed as having special educational needs. It is vital you and your child are not ashamed of this. There are great benefits to having SEN.

SENCO Special Educational Needs Coordinator.

SLD Severe Learning Difficulties.

Special Schools State schools in England and Wales which are provided by LEAs for certain children with special educational needs.

Specialist Schools Don't confuse these with special schools. They are very different. This type of school includes technology, languages, sports and art colleges operating in England.

Statement of Special Educational Needs If School Action and School Action Plus fail to solve a pupil's learning difficulties then he or she will be assessed again by the school and LEA and may be given a Statement of Special Educational Needs. Only three per cent of pupils receive such a statement. The statement is a legally binding document and is reviewed every year.

UCAS Universities and Colleges Admissions Service. The central agency for processing applications for undergraduate courses. It may well be worth checking the UCAS website before making final decisions on A levels, as the website will inform you about what A levels are necessary for specific degree courses (see: www.ucas.com).

Notes

Chapter 1: Getting your child into a good school

1   www.dfes.gov.uk/sacode
2   www.bbc.co.uk/dna/actionnetwork/A1181792
3   Parts of this article appeared in the *Sunday Telegraph*, 18 January 2004, (www.telegraph.co.uk/opinion/main.jhtml?xml=/opinion/2004/01/18/do1802.xml)
4   Elizabeth Grahamslaw, *A Parents' Guide to Primary School*, Virgin Books.
5   Adam Luck and Michael Shaw, *Times Educational Supplement*, 23 June 2006
6   Natasha Walter, 'On A Wink and A Prayer', *Guardian*, 14 July 2006
7   John Crace, 'How heads bend the rules', *Education Guardian*, 25 April 2006
8   'Pupils aged just eight in 11-plus cramming', *Times Educational Supplement*, 22 September 2006

Chapter 2: Getting the most out of your school

1   Research carried out by Debi Roker, Kerry Devitt and Amanda Holt of the Trust for the Study of Adolescence, funded by a grant from the Calouste Gulbenkian Foundation: www.tsa.uk.com
2   DfEE guidelines
3   'Too Cool for School', *Sunday Times*, June 2006

Chapter 3: How to tackle the big problems

1   'What Parents Worry About', *Times Educational Supplement*, 2 June 2006
2   Parts of this article appeared in the *Mail on Sunday*, 26 September 2006 © Francis Gilbert
3   Keith Sullivan, *The Anti-Bullying Handbook*, OUP
4   Ted Jeory (ted.jeory@archant.co.uk), *East London Advertiser*, 27 October 2005
5   'Cyber Bullying', *Sunday Times*, 4 June 2006
6   *Sun*, 20 August 2005

7   The Institute of Alcohol Studies: www.ias.org.uk/publications/alert/
    05issuer/alert0501_p8.html
8   Michael Shaw, 'Violence at school gates over cartoons', *Times
    Educational Supplement*, 10 March 2006
9   Caroline Roberts, 'Gangs', *Times Educational Supplement*, 23 June 2006

Chapter 4: Does your child have special needs?

1   Section 312 Education Act 1996
2   Special Educational Needs – Code of Practice, November 2001, p. 37
3   Parts of this article appeared in the *Daily Telegraph*, 21 November 2004
    © Francis Gilbert
4   'Vocational ghetto for SEN pupils', *Times Educational Supplement*, 24
    March 2006

Chapter 5: Getting involved with your child's education

1   Read the conclusions of Charles Desforges' important research at: www.
    dfes.gov.uk/research/data/uploadfiles/RB433.pdf
2   *Times Educational Supplement*, 31 March 2006
3   www.estyn.gov.uk/inspection_reports/DylanThomas_sec.pdf
4   *Times Educational Supplement*, June 2006

Chapter 7: When schooling causes conflict

1   news.bbc.co.uk/1/hi/uk_politics/3229453.stm
2   news.bbc.co.uk/1/hi/uk_politics/3229453.stm

Chapter 8: What makes a good school

1   Story from BBC NEWS: news.bbc.co.uk/go/pr/fr/-/1/hi/education/
    4356081.stm
2   William Stewart and Warwick Mansell, 'Are Academies really a
    success?', *Times Educational Supplement*, 10 March 2006
3   'The People versus Academies', *Education Guardian*, 13 June 2006
4   'Single-sex schools no benefit for girls', Distraction by boys a myth says
    study, *Observer*, 25 June 2006
5   *Times Educational Supplement*, 21 May 2004
6   news.bbc.co.uk/1/hi/education/3672404.stm
7   www.telegraph.co.uk/news/main.jhtml?xml=/news/2002/07/05/
    nblair05. xml

Chapter 9: Getting the most out of the National Curriculum

1   www.standards.dfes.gov.uk/rosereview/
2   *Times Educational Supplement*, 24 May 2006
3   Adi Bloom, 'Reading is easy listening on farm', *Times Educational
    Supplement*, 23 June 2006

4 'Some sound reading advice', *Sunday Times*, 26 March 2006
5 Diane McGuinness, *Why Children Can't Read and What We Can Do About It*, Penguin
6 Read the conclusions of Charles Desforges' important research at: www.dfes.gov.uk/research/data/uploadfiles/RB433.pdf
7 Hilary Spurling, 'The Writing's on the Wall', *Sunday Times*, 26 March 2006
8 Tony Gardiner, 'Opinion', *Times Educational Supplement*, 10 March 2006
9 John Crace, *Education Guardian*, 27 October 2006
10 Laura Clout, *Daily Telegraph*, 5 June 2006
11 'What Parents Worry About', *Times Educational Supplement*, 2 June 2006

Bibliography

ELIZABETH GRAHAMSLAW, *A Parents' Guide to Primary School*, Virgin Books (www.virgin.com/books). A very approachable, no-nonsense guide to primary schools.

BARRY DIXON, *Education – A Carer's Handbook*, The National Teaching & Advisory Service (www.ntas.org.uk).

BARRY DIXON, *Education – A Social Workers' Handbook*, Katherine Palin (ed.), The National Teaching & Advisory Service (www.ntas.org.uk). Of all the education books I read I found these two books (by Barry Dixon), aimed at giving information for professionals supervising and looking after children in care, the most succinct and easiest to dip in and out of. Perhaps they could be made more freely available?

The Good Schools Guide, Lucas Publications (www.goodschools guide.co.uk). Make sure you read the latest edition and read it in the library because it is very expensive. It contains useful information on all the top schools in the country. However, it is not always accurate, often being biased in favour of independent schools. If you can cope with trawling through the latest Ofsted report this will be more informative.

BILL LUCAS and DR STEPHEN BRIERS, *Happy Families*, BBC Books, 2006. This is a more general book about being a good parent, but so much of its advice is applicable to schools. There is a must-read comic strip section in the middle (pages 102–113) about different parenting styles.

HILARY WILCE, *Help Your Child Succeed At School*, Piatkus Books (www.piatkus.co.uk), 2004. This is a level-headed and calm guide to all aspects of your child's schooling. It has a superb chapter on 'Nutrition and Success' which is all the more relevant now in the light of the Healthy Schools Initiative.

MIRANDA PERRY, *How to Choose a State Secondary School: A Complete Guide to Choosing the Right School for Your Child*, Oleander Press (www.oleanderpress.com). This is an unbelievably comprehensive book on all the different strategies for spotting good schools. I found it too exhaustive. Its chapters on how to decipher Ofsted reports, the league tables and school prospectuses are very good though. It is a book that can be dipped in and out of.

JOHN O'FARRELL, *May Contain Nuts*, Black Swan (www.books attransworld.co.uk), 2005. A hilarious novel about a pushy parent in south London who learns to love the state schooling system. The uptight mum is so anxious at one point that she disguises herself as a school child and sits an exam!

PETER HYMAN, *One Out of Ten*, Vintage, 2005. This is definitely the most fascinating recent book on the role politics plays in education. It is written by a former speech writer for Tony Blair who became a teacher in one of the roughest comprehensives in London. Ignore all the slavish praise of Tony, and you'll find an eye-opening book full of great advice and insight. It is a very handy guide for any parent who sends their child to an inner-city school.

Special Educational Needs: Code of Practice, date of issue November 2001, Ref: DfES 581/2001. Copies of this can be obtained for free from: DfES Publications, PO Box 5050, Sherwood Park, Annesley, Nottinghamshire, NG15 0DJ. A free but definitive edition of the law regarding SEN pupils. It is not light reading but is definitely worth it if your child has significant SEN issues.

Index